PRODUCT STRATEGY FOR HIGH-TECHNOLOGY COMPANIES

PRODUCT STRATEGY FOR HIGH-TECHNOLOGY COMPANIES

How to Achieve Growth, Competitive Advantage, and Increased Profits

Michael E. McGrath

McGraw-Hill

New York   San Francisco   Washington, D.C.   Auckland   Bogotá
Caracas   Lisbon   London   Madrid   Mexico City   Milan
Montreal   New Delhi   San Juan   Singapore
Sydney   Tokyo   Toronto

McGraw-Hill

A Division of The McGraw·Hill Companies

Library of Congress Cataloging-in-Publication Data
McGrath, Michael E.
    Product strategy for high-technology companies: how to achieve
growth, competitive advantage, and increased profits / Michael E.
McGrath.
        p.   cm.
    Includes index.
    ISBN 0-7863-0146-5
    1. Strategic planning.   2. Product management.   3. High technology
industries—Management.   4. Industrial management.   I. Title.
HD30.28.M3837   1995
658.4'012—dc20   94–27340

Printed in the United States of America.
        8 DOC 10 9

To my wife Diane
and children: Jill, Mike, Chris, and Molly

Preface

In more than 20 years of consulting to high-technology companies, I continually experienced the difficulty they were having with product strategy. This was not because they were incapable; I believe high-technology executives are some of the most capable in all industry. It was caused, I concluded, by the unique challenges of a technology-driven business.

They needed a new approach to manage these unique challenges. In some cases, existing concepts could be modified, refocused, or emphasized differently. In other cases, entirely new concepts were necessary. These concepts also had to be translated into specific strategies. The purpose of this book is to define the concepts and resulting product strategies that are needed by high-technology companies.

These concepts and strategies were developed empirically from experiences of high-technology companies. They are more practical than theoretical, although they will push high-technology management to the cutting edge in product strategy. All are practical enough to be implemented, but implementation will require some effort.

In defining these concepts and strategies, I had the advantage of Pittiglio Rabin Todd & McGrath's (PRTM) considerable experience and involvement in the high-technology industry. As the leader in management consulting to this industry, PRTM has a broad perspective on the management of high-technology companies, including the issues of product strategy.

Product strategy is one element of the overall product development process and needs to be managed within that context. Over the last eight years, PRTM has implemented a high-performance product development process, called PACE (Product And Cycle-time Excellence), in 75 large high-technology companies. This process was described in a book that I wrote with Michael Anthony and Amram Shapiro, *Product Development: Success Through Product And Cycle-time Excellence (PACE)*. In most of these 75 implementations, companies identified product strategy as their primary problem once the fundamental elements of the product development process were running smoothly.

This book is written primarily to help executives, product development teams, product managers, and others involved in determining or applying product strategy. Secondarily, it may also be helpful to outside directors of high-technology companies, and investors, as well as students and others with a desire to learn about product strategy.

Product strategy is both complex and fluid. I concluded that one of the reasons companies had such difficulty with it was that they just did not know how to do it. This was not due to lack of ability or desire but because this complex, fluid process had not been sufficiently defined. There are other books, as well as many articles and research papers, on various aspects of product strategy. However, an executive could not possibly review all of these, select what applies, modify the techniques to fit high-technology products, create new techniques where needed, and summarize what needs to be done. Additionally, all of this needed to be translated from theory to practice.

To serve as a useful reference to high-technology companies, this book goes beyond the underlying concepts of product strategy and into its structure, techniques, and specific strategies. In PRTM's experience, this additional step is essential to actually implementing new concepts. The attempt to be as specific as possible risks the criticism that some of this may not apply exactly to all companies. That should be assumed. Each company should use what applies and modify it to fit specific needs.

The book contains numerous examples since I believe that illustration is the best way to describe something as complex as product strategy. All examples are from the public domain or are significantly disguised. None are taken from proprietary client information. In selecting examples, I tried to illustrate product strategy in as many high-technology industries as possible while at the same time using examples that were technically understandable. For sake of definition, high-technology is considered to include computers and electronic systems, software, data and telecommunications, advanced materials, specialty chemicals, biotechnology, medical products, pharmaceuticals, and aerospace. These industries represent approximately 75 percent of all R&D investment and are PRTM's client base of experience.

Some of the concepts, techniques, and strategies may also apply to other industries, particularly those with similar characteristics. However, this should not be taken for granted.

After the introductory chapter, the book is structured into sections following the framework developed for product strategy. Chapter 13 is particularly noteworthy in that it defines product strategy as a process. Product strategy is a process. Although I had previously suspected this, it was not until I completed all of the preliminary work on the structure, techniques, and strategies that I was able to confidently make this statement. The implications are significant. If a company can define and implement a process for product strategy, it can control the quality of its product strategy by managing this process. Good product strategy is unlikely from an ineffective product strategy process. Better product strategy results from a better product strategy process. Exceptional product strategy may result from a world-class product strategy process.

And exceptional product strategy is what it will take to be successful in the future—at least in the high-technology industry. I estimate that $5 billion to $10 billion is wasted each year because of product strategy deficiencies. Companies can no longer afford these mistakes. Global competition is accelerating, and fewer high-technology companies will succeed. The pace of technology is relentless. New technology is emerging at an increasing rate. Those that cannot keep up will simply be put out of business.

While an exceptional product strategy alone is not sufficient for success, it is necessary. Without the correct strategy, a company will have limited success or possibly fail no matter how well it manages other aspects of its business. With an exceptional product strategy, a company has unlimited potential.

Acknowledgments

I would like to acknowledge the contributions of many to this book. As always, the contributions of PRTM's clients have been extremely important. In working with many of the best companies in the high-technology industry, PRTM has the opportunity to tackle some of the most challenging problems and push the envelope of management processes. This book is part of that effort.

The writers and editors of the popular business press and technical journals, whose efforts usually go unrecognized, should be acknowledged. In doing the research for this book, I read thousands of their articles, which contributed to the examples and overall perspectives in this book. This also gave me an appreciation for the contribution they make to business management. Likewise, prior research and publications by academics and others have contributed to many of the concepts.

The Directors and consulting staff of PRTM contributed their time, experience, and talent to the completion of this book. It is impossible to thank everyone individually, since PRTM's team approach blends the experience of all. However, I would like to single out the contribution of Jon McKay, whose detailed review of the early manuscript and suggested additions proved valuable. I would also like to acknowledge my appreciation to my administrative assistant, Jil Sinon, who somehow managed to keep all this together as I wrote it.

Finally, I would like to thank my family: Diane my wife, and my children Jill, Mike, Chris, and especially Molly for waiting until I finished this book to arrive. Their support and tolerance during my adventures such as this go beyond what should be expected of anyone.

Michael E. McGrath
Director, Pittiglio Rabin Todd & McGrath
Weston, Massachusetts

Contents

Chapter One

Unique Challenges of Product Strategy in High-Technology Companies

M anaging a high-technology company is a little like participating in an adventure story. It is fast-paced, exciting, surprising, and dangerous. The right moves can lead to tremendous success. The wrong moves can quickly result in disaster. Nobody is really sure what lies ahead. Those with vision, insight, and perseverance can succeed. They can survive mistakes, but only if they are nimble enough to adjust in time.

Formulating product strategy in a high-technology company is like trying to anticipate what is going to happen and deciding where to go in this adventure. High-technology product strategy is not an adventure for the faint of heart. Nor is it for those who do not clearly know what they are doing. To be successful—perhaps even to survive—a company must master product strategy and skillfully navigate through competitive challenges, or the adventure will go astray. History shows that it is the proper development, application, and management of product strategy that separates long-term winners from losers.

Bill Gates started Microsoft in 1975 at age 19 and expanded it to a $4 billion software giant in less than 20 years by skillfully applying product strategy to new, rapidly emerging markets. Microsoft's expansion strategy leveraged its core competencies, enabling it to expand from early computer languages to operating systems, applications, and other related products. Microsoft continually differentiated its products to achieve competitive advantage. Windows provided clear ease-of-use advantages. Microsoft Office provided an integrated suite of products that was difficult for competitors to copy.

Although it took longer, 3M followed a similar expansion strategy to develop more than 50,000 products and over $13 billion in revenue by 1992. Building on technical competencies in disciplines such as adhesives, bonding, abrasives, and materials, 3M continuously expanded into new product platforms, including masking and cellophane tapes, magnetic recording tapes, thermofax copying machines, industrial adhesives, reflective materials, tartan surfaces, medical products, and its famed Post-It notes.

In high technology, innovation can create new markets and fuel growth. Intel, for example, identified a product opportunity for the microprocessor in 1969, while solving the problem of a calculator circuit. It used this innovation to build a $6 billion business. However, continued success from an innovation requires constant attention to product strategy. Intel was good at this, continually introducing new platforms and product lines, each more successful than the previous one. Competitors could not keep up with Intel, and it captured more than 70 percent of the microprocessor market by 1993, becoming the world's largest semiconductor manufacturer in the process.

Developing new technology provides companies the opportunity to distinguish their products. Apple Computer successfully applied vectors of differentiation in its product strategy to distinguish its products from those of other early personal computer companies. Its Macintosh computers are a classic example of product differentiation, and its differentiation strategy for the PowerBook product line resulted in first-year sales of more than $1 billion. Apple also provides examples of mistakes in product strategy with several unsuccessful products and its failure to extend the vector of differentiation of its Macintosh platform.

High-technology product strategy cannot be static. Companies need to adapt their product strategy as the market and competition shifts. Compaq Computer's strategy of product differentiation succeeded, while other computer companies, such as Fortune Systems, Victor Technologies, Kaypro, and Osborne Computer, failed. It used first-to-market strategies to introduce a portable computer in 1982 and the first Intel 386-based systems in 1986. Then Compaq stumbled as low-cost competitors such as Dell began to steal market share. On the brink of disaster in 1991, Compaq reacted in time by adopting a price-based product strategy supported by competencies in low-cost operations. In 1993, it was the most successful personal computer company and well positioned for the future.

Scientific advances can create opportunities for entirely new high-technology markets. For example, Genentech used the new science of genetic engineering in 1982 to create the first biotechnology product approved by the FDA. From this, it created a strong research capability based on gene splicing and became one of the fastest growing biotechnology companies. Along the way, Genentech found that there is even competition in innovative products. It fought a classic battle to define the differentiation of its Activase product (blood-clot dissolver) against a competitive product which sold for 90 percent less.

In high-technology markets, new technology can also replace older technology, destroying existing markets in the process. Wang Laboratories was a popular success story in the 1970s and 1980s. In the mid-1970s, it abandoned the calculator market and introduced the first screen-based word processor. Along with its minicomputer product line, this fueled Wang's growth to $3 billion in revenue and 31,000 employees by 1988. Then personal computers displaced special-purpose word-processing systems, and Wang responded too slowly and with the wrong strategy. It filed for bankruptcy in 1992, reducing employment to approximately 6,000 in 1993. Had Wang adjusted differently to changing technology, it might have become a very successful application software company.

Failure like Wang's is common for high-technology companies. For example, most of the minicomputer companies of the 1970s eventually failed. Of the 60 companies founded to build minicomputers, 44 were no longer in business by 1990, 13 resorted to niche or specialty products, and three (Digital Equipment, Data General, and Tandem) were still in business. Of the 32 companies that entered the minicomputer market from existing businesses, Hewlett-Packard and IBM were successful, 27 ceased manufacturing, and three (Hughes, Raytheon, and Texas Instruments) resorted to building special-purpose minicomputers.[1]

Product strategy success and failure frequently occur in the same company. IBM had a knack for this, demonstrating numerous examples of each during the 1980s. In one business segment alone, personal computers, it built a dominant position, failed to capitalize on this position, and then lost out to competitors because its product strategy failed. Yet in 1993, IBM changed its personal computer product strategy and strengthened its competitive position.

Product strategy in high-technology companies presents many unique challenges not faced by companies in other industries. These challenges make product strategy both more critical and more difficult at the same time. It is more critical because continual technological change forces more frequent strategic decisions. If a high-technology company stops to rest on its success, a change in technology can cause it to fall hopelessly behind. If a company moves quickly, it can use changing technology to achieve competitive advantage.

Product strategy is also much more difficult in high-technology companies. Technology is complex. It advances rapidly, changing competitive advantages in the process. Product and market life-cycles are short. Markets with short life-cycles mature rapidly, and competitive advantages shift throughout the life-cycles. It is this combination—the criticality and the difficulty of product strategy—that makes it exciting. Those who are good at it succeed in the adventure; those who are not fail.

PRODUCT STRATEGY CHALLENGES IN HIGH-TECHNOLOGY COMPANIES

High-technology companies face unique challenges stemming from the complications of products and markets that are technology driven. There are four major challenges that high-technology companies need to meet:

- Constantly building new markets.
- Managing short and rapidly changing product and market life-cycles.
- Harnessing emerging technology.
- Adapting to collapsing markets.

Individually, these challenges make it difficult to establish a successful product strategy. Collectively, the task becomes intimidating.

Constantly Building New Markets

High-technology companies are constantly building new markets. As innovators of new markets or as early entrants into emerging markets, they build markets that did not previously exist. In some cases, a market may be totally new, and its construction begins from the ground up. In other cases, it may be changing and is under reconstruction. Rarely do high-technology companies have much time to live in a market. They cannot simply redecorate it. They never have the luxury of sitting back and enjoying it for very long. If they do, then someone else will tear down the market around them while they are sitting in it.

Constantly building new markets is exciting, fast-paced, and exhilarating. New customers are discovered. Growth is rapid. New competitors appear. Innovative high-technology products build markets that never existed before. They create a demand for something that people did not know they needed. For example, video-compression and audio-correction technologies created the video-conferencing market. Companies could hold meetings with participants thousands of miles apart, and video conferencing became a regular part of business.

New technology creates exciting opportunities for innovation. What was once impossible becomes possible. Products that were previously not necessary become indispensable.

Computer technologies and mechanical engineering created ATMs (Automated Teller Machines), and by the 1990s ATMs were a normal part of life that most people took for granted. In the United States alone, there were almost 500,000 ATMs in use by 1993, and as a result, the number of bank tellers declined by approximately 60,000 from 1989.[2]

The home-video market was created in the 1970s, and by 1993 the market for VCRs and video tapes was almost $20 billion. In 1993, Hollywood studios made $5.1 billion from video tapes compared to only $2.5 billion from the box office.[3] Software technology and microprocessors created video games, which by 1993 became a $6 billion market, larger than the market for television.

Sony created an entirely new market with its Walkman by combining earphone technology and compact cassette players. Sony anticipated that many people would enjoy listening to good stereo sound from a portable tape player, even if it was unable to record. Walkman products became extremely successful.

Though exciting, continuously building new markets is also exhausting and risky. The building never stops. High-technology companies continually need to speculate on new markets. They need to anticipate how potential customers will use potential products. They need to make assumptions regarding competitors that are in turn making their own speculations on the market. This puts tremendous pressure on product strategy since strategic decisions are most critical at the outset of a new market.

Managing Short and Rapidly Changing Life-Cycles

Short product life-cycles are a well-defined characteristic of high-technology products. However, the problem is actually quite a bit more difficult than this characteristic implies. Short product life-cycles alone are not the biggest problem; the short market life-cycles are more difficult to manage.

Market life-cycles are short for the same reasons product life-cycles are: New or emerging technology drives the market in a different direction. Market life-cycles are not only short, but they also change rapidly. A high-technology market can go from the development to growth stage in two years, and then into the maturity stage less than two years later. Another year later, it could be in decline. Throughout this rapid progression, prices drop, and differentiation advantages change.

Product life-cycles for most high-technology products are notoriously short—and in some cases getting even shorter. The life-cycle of microprocessors, for example, is approximately 3.5 years. A personal

FIGURE 1–1

Intel Microprocessor Life-Cycles. *This illustrates successive product platform life-cycles for microprocessors. Each new one is more successful but is quickly replaced.*

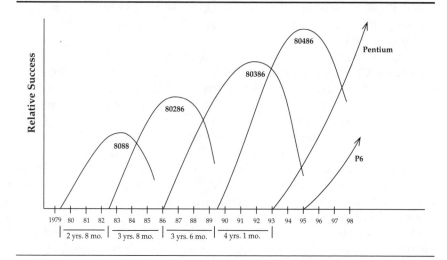

computer product is competitive for nine months or less. Feature-based consumer electronics may last for only a few months. The pressure to come up with a winning product strategy on each product life-cycle change is especially difficult when this happens every 18 to 24 months.

Figure 1–1 illustrates product life-cycles for microprocessors, using the Intel microprocessor product lines as an example. Each of these is a distinctly different product platform; within each platform there are a number of product variations (devices with differing speed or power consumption) and product-line extensions. Within 3.5 years, these were replaced by more powerful products.

Short-life-cycle products become obsolete quickly, putting pressure on product strategy to predict their decline in time to plan a replacement product. Sometimes a replacement product needs to be planned even before its predecessor is released to market.

Companies that successfully manage short product life-cycles can achieve competitive advantage. IBM, for example, introduced the IBM PC in August of 1981, and then replaced it with the XT in early 1983, only 18 months later. IBM began working on the XT even before it introduced the PC. It then replaced the XT with the AT in August of 1984, again only 18 months later. By 1984, IBM's PC revenue was $4 billion, and it dominated the market for personal computers.

Short product life-cycles require a company to make product strategy decisions more frequently. If the decisions are right, then it wins—but only for a short time. If they are wrong, then the competition wins. IBM also provides this example. After the success of its AT, IBM made a strategic error on the next life-cycle change, letting Compaq take advantage of the increased power of the Intel 80386 in 1986, while it delayed and tried to develop a "clone-killer" strategy. By the end of the decade, IBM lost its dominant position and 20 percent of its market share. This loss was equivalent to more than $5 billion per year in revenue.

Competitive advantage in high-technology markets is difficult to maintain for very long because the markets mature rapidly and alter advantages. For example, technology changes cause shifts in the competitive advantages of differentiation, making a sustainable advantage very difficult. A clear differentiation advantage today can be eroded tomorrow.

Tandem Computer and Stratus Computer experienced the impact of such a change. They differentiated their computer systems from the rest of the computer industry by fault tolerance, since their computers kept running despite the failure of any component or subsystem. Fault tolerance clearly differentiated their computer systems, making these systems attractive for applications such as banking and airline reservation systems where continuous availability was critical. This differentiation also insulated them from the early turmoil in the computer industry. However, advanced technology and increased reliability in general computers reduced the differentiation of fault-tolerant computers. As the distinction became smaller, Tandem and Stratus needed to increasingly compete on other factors such as performance, software, and open systems.

Changing technology can also introduce a new basis for differentiation. The computer industry, for example, moved from proprietary to open systems, causing turmoil at companies such as Data General, Wang, Prime, IBM, and Digital. They had to differentiate their computer products on something other than microprocessors or operating systems.

Declining prices is another phenomenon of rapidly maturing markets. Price declines in high-technology products have become legendary. Computers that once cost millions of dollars now cost thousands. Calculators originally priced at more than $1,200 were later so cheap that magazine publishers gave them away free as promotional items. The prices of some expensive medical drugs were eventually reduced to less than 10 percent of their original prices.

Imagine the challenge in the auto industry if the price of new cars dropped to under a thousand dollars. What if a new house cost $3,000 and could be furnished for less than $100? Imagine the implications. How would the food industry adjust if the price of food dropped 20

FIGURE 1–2

Price Decline of VCRs[4]. Illustrates the rapid decline in price for VCRs.

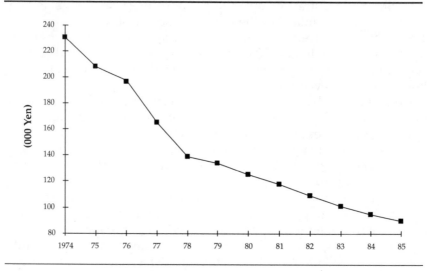

percent annually? How would the oil industry react if an alternative fuel cost half as much? Price declines such as these are commonplace in high-technology markets.

For example, as is illustrated in Figure 1–2, VCR prices declined precipitously from ¥231,000 to ¥90,000 ($41,050 to $410)[5] in a little over a decade. This price drop of more than 60 percent was due to advances in component technology, manufacturing process improvements, and higher volumes. Price-based competition increased as VCRs became commodities when competitors were unable to differentiate them. The drop in price also expanded the market as more customers were able to afford VCRs.

Rapidly declining prices are common in high-technology products. Technology advances. Products become undifferentiable. Prices decline. Volume increases. Prices decline even further. This occurs in most high-technology markets. The price of electronic calculators, for example, dropped 98 percent from ¥182,000 ($825) in 1967 to ¥4,000 ($18) in 1979. At the same time, production volume increased from 100,000 units to 6 million units.[6]

High-technology companies use product strategy to manage short and rapidly changing life-cycles. Platform strategy manages the succession from one platform to the next. Differentiation and price-based strategy define and revise the primary basis for competition throughout the life-cycle.

Harnessing Emerging Technology

The underlying challenge of product strategy is to harness emerging technology. High-technology products are technology driven. They are feasible because of new technology, and they achieve competitive advantage from emerging technology. Harnessing this technology is the key to success. Harnessing is a more appropriate description than applying since the task involves both bringing emerging technology under control and directing its force.

The technologies behind products such as clothing, furniture, steel, books, and food are relatively straightforward. They are generally understood with a little experience and do not change frequently. The technologies underlying high-technology products, on the other hand, tend to be complex, and they tend to change continuously.

Technologies that go into making biotechnology drugs, advanced materials, medical instruments, or fault-tolerant computers are not easy to understand. Some products even incorporate multiple complex technologies, and one individual cannot understand them all. Furthermore, much of the experience in emerging technologies becomes obsolete in a short time.

As an example, take a data communications product that does data management and interconnection for a computer network. The underlying electronics technology includes analog to digital conversion, microcomputing for the intelligence in the system, data storage, and application-specific integrated circuits (ASICs). Software technology includes microcode for the microprocessors, data compression algorithms, application software, and network-management software. The communication interfaces and protocols are numerous, varied, and change almost yearly. Finally, the packaging for the product requires an understanding of configuration flexibility, heat suppression, and user-friendly interfaces.

All of these technologies are individually complex. All are changing rapidly. Yet product strategy for a data communications product needs to encompass the critical elements and trends for all of these technologies. Mastering these to the point of making them core competencies can take years.

Products based on technology can also be replaced by substitute products made from an entirely different technology. Because of this, a company needs to understand not only its own technologies, but other potentially threatening technologies as well. For example, new materials and process technologies created a worldwide contact lens market that exceeded $1 billion, replacing a portion of the traditional eyeglass market. Then, just when contact lens production stabilized, new technology created a substitute product, the disposable contact lens. Led by Johnson & Johnson's Acuvue disposable contacts, this new technology captured a significant share of the contact lens market.

Medical diagnostics provides another example. Diagnostic products based on advanced chemical technologies enabled increased accuracy in the diagnosis of disease and illness, making major improvements in the practice of medicine. Then biotechnology advances changed the medical diagnostic market. Technologies such as PCR[7] amplify a few DNA molecules of a virus to billions enabling them to be accurately identified. This new technology could diagnose a disease such as tuberculosis in several hours rather than the six weeks required for a traditional result from bacterial culturing.

Developing technology-driven products involves complex choices for alternative designs, functions, and technologies. These choices are complex because the technology is emerging and the markets are new. Frequently, there are alternative ways to implement a technology, and in some cases there are choices regarding which technology to select.

Additionally, it is usually not clear what the market will value in a new or improved technology. Meeting customer expectations is particularly challenging when the customer does not know what the technology can do. This requires product developers to anticipate customer requirements even before customers have had a chance to understand how they would use the product.

High-technology products, particularly those that create new markets, also blaze trails into new territories where there are no standards. There may be no standards for compatibility of formats, as happened with Beta versus VHS video tapes. There may be no standards for the interaction of different systems, such as was initially the case in video conferencing equipment. There may be no standards for preferred platforms, such as in computer operating systems. Standards—or lack of them—has been a historical problem for products based on new technology. For example, Edison and Westinghouse battled over an AC or DC standard when they introduced electric lighting.

Standards are critical whenever there is a requirement for interoperability—that is, when different products need to work together in a system. This is necessary for many high-technology products. Application software needs to work with the computer platform, operating system, and peripherals. Video games work only on specific game players. Communication devices need the same protocols to communicate. Biological specimen collection containers must be compatible with processing instruments.

Product strategy determines how to harness technology. It selects which opportunities to pursue and decides how to apply technology to achieve competitive advantage.

Adapting to Collapsing Markets

Eventually all high-technology markets collapse. (There may be exceptions to this statement, but they are few.) Some high-technology markets age gracefully, becoming low-technology markets that are no longer technology driven. A few may decline over a long time. Most high-technology markets eventually collapse, replaced completely by new technology.

A market could be large and successful today, but gone tomorrow. The primary cause of this phenomenon is new alternative technology. Alternative technology can provide advantages so significant that customers begin to use a different type of product. The precipitous decline of IBM's large-scale systems business provides what is perhaps one of the most dramatic examples of a collapsing market.

IBM dominated the market for large-scale computer systems since the 1960s, which drove the company's growth through the 1980s. Starting in 1990, however, this market began to collapse, eroded by high-powered workstations and networks of smaller computers. As is shown in Figure 1–3, IBM's large-scale systems business dropped off a cliff, falling 50 percent, or almost $6 billion, from 1991 to 1993. The impact was even more severe on gross profit margins, which declined from 70 percent to 40 percent at the same time revenues were declining. The combined impact was an estimated drop in IBM's mainframe computer gross profit from $8.5 billion to $2.5 billion.

The loss of $6 billion in gross profit in two years can cause significant problems for any company, even IBM. As a result, it needed to refocus its strategies and significantly cut overhead. The drop in mainframe revenue also shifted the thrust of its business. By 1993, IBM's personal computer revenue (almost $10 billion) exceeded its mainframe revenue, and by 1995 mainframe revenue was expected to become relatively small compared to personal computer revenue. The personal computer business is very different from the mainframe business. It has different economics, a different competitive model, and requires different product strategies to be successful.

This example illustrates why high-technology companies need to be insecure, perhaps even paranoid, regarding the long-term prospects for their markets. Ironically, it is the market leader that needs to worry the most.

IBM was not alone in facing this phenomenon of collapsing high-technology markets. Wang experienced it in word processing. In the late 1970s, Wang established a dominant position in word-processing systems; most large companies were using Wang word processors to increase their typing productivity. With the arrival of PCs, however, special-purpose word-processing equipment became too limited and

FIGURE 1–3

IBM Mainframe Revenue and Gross Margin.[8] In two years IBM's mainframe revenue dropped by 50% and gross profit declined by almost 70% (1995 data estimated).

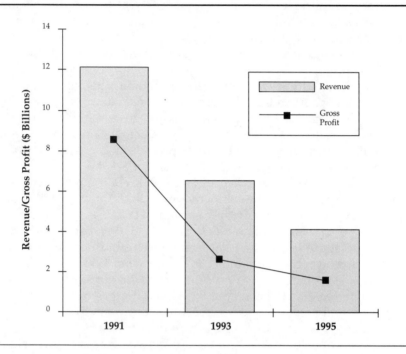

too expensive. Wang failed to move with the new technology. But what if it had converted its word-processing software to work on IBM and Apple PCs? Perhaps today Wang would be a large successful software company like Lotus or Microsoft.

In some cases, a market can fade because it becomes saturated. When a new technology creates a market, there is rapidly growing demand for the resulting products. However, the market eventually becomes saturated when most of the potential customers buy the product and have no need to buy another. The automotive radar-detector market suffered this fate. Created by technology, it grew to more than $200 million (retail) during the 1980s. Eventually, the market became saturated and began to contract in the 1990s as manufacturers ran out of ideas for improving their products sufficiently enough to get customers to replace the detectors they already owned.

A change in the desirability of a technology can also be behind the decline of a market. CFCs (chlorofluorocarbons) were hailed as a technological advance in the 1930s. They were safe (nontoxic, nonflammable), energy efficient, and cheap. However, scientists discovered that

CFCs were depleting the ozone layer. Governments and industry initiated actions to replace CFCs, and the $1.5 billion market for CFCs was on its way to elimination. By 1993, U.S. taxes on CFCs increased the cost to more than $5 a pound, providing an incentive to switch to other alternatives such as 134a and HCFCs. As is the case whenever the market fades, the market leader—in this case DuPont—had more to lose, while new competitors had more opportunity.

Companies do not so much manage the decline of their markets, as they adapt to it. They have some control over it, but usually not enough to manage the timing of the decline. Instead they need to expect the decline, anticipate the consequences, and have other products ready to replace the lost revenue. They do this through product strategy.

MANAGING PRODUCT STRATEGY

Because of these unique challenges, product strategy is much more difficult for high-technology companies than it is for companies in more stable industries. This may partially explain why most high-technology companies are not really very good at product strategy. In fact, in conversations with CEOs of high-technology companies, almost none of them were satisfied with their product strategy. Most saw it as a weakness they needed to correct. This void creates an opportunity for companies to better manage product strategy and outmaneuver their competitors.

Product strategy must be organized into a framework in order to be better managed. This enables a clearer definition of the different aspects of product strategy and how they fit together. The framework described here includes a structure for product strategy as well as specific generic strategies. The specific generic strategies can be grouped into competitive strategy and growth strategy. These can be combined to build an integrated framework, which leads to managing product strategy as a process.

Structure of Product Strategy

Product strategy can be visualized, as shown in Figure 1–4, as a four-level structure: vision, product platforms, product lines, and individual products. Each level in this hierarchy has distinctly different characteristics. The development of product strategy tends to flow from top to bottom and from the general to the more detailed and specific.

Hierarchically, strategic vision is at the top level of the product-strategy pyramid. Product platforms are derived from this vision, as it guides the nature, timing, and competitive positioning of product

FIGURE 1–4

The Four-Level Structure of Product Strategy. Illustrates the flow and development of product strategy.

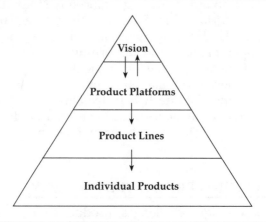

platforms. A vision of growth through price leadership, for example, delineates a low-cost platform and competitive positioning based on price. Product lines are based on product platforms, and individual products are released over time as part of a product line. The top three levels of this pyramid are the primary strategic levels. The bottom level is the execution level where product development takes place.

Strategic Vision (Chapter 2).   Product strategy starts with a clear strategic vision. Without a strategic vision, there is confusion about where to go and what to do. Product strategy forms randomly. With a clear strategic vision, everyone in a company knows where the company is going, how it will get there, and why it will be successful. Product strategy will be more clearly focused and crisply executed.

High-technology companies exhibit differing proficiencies for strategic vision. Some have clear and exciting strategic visions. Others have defective vision; typically because they have not focused it properly. Chapter 2 describes the types of visions and the ingredients needed for a successful strategic vision. It summarizes how strategic vision is developed and when it needs to change.

Product-Platform Strategy (Chapter 3).   Product platforms, not individual products, are the primary level for product strategy in high-technology companies. Platforms provide the foundation for multiple products in a product line, and the characteristics of a platform usually determine the success of the individual products that come from that platform. By separating product-platform strategy from product-line strategy and individual products, senior executives can focus more time and attention on the decisions that will primarily determine future success.

Product platform strategy involves deciding what platforms to develop, how to develop them, and when they should be developed. For high-technology companies, the strength of a product platform is directly rooted in its defining technology and related core competencies. Successful product platform strategy has some necessary ingredients. Failure to consider one or more of these ingredients has been the underlying reason behind many of the problems facing high-technology companies. In addition to describing these ingredients, Chapter 3 illustrates platform strategy with examples and a case study.

Product-Line Strategy (Chapter 4). Individual products are part of a broader product line, which is usually derived from a common platform. Product-line strategy is a time-phased conditional plan for the sequence of developing these individual products within a product line.

The primary objective of product-line strategy is to cover a market by penetrating multiple market segments. Here also, there are several elements that are necessary for a complete product-line strategy. Failure to consider these does not have as significant an impact as incomplete platform strategy, but it does restrict the potential success of the product line. The role of product-line strategy and the elements required are described in Chapter 4. These are illustrated with a case study using the Intel 486 product line.

Competitive Strategy

There are two primary strategies for competitively positioning products: product differentiation and price-based strategy. A company will typically emphasize one over the other, but both are in action at any given time. In addition, there are several supporting strategies: time-based strategy, product globalization, and cannibalization. These are not always needed, but can support the primary strategies in certain situations.

Product Differentiation (Chapter 5). Product differentiation is the preferred competitive strategy of high-technology companies. When successfully differentiated, a product can command a premium price because it provides a higher added value to customers. Differentiation positions products competitively in a market and segments the market based on customer differentiation preferences.

In high-technology products, differentiation is best achieved through vectors instead of individual points, such as a new feature. Vectors of differentiation establish and progressively improve a consistent theme of differentiation, such as ease of use. This raises differentiation to a strategic-level rather than a design-level decision. Chapter 5 introduces the concept of vectors of differentiation.

High-technology companies have successfully employed a range of differentiation strategies, and specific generic strategies have been developed from this experience. These strategies are summarized in the chapter.

Price-Based Strategy (Chapter 6). The second primary strategy for competitively positioning products is price based. All companies have a price-based strategy, but most ignore it as a strategy. Instead they manage it tactically, suffering strategic consequences as a result. Price-based strategies can be offensive or defensive. Chapter 6 summarizes the underlying concepts of price-based strategy and defines both offensive and defensive generic strategies. It illustrates the application of price-based strategy with a case study on Compaq Computer.

Offensive price-based strategies require a company to exploit all sources of cost advantage. The major sources for this are also summarized in the chapter.

Time-Based Strategy (Chapter 7). Time-based strategy is a supporting competitive strategy. It is becoming increasingly popular because it creates an advantage of being the first or the fastest. Although related, these are very different. These advantages lead to two types of time-based strategy: first-to-market or fast-follower strategies. Chapter 7 summarizes generic strategies for each.

Time-based strategies can also be risky and can backfire if inappropriately applied. No matter what time-based strategy is used, a company must have a superior product development process, or it will be starting a game that it cannot win.

Global Product Strategy (Chapter 8). For many high-technology products, the economic advantage of a global product strategy can be so significant it can completely overshadow products from local or regional competitors. This advantage emphasizes the importance of globalization in product strategy. However, there are many reasons why products are difficult to globalize.

Understanding these issues as well as the interdependence of the elements of global strategy leads to four generic global product strategies. These issues and strategies are described in Chapter 8.

Cannibalization Strategy (Chapter 9). Cannibalization is a recurrent strategic issue for high-technology companies, as emerging technology drives them to continuously upgrade and replace their existing products. Cannibalization is a controversial strategic issue that comes into play when a company's new product will be successful at the expense of another of its own products. In some cases, cannibalization should be avoided; in other cases avoiding it encourages competitive attack.

Chapter 9 deals with this issue of cannibalization and summarizes offensive and defensive cannibalization strategies. It also describes an analytical approach for evaluating product strategy in cases where there is cannibalization.

Growth Strategy

Excepting opportunities in existing markets, growth comes from expanding into other markets and innovating new markets. There are two types of growth strategies. The first focuses efforts on expansion paths into new markets. The other cultivates innovation.

Expansion Strategy (Chapter 10). High-technology companies frequently grow by pursuing a strategy of expanding into new markets. This was the fundamental product strategy behind the success of companies like Microsoft, 3M, and Johnson & Johnson. Leveraging core competencies is the key to expansion into new markets. Leverage also provides the basis for a framework that can be used to plan, evaluate, and prioritize expansion opportunities.

Chapter 10 introduces this framework and shows how it can be used to define and evaluate expansion paths. It also discusses how expansion opportunities build upon core competencies. Microsoft's expansion over a 13-year period is used as a case study to illustrate this framework. The framework also provides guidelines for evaluating expansion through joint ventures.

Innovation Strategy (Chapter 11). The ideal of innovation is to apply new technology to create a new class of product, one that establishes an entirely new market. Chapter 11 examines the ingredients of innovation, and this leads to generic innovation strategies. Innovation strategy can be opportunity driven, prediction driven, or technology driven.

Several barriers to successful innovation need to be considered. These are also summarized in Chapter 11. Innovation is illustrated through examples and a case study on the Apple Newton.

FIGURE 1–5

An Integrated Framework for the Elements of Product Strategy. Illustrates the
interrelationship of the elements.

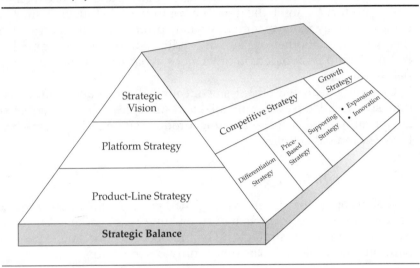

Integrated Framework

When all of these elements are pulled together, they create the integrated framework illustrated in Figure 1–5. It shows the three structural levels of product strategy on one dimension. Strategic vision is
not only the top level of the structure, it also provides the top level for
other strategies. Competitive strategy and growth strategy are aspects
of both platform and product-line strategy.

The structure and strategies that make up this integrated framework
are supported by a foundation of strategic balance. This manages the
emphasis that is placed on each of these to achieve an appropriate balance. This integrated framework leads to the conclusion that product
strategy can be managed as a process.

Strategic Balance (Chapter 12). Strategic balance can be
viewed as the demand management process for new product development. A company, especially a high-technology company, cannot exploit every opportunity. It does not have sufficient resources.

Chapter 12 describes the process of strategic balance among the major trade-offs that most high-technology companies need to make. It
also introduces the R&D Effectiveness Index as an overall metric of
product development. These are all illustrated in a case study on
achieving strategic balance.

The Process of Product Strategy (Chapter 13).   Product strategy is a process. As a process, it can be managed and improved. A better process of product strategy creates better product strategy. The process consists of two dimensions: structure and skills.

Chapter 13 describes the process of product strategy based on the structure in the integrated framework illustrated in Figure 1–5. It summarizes how the individual elements relate in a process context and how product strategy skills develop specific strategies. It also describes the timing and responsibilities for product strategy. Finally, the chapter shows how the product strategy process relates to other product development processes and how core competencies leverage or restrict product strategy.

Strategic Thinking (Chapter 14).   Successful product strategy requires strategic thinking. The final chapter is intended to stimulate this type of thinking. It describes activities that masquerade as product strategy, but should not be confused as product strategy. It also highlights other models for strategic thinking from military strategy, game theory, sports strategy, and decision-making theory.

SUMMARY

Product strategy for high-technology companies involves unique challenges—challenges not faced by other companies that do not have technology-driven products. These can be grouped into four major challenges: constantly building new markets, managing short and rapidly changing product and market life-cycles, harnessing emerging technology, and adapting to collapsing markets. Understanding these unique challenges is the starting point in developing successful product strategy.

An integrated framework is necessary for managing product strategy. This framework summarizes the structure of product strategy as well as the organization of competitive and growth strategies that are used in the remainder of this book.

NOTES

1. C. Gordon Bell, *High-Tech Ventures* (Reading, MA: Addison-Wesley, 1991), p. 175.

2. Thomas A. Stewart, "The Information Age in Charts," *Fortune,* April 4, 1994.

3. Steve Fainaru, "Endangered Species," *Boston Globe,* January 16, 1994.

4. Japan Electronics Industry Development Association, as published in Gene Gregory, *Japanese Electronics Technology: Enterprise and Innovation* (Tokyo: The Japan Times Ltd., 1986).

5. Converted at a 1980s rate of ¥220/$.

6. Japan Electronics Industry Development Association, as published in Gene Gregory, *Japanese Electronics Technology: Enterprise and Innovation* (Tokyo: The Japan Times Ltd., 1986).

7. PCR (Polymerase Chain Reaction) is a biological technique for reproducing at will a specific fragment of DNA without cloning.

8. Ira Sager, "Lou Gerstner Unveils His Battle Plan," *Business Week,* April 4, 1994.

Chapter Two

Strategic Vision

T he old axiom "If you don't know where you are going, then any road will take you there," applies to product strategy as well. If a company does not have a clear strategic vision of where it wants to go, then any product strategy will take it there.

Product strategy begins with a clear strategic vision. Strategic vision provides the context and direction for product strategy. It guides those developing the specific elements of product strategy by telling them where the company is going, how to get there, and why the company can be successful.

Companies with an exceptional strategic vision can achieve unusual success. They clearly know where they are going and how they will get there. They are confident that they will be successful, and they move decisively. There is no debate or argument about contradictory directions. There are no ambiguities about where they are going. There is no confusion about what to do or how to do it. They determine their product strategies to achieve their visions and then execute these strategies.

Some of the biggest successes in industrial history were created by people with exceptional vision. Joseph Wilson saw the vision of copying machines in Chester Carlson's xerography. Tom Watson saw the future in computing, even though his initial view of it was somewhat limited. Bob Noyce of Intel saw the future potential of microprocessors. Henry Ford envisioned a process that would put a car in every garage. Bill Gates saw better than anyone else that the explosion in microprocessors would open a vast array of opportunities for computer software.

Even these visionaries, however, could not always see clearly into the future. Tom Watson turned down Carlson's xerography because he did not see future opportunity for it. Henry Ford did not see the need for more than one color or model of automobile.

New high-technology ventures usually have a clear vision. In start-up companies, the original founder was typically a visionary who started the company based on this vision. For example, Ken Olsen's vision of a "minicomputer" in the 1950s led to the launch of Digital Equipment Corporation. He developed the first small, low-cost computer and introduced a keyboard and video screen that interacted directly with the computer.

When they achieve their original visions, some visionaries are able to evolve or change the direction of their original visions, but this is not always the case. Digital Equipment and Wang Laboratories suffered from successful visions of the minicomputer that later became obsolete.

Some high-technology companies seem to lack any strategic vision. They may have one good product idea, but then they do not know where to go next. Inevitably they fail. Companies without strategic vision are "flying blind" strategically. They fail to see the impact of emerging technologies or shifts in the market. Some cannot see because they have deficient vision. Others have a vision, but it turns out not to be real. They see a mirage.

For most companies, a reasonably clear strategic vision is adequate. It does not need to be exceptional, but it cannot be deficient. A reasonably clear strategic vision contains several critical ingredients.

Strategic vision is executed through platform strategy. The CEO of a major software company had a clear vision of the future for his company. He knew that it had to change. It had to develop a lower-cost platform to fend off competition and expand into a growing market segment. However, he had no idea how to execute his vision through platform strategy. Nothing happened. Out of frustration, he wrote a 53-page memo to all the employees outlining his vision, including how competitors could defeat the company. That did not work either.

The problem was not disagreement with the CEO's vision. Everyone agreed and shared his frustration. The problem was that the company did not understand product strategy and did not have a process for linking the CEO's vision to new products.

This includes reconciling the vision to the implied constraint of the company's budget for R&D spending. If the platform strategy cannot implement this vision within the budget constraint, then the company has a strategic dislocation. Either the vision or the budget must be adjusted. This is where reality sets in. Yet, many companies do not do this strategic reconciliation. They initiate product development, then explain their failure to achieve the vision on not investing enough or blame engineering for not developing products faster.

The way a company sees the future is the key to strategic vision. All companies see the future differently. Some see it much more clearly than others.

TYPES OF VISION

There are several types of vision (see Figure 2–1). Deficiencies in strategic vision are often correctable, but first a company must recognize them.

FIGURE 2–1

Types of Strategic Vision. *A summary of the characteristics of each type of vision.*

Blind Vision	• No strategic vision • Confused or contradictory visions • A statement of goodness • Bad vision • Asleep
Shortsighted Vision	• Too focused on short term • Do not see future opportunities • Failure to see technical discontinuities
Tunnel Vision	• Narrow view of future • Ignore other new technologies or market shifts
Vision a Mirage	• Opportunities are illusory • Trying to create new market that never emerges
20/20 Vision	• Envision the future clearly enough • A reasonable strategic vision • Average vision, not superior
Peripheral Vision	• Integrate surrounding technologies and related market trends to create new opportunities
Foresighted Vision	• Able to see and take advantage of opportunities that others do not see • Position in anticipation of opportunities

Blind Vision

Some companies appear to be completely sightless when it comes to their vision of product strategy. They hit the wall without ever seeing it. Because they lacked a vision that showed them what was ahead, they were blind to what would or could happen. There are different degrees of blindness in strategic vision. Some companies seem to be totally blind, while others may be partially blind. Still other companies are not really blind at all, they just have their eyes closed for a while. Perhaps they are asleep.

Companies are strategically blind for different reasons. Some companies may think they have a strategic vision, but what they really have is a statement of goodness. Prime Computer, for example, stated in 1988 that it had a "clear goal: to make money for its customers, and through that, for its owners." Granted, some within Prime may have had more specific visions of where it was going, but theirs was not the company's vision. Prime was a cash-starved company with few core competencies in a market that was deteriorating. It eventually went bankrupt and spun off its only real technology of value, the Computervision business it had previously acquired.

Some companies just do not seem to have any strategic vision. Maybe they forgot to do it, or they did not think it was important. Perhaps the CEO had a vision, but he did not share it with the rest of the company. In that case, he may not be blind, but the rest of the company is. Bachman Information Systems is an example of a company that lost its vision. It achieved meteoric growth and went public based on the success of its mainframe-oriented software. Ranked nineteenth among *Inc.* magazine's fastest growing companies in 1992, Bachman grew from $13 million in 1990 to $48 million in 1992.

However, Bachman did not see the changes that were taking place in the mainframe market, and revenue collapsed in 1993 as PC-based client-server computing began to replace mainframe computing. The trend had been visible for several years, but the company did not see it. "I should have had my periscope up faster and seen this happen," was the way that CEO Arnold Kraft described his lack of vision. Former employees believed that the company's close ties to IBM, which was a stockholder and joint developer, blinded the company to the shift to distributed computing.[1]

A company may have a vision of its future, but this vision has a blind spot, typically an issue or assumption about which it is markedly ignorant. For example, one company making advanced composite materials failed to acknowledge the advantages of an alternative technology. However, a competitor did see it and was able to achieve a significant competitive advantage.

The Bachman example illustrates a classic case of blindness in product strategy. It also shows how it can happen so easily. A company assumes that a critical characteristic in its future is unchangeable, thereby blinding it to any change in that characteristic. In the case of Bachman, it was blinded to the decline of IBM-dominated mainframe computing.

Some companies are essentially blind because they have too many visions. Dozens of different and incompatible visions may be scattered throughout the company. Individuals may have beliefs about where they think the company should go, but there is no collective vision. There is no leadership. For example, a major electronics conglomerate gave up on developing a strategic vision. Its CEO stated that it was going to be "customer led." This resulted in each division working on so many different products that repetition, duplication, and wasted development dollars became a way of life. It does not take long to get in trouble when there is insufficient leadership.

These companies become "decision proof" concerning product strategy. They launch many initiatives, but are unable to make the tough decisions necessary to select a strategy and set priorities. As a result, product development activities tend to drift in frustration. Typically, the problem of being decisionproof is a symptom; the real cause is a lack of strategic vision. There is no agreement on where the company is going.

Shortsighted Vision

Some companies tend to be shortsighted; they lack the foresight to see sufficiently far enough into the future. As a result, they miss opportunities or do not see changes that are going to affect them.

Some of the biggest success stories in history involve opportunities overlooked by other companies unable or unwilling to perceive new product opportunities. Even though they were in similar businesses, they may be blind to new possibilities. Kodak, for example, was not interested in Edwin Land's instant camera invention in 1947, so Land founded Polaroid Corporation.

Another shortsighted company was Ampex Corporation, which invented the video tape recorder (VTR) in 1956. Even at an initial price of $50,000, the VTR became a big success with broadcasting companies. Ampex had a strong patent position and actively improved the VTR product with solid-state circuitry and color capability. However, it did not have a sufficiently clear vision of the possibilities for the VTR in the consumer market, choosing instead to focus on the broadcast market and to diversify outside of VTRs. It lost the opportunity to be a participant, or possibly even the leader, in the multi-billion dollar consumer VCR market.

Failure to see technological discontinuities is typically attributed to shortsightedness. Discontinuities are points where the improvement of one technology begins to diminish, and another takes its place. DuPont was successful in introducing nylon tire cord technology to displace rayon in the 1960s. Later, however, it did not see the technological discontinuity coming when polyester fiber technology proved to be superior to nylon, and it lost out to Celanese.

Tunnel Vision

Like someone with tunnel vision, a company can take a very narrow view of the future. Its peripheral vision is eliminated, and it ignores the impact of new technology, industry standards, competition, or the way a market is changing. Tunnel vision can be fatal to high-technology companies, as happened with Adam Osborne and Osborne Computer, which back in 1982 was one of the fastest growing companies in American history.

In the late 1970s, Adam Osborne was considered by many to be a visionary of the fledgling microcomputer industry. He published his views on its technology and markets in books and magazine articles. In 1981, he introduced the Osborne 1, a portable computer with bundled software that sold for $1,795. His vision was a computer for the masses—not the best computer, but one that was adequate and priced to sell in volume. He saw himself as the Henry Ford of the new microcomputer industry. The Osborne 1 proved to be a hit. Sales took off, and Osborne predicted that his company would reach $1 billion in sales by 1984. But Osborne's tunnel vision reinforced his self-perception that he could do no wrong, and he failed to see the looming impact of other changes taking place in the industry.

In 1981, IBM, which Osborne had repeatedly put down as an obsolete company, introduced its PC based on a 16-bit microprocessor that was faster than Osborne's 8-bit microprocessor. Osborne predicted that, "IBM will soon be out of the business completely."[2] However, the DOS operating system developed by Microsoft made Osborne's CP/M operating system obsolete. IBM's computer screens and disk drives were superior to those of the Osborne 1. Other companies, such as Compaq Computer, improved on Osborne's original strategy by making IBM-compatible portable computers. Sales of Osborne computers dropped precipitously in 1983. By September, the company had to lay off almost all of its employees and filed for Chapter 11 bankruptcy.

Bill Lowe of IBM also suffered from tunnel vision when he maintained an IBM-centric view of the future. In 1985, he gave Microsoft the rights to sell the jointly developed DOS operating system to other manufacturers in return for IBM's free use of it on IBM PCs. IBM, after all, had 80 percent of the DOS market. Microsoft's Bill Gates saw that this would change. By 1992, IBM's share of the market dropped to 20 percent, and IBM had given away its share of a $2 billion market for PC operating systems.[3]

Bill Gates also saw how IBM could prevent the PC from becoming a commodity business, and he even shared that vision with IBM CEO John Akers in 1984. Gates' vision for IBM was to use its semiconductor expertise to differentiate its microprocessors from those that Intel was making available to clone manufactures. Then IBM could produce operating system improvements to take advantage of the special features that it built into its chips.[4] Akers shared Bill Lowe's tunnel vision and ignored Gates.

Vision a Mirage

Sometimes a company looks into the future and sees an exciting opportunity, but it turns out to be as illusory as a mirage. High-technology companies frequently try to create entirely new markets, and sometimes these new markets fail to appear.

In 1980, SOLVation Inc. envisioned the emergence of PC-based information systems for small businesses. It saw a market opportunity even larger than the $10 billion systems market for computing in mid-sized companies. As part of its vision, SOLVation saw low-cost customized application software, on-line support, and total turnkey solutions for specific industries, all at 5 percent of the price of minicomputer-based information systems.

To implement its vision, SOLVation pioneered the development of several new technologies. Innovative on-line support enabled SOLVation support staff to operate customer computers remotely to tutor customers or diagnose problems. It created software application generators using large, powerful computers to develop and customize software for individual customers. Finally, it configured turnkey systems with complete applications software for small accounting firms, advertising agencies, and manufacturers. SOLVation sold its systems at a competitive price on three computers: one of the first multi-user systems; IBM PCs; and through a joint venture with Sony, the Sony personal computer.

Four years and $16 million later, SOLVation failed. Its vision turned out to be a mirage because the market it envisioned never emerged. Instead, small businesses were content to use Lotus 1-2-3 spreadsheets as their introduction to computers. Even ten years later, there was no significant market for serious computer applications in small business.[5]

20/20 Vision

A 20/20 strategic vision represents the average capability. With a 20/20 strategic vision, a company can see sufficiently into the future to clearly express where it wants to go and how it will get there. Its vision incorporates a sufficient understanding of technological trends and market opportunities. The company can then act in such a way as to get to where it wants to go.

Understanding technological trends includes focusing on critical technologies that affect the company's product strategy. To do this, a company needs to identify its key technologies. Valid Logic saw the coming trend in open systems and adapted its circuit board design software to work with the UNIX operating system. Mentor Graphics, its leading competitor, stayed with the Apollo proprietary closed-operating platform and did not convert to UNIX until four years later. This cost Mentor significant market share.

In some high-technology industries, and at some points in time, a 20/20 vision is sufficient to be successful. For example, 20/20 vision may be sufficient in the growth and maturity stages of a market but not in the development stage. Depending on its expectations, a company can decide whether 20/20 vision—average strategic vision—is sufficient.

Peripheral Vision

A company with peripheral strategic vision is aware of surrounding technologies, emerging trends, and potential opportunities. A company without a peripheral strategic vision simply sees straight ahead. Wang did not have the peripheral vision to see the impact of the personal computer surge coming at it from the side. Its vision focused on minicomputers and stand-alone word-processing systems.

Digital Equipment, on the other hand, eventually saw the threat of open systems and alternative architectures in redefining its strategic vision in 1993. Bob Palmer, Digital's CEO stated that its strategic vision was to be "the leader in open client-server systems that deliver customer solutions."

Dave Mahoney, CEO of Banyan Systems, one of the leading makers of networking systems, used his peripheral vision to see the emerging trends in computer hardware. Banyan repositioned itself as a software company and converted its software to run on standard computers, eliminating its proprietary computer manufacturing operations. As a result of Mahoney's peripheral vision, Banyan continued its increasingly profitable business and avoided the trend that crippled many similar companies.

Foresighted Vision

Foresighted companies take advantage of opportunities that others have not yet seen. They position themselves to solidify skills that will be needed in the future and are able to move earlier than competitors to take advantage of new opportunities.

Bill Gates at Microsoft, for example, saw how quickly microprocessors would emerge and understood the need for graphical user interfaces. He saw that combining these would create new software opportunities. This enabled him to shape product strategies based on this foresight.

Foresighted vision does not necessarily result in invention. Bill Gates of Microsoft and Craig McCaw of McCaw Communications each saw a pattern emerging in their markets. Gates saw a world where microcomputers could do almost anything, and McCaw saw the future of wireless communications. However, neither invented the products that made him rich.

PURPOSES OF STRATEGIC VISION

Strategic vision, whether good or bad, serves several essential purposes. Understanding these helps to shape the vision.

1. *Focuses the efforts of those responsible for identifying new product opportunities.* The strategic vision tells them the direction they should look for new opportunities. With a strategic vision, they begin to consider the right opportunities almost subconsciously. Without a vision, they come up with diverse ideas for new products that are not consistent with the company's strengths or direction. While potentially creative, a myriad of inconsistent opportunities distracts a company and dilutes scarce resources.

For example, one consumer electronics company pursued an opportunity in broadcasting because someone thought it could be profitable. After investing a significant amount of time and money to initiate development, the company decided that the opportunity did not fit its strategy. In the meantime, it had neglected other opportunities that took advantage of its skills. Competitors focused on the directly related opportunities and benefited from the company's distraction.

2. *Establishes a framework for platform strategy.* Strategic vision provides the framework for product platform strategy. It guides the nature, timing, and competitive positioning of product platforms. Without a strategic vision, platform strategy is unguided. One company's dilemma illustrates this problem.

"*I think we need to develop a new product platform,*" the VP of Engineering told the CEO as they discussed the upcoming R&D budget.

"*What kind of platform?*" the CEO asked.

"*I don't know. Who is supposed to identify these?*"

"*Tom, the VP of Marketing is—I think,*" replied the CEO.

"*He's entirely focused on selling current products. He doesn't think strategically.*"

"*New platforms are driven by technology. What new platforms can be created by emerging technology?*" the CEO asked.

"*There are hundreds.*"

"*We need to find out how other high-technology companies solve this problem,*" the CEO concluded.

In another example, a minicomputer company sent a team off site to conceptualize the next generation products. With virtually no direction from or communication with top management, the team spent two months being creative, pushing the technology envelope. They came back with a de-facto mainframe product concept that was a complete departure from the company's direction into a smaller, more competitive system. The proposal was rejected, and the team was requested to start from scratch, guided by a clearer divisional product vision.

3. *Guides product development activities.* The people working directly on new products are more successful if they know where the company is going and how it expects to get there. This helps them to make design-level decisions consistent with the strategic vision. A clear strategic vision helps align product development activities in a common direction. Activities can be shared across similar projects, and individual products can be better linked.

If those developing products do not understand the company's vision, they guess at it or make it up themselves. This leads to organizationally inverted responsibilities. The product developers determine the company vision because the CEO and senior staff are too busy fighting fires and making detailed product design decisions.

Strategic vision also motivates people to work harder. If the engineers have faith that management knows where it is going and has its eye on the future, they will put in the extra effort to ensure that the company gets there with new products. Nothing helps a development team to jell quicker than a crisp, well thought out strategic vision. However, if a development team lacks confidence in a company's vision, it is difficult to keep them there after 5:00.

4. *Provides general direction for technology development.* A clear strategic vision helps to set the general agenda for technology development. It suggests the core competencies that will enable a company to succeed. Xerox, for example, invented a dry-processing film called Verde-Film to replace the traditional darkroom chemical-processing process. The film was targeted for use in the $2 billion printing industry for imagesetters and scanners because it can print only one color at a time. While use of this technology in full-color 35mm consumer film application was feasible, it was not consistent with Xerox's vision. Dr. Hardy Sonnenburg, head of the Xerox lab that developed the new film, said, "To produce such a film does not fit in with our corporate profile, which is in the document business."[6]

5. *Sets expectations for customers, employees, and investors.* These groups help a company achieve its vision. Employees provide the effort. Investors provide the money. Customers join the company on the journey by buying its products.

A strategic vision is the best way to communicate to these groups where the company is going. If they believe in the vision, they will enthusiastically support the company. If they do not, they may abandon it. However, without a vision their support may be unpredictable.

Communicating the strategic vision creates a dilemma. If a company tells everyone its strategic vision, competitors will also learn about it. This points out one of the differences between strategic vision and product strategy. The vision does not describe specific details. While it can be of some help to competitors, it is not specific competitive intelligence.

INGREDIENTS OF STRATEGIC VISION

Strategic visions vary depending on the company, its products, its markets, and its beliefs. Unfortunately, many visions are too general, sounding more like a statement of goodness than real strategic vision. The following is an example:

Our strategy is to develop products that truly fulfill customer needs by exploiting our skills and abilities to the maximum level. We will do this with high-quality products that provide a substantial competitive advantage.

This does not provide any direction at all for product strategy. It could apply to any type of business: supercomputers, soap, or insurance. Yet it is typical of a company that confuses general goals and strategic vision. Compare that vision statement to the following from Compaq Computer in 1993:

Compaq's goal is simple: We want to be the leading supplier of PCs and PC servers in all customer segments worldwide. We intend to accomplish this goal by leading the industry in developing new products, pricing competitively, controlling costs, supporting customers, and expanding distribution. Compaq understands the dynamics of the industry and is poised to move decisively to exploit new opportunities

Compaq's strategic vision provides a clear focus for its product strategy. The vision describes where product strategy is aimed: PCs and PC servers in all market segments throughout the world. This aim is clear, but not too limiting since it provides opportunity for expansion into many markets. The vision also describes how Compaq will get there: by having a better product development process than its competitors, by competing strongly with a price-based strategy, by managing costs, and by having good customer support. This clearly focuses product-platform and product-line strategies.

Finally, Compaq's vision provides an understanding of why it will be successful: because it will understand the dynamics of the industry. This is not specific, but with rapidly changing technology, it is dangerous to be too specific. The vision indicates that Compaq expects to manage these changes in technology better than its competitors.

A complete strategic vision statement such as Compaq's answers three questions relative to the product strategy of a company:

- Where is the company going?
- How will it get there?
- Why will it be successful?

Where?

This ingredient of strategic vision describes the opportunity. It needs to be as specific as possible, while not limiting the opportunity to a single product or market segment. "We aim to take advantage of growth opportunities" is obviously too broad. It does not provide much direction on where product strategy should be directed. Growth opportunities could include computer chips or potato chips.

On the other hand, statements such as, "We aim to provide diagnostic tests for tuberculosis," limits the company to a single product line. This may be appropriate if the company has no desire to expand into other markets, but otherwise it is restrictive. The key to answering the question, "Where is the strategy going?" is in finding the right balance between short-term objectives and longer-term opportunities. The following is a good example:

Our strategy is to provide computer-based tools for improving programmer productivity.

This vision describes in reasonably specific terms the types of products that the company will develop (programmer productivity tools), while not restricting them to a specific type of tool. Products could include tools for automated design, system analysis, or object-oriented programming. The vision also stresses the product focus—software productivity. This provides a common theme for new products, stated in terms of customer value. Notice that the vision intentionally omits any restriction of computer platform. "UNIX software development tools," is an entirely different vision. The vision stated here provides strategic flexibility regarding computer platforms.

How?

The next ingredient of strategic vision describes how the company will get where it wants to be. In high-technology companies, this ingredient frequently defines the technology trend that is most important. NEC's vision, for example, was to exploit the convergence of communications and computing, taking advantage of the emerging trend that it thought was most important.

Here again, the need is to be specific without restricting resulting strategies. "By taking advantage of the new 386 microprocessor," for example, is a limited vision. It describes how to get there for now, but it does not provide any guidance on what to do next. The "how" ingredient needs to be robust enough to last beyond the next product, as is illustrated in the following, building on the previous example:

Our strategy is to provide computer-based tools for improving programmer productivity. **These tools will take advantage of increasing computer power.**

This vision provides the direction to develop these productivity tools. Computer power is increasing rapidly, and the company intends to take advantage of this trend in its products. When combined with the previous ingredient of the vision, this defines the opportunity: Increasing computer power will provide new uses, perhaps new markets, for software productivity tools.

Why?

The third ingredient defines why the company will be successful in getting to where it wants to go. Usually this is based on the unique added value provided to the customer. This ingredient of the vision sets the stage for competitive strategy. For a company competing on price, the strategic vision would include something like, "by being the price leader and low-cost producer." For a company competing with a strategy of differentiation, the vision would provide direction for potential vectors of differentiation. Digital Equipment's vision, stated earlier, of being the leader in client-server computing was supported by the belief that it had more technical understanding and a better foundation than its competitors.

The basis for competitive advantage needs to be reasonably clear. "Our products will use appropriate technologies to fulfill customer needs and provide the highest quality," does not instill a great deal of confidence that the company really knows how it will be successful.

The following is an illustration of answering the "why" question based on the earlier example:

Our strategy is to provide computer-based tools for improving programmer productivity. These tools will take advantage of increasing computer power **to provide ease of use.**

This declares "ease of use" as the vector of differentiation. All product platforms and individual products will be positioned based on "ease of use," and the company will segment the market based on this vector.

STRATEGIC VISION FORMAT

The format for strategic vision seems to hold a particular interest for many. Is it a slogan? A sentence? A paragraph? A presentation? A book?

While the format is not as critical as the content, brief is better. If a strategic vision can be expressed briefly, then it can be communicated more clearly. A few sentences usually seem to be the best format. The previous examples of Compaq Computer and the software productivity tools company used this format.

The strategic vision at Xerox is communicated by its slogan, "The Document Company." This works effectively, providing a clear but flexible view of where Xerox is going. A very brief vision statement such as this periodically needs to be explained in a little more detail to make it actionable.

A strategic vision can also be more detailed, particularly when a company believes that it must describe some specific details of product strategy. In this case, it is a hybrid between a statement of product strategy and a strategic vision, since it actually outlines the product strategy. There are some drawbacks to this format. It limits flexibility and creativity by excluding what could be exciting alternatives. Also, it provides others with some meaningful competitive intelligence.

However, in some cases, more strategic details need to be communicated. For example, independent dealers and software developers may need to understand a computer company's strategic direction. If they do not understand the direction, they may abandon the company for another. This is probably what Apple Computer had in mind in 1992. Figure 2–2 illustrates how it used this detailed format to express its strategic vision of product strategy.

A strategic vision should not be conveyed only through a single format. A CEO can and should expand on the company's vision and explain it from time to time in presentations to employees, at strategy sessions, and in annual reports. The brief vision statement becomes the theme for more in-depth explanations. These explanations may vary as the circumstances change since even the CEO may interpret the vision differently over time. The vision should be living and robust.

CHANGES IN STRATEGIC VISION

Strategic vision changes as technology, competition, and customer expectations change. Sticking to an obsolete vision for too long will guide a company's product strategy in the wrong direction. Changing a vision too frequently is very inefficient. "Gee, I changed my mind again. I guess everything that you have done is wasted; let's try going in this direction for a while," does not instill confidence in leadership.

FIGURE 2–2

Apple Computer's Strategic Vision of Product Strategy. *Example of a more detailed strategic vision.*[7]

Phase 1: *Market-Share Strategy*	• Reduce the time it takes to bring new products to market • Lower prices on Macintosh products to attract more customers • Broaden the Macintosh family
Phase 2: *Enterprise Computing Strategy*	• Establish Apple as a key player in client/server computing • Expand Apple's product line by creating powerful servers • Work with key partners to provide better ways to integrate Macintosh into large-enterprise networks • Work with IBM to develop PowerOpen — a new open-systems, UNIX-based platform
Phase 3: *Emerging Technologies Strategy*	• Move Macintosh to RISC technology; work with IBM and Motorola to develop PowerPC — a line of RISC-based micro-processors for Macintosh and IBM systems • Take a leadership role in emerging technologies, such as object-based systems, multimedia, and personal-information systems

Strategic vision can be changed in several ways. It can be clarified, as the company moves closer toward achieving its original vision. It can evolve, as the company learns more about itself and its markets. Eventually, most high-technology companies need to change their vision. They may be close to achieving their original vision and need a new one, or technology may change significantly enough that their original vision is no longer exciting or profitable. Whatever the reason, all strategic visions eventually need to change.

Clarification

A clarification of strategic vision is not a change in direction. It is merely a matter of bringing the vision more clearly into focus so that the company can achieve it more productively.

Xerox clarified its vision as it entered the 1990s. Previously, it had focused on significant tactical objectives, increasing quality to improve its performance in the marketplace. However, as it entered the 1990s, it became more strategically focused. Xerox developed a clear vision of the future with a single-minded purpose: to be *The Document Company*. It believed that despite, or possibly because of, changing technology, the need for document-based office productivity would increase. Xerox then focused all of its research, product development, and marketing around achieving this vision. It diminished or reduced nonrelated activities and even got out of the financial services business.

Evolution

Strategic visions can also evolve. If the vision evolves properly, a company can adjust the where, how, or why, while still maintaining momentum.

The direction of Bill Foster's vision at Stratus Computer evolved as the company's market and competition changed. Initially, the company's vision was "fault-tolerant" or redundant computing. Later, it became "high availability." This adjustment was made because computer hardware redundancy became less important, while a high-availability software architecture became more important.

By 1992, the vision evolved into "continuous availability." This evolution was necessary to crystallize the difference between its products and general-purpose computers that were incorporating aspects of fault resiliency or high availability. The distinction between "high" and "continuous" was essential to the evolution of the vision. By 1993, Stratus evolved its vision to be "the leading supplier of comprehensive solutions where availability is a critical need." This completed its evolution to include computer software as well as computer hardware.

Change in Direction

Companies need to change their vision when it becomes obsolete, hopefully before an obsolete vision gets them into trouble. Changing the vision redirects the company in an entirely new direction, and because of this the change can be traumatic.

Conner Peripherals set the growth record for a new company, exceeding $100 million in revenue for its first year. It achieved this success by being the technology leader, introducing increased capacity and performance in its disk drives, which were sold to personal computer manufacturers such as Compaq. The Conner vision was narrowly focused on advanced-technology disk drives custom designed for PC manufacturers. These were developed around a philosophy of "sell-design-build," which guaranteed high volume sales for customized products. But this vision ran out of gas and could no longer provide Conner with the growth it wanted.

In 1992, Conner Peripherals embraced a new vision to transform itself into a "leading supplier of total storage solutions for the computer industry by providing a comprehensive offering of disk drives, tape drives, storage management software, and value-added distribution." By diversifying across many related businesses, Conner hoped to take advantage of the individual growth curves of these market segments.

RESPONSIBILITY FOR STRATEGIC VISION

Responsibility for strategic vision rests clearly with the CEO or head of the business unit. This does not mean that he or she develops that vision without input from others. On the contrary, it is usually a mistake to develop a vision in a vacuum.

Strategic visions are developed at the business-unit level, not the corporate level. The business-unit level is where product strategy is formulated from that vision. Trying to develop a strategic vision at the corporate level of a large diversified company is ineffective. The business units are usually too different to pursue the same vision. Lou Gerstner, CEO of IBM, was not far off when after six months on the job he was pressured to give his vision for IBM. He said, "Our mission is to be the most successful information-technology company in the world." . . . "O.K., you wanted a vision statement. Fine, we got it—now let's go back to work."[8]

At the corporate level of a large diversified company, the vision is more general. Perhaps it could be considered a vision for the business-unit visions. It is one that is not directly intended to provide the basis for product strategy. Something like Lou Gerstner's "vision" may be appropriate.

Sometimes a CEO's philosophy can serve as the basis for a strategic vision of product strategy. For example, T.J. Rogers of Cypress Semiconductor has never left anyone in the dark about what he thinks, and his philosophy is clear: "If it doesn't make for faster circuits, happier customers, or more motivated employees, we don't spend a nickel on it." While this does not provide a complete vision, it certainly is clear philosophy, which fulfills many of the purposes of a strategic vision.

SUMMARY

Strategic vision is the starting point for product strategy. It provides the context and direction by describing where the company is going, how it expects to get there, and why it can be successful.

Strategic vision varies widely among high-technology companies. Some have defective vision; others have exceptional vision. Defective strategic vision includes blind vision, shortsighted vision, tunnel vision, and seeing a mirage. Normal strategic vision is classified as 20/20. Some companies are exceptional because they have a peripheral vision or a foresighted vision.

While the format can vary, a strategic vision includes specific ingredients that describe the where, how, and why of the vision. A vision will also change over time. This change can be a clarification, an evolution, or a complete change in direction. Strategic vision should be set at the business-unit level, and the CEO of a company or business unit is responsible for its vision. The resulting product strategy is aimed at achieving this vision.

NOTES

1. Maria Shao, "Bachman Information Systems Recasts Itself After Crash," *Boston Globe,* May 2, 1993.

2. Phil Patton, "Champion of the Adequate," *Audacity,* Spring 1993.

3. Paul Carroll, *Big Blues: The Unmaking of IBM* (New York: Crown Publishers, 1993), p. 90.

4. Paul Carroll, *Big Blues: The Unmaking of IBM* (New York: Crown Publishers, 1993), p. 111.

5. The author confesses to be the architect of the SOLVation vision as the company's CEO.

6. Christopher Lloyd, "Film Developers Without Chemicals," *Sunday London Times,* November 7, 1993.

7. Apple Computer, 1992 Annual Report.

8. Judith H. Dubrzynski, "An Exclusive Account of Lou Gerstner's First Six Months," *Business Week,* October 4, 1993.

Chapter Three

Product-Platform Strategy

P roduct-platform strategy is the foundation of product strategy, especially in high-technology companies, which have multiple products related by common technology. It defines the cost structure, capabilities, and differentiation of subsequent products. By separating product-platform strategy from product-line and individual product strategy, a company can concentrate its focus on strategic issues.

A product platform is not a product. It is a collection of the common elements, especially the underlying core technology, implemented across a range of products. In general, a platform is the lowest level of relevant common technology within a set of products or a product line. These common elements are not necessarily complete in the sense that they are something that could be sold to a customer. A product platform is primarily a definition for planning, development, and strategic decision making.

The nature of product platforms varies widely across industries and product applications. For example, the platform for a personal computer is the microprocessor combined with its operating system, such as the Apple Macintosh, Intel/Windows, or Digital Alpha/Windows NT platforms. The packaging, power supply, computer memory, disk drives, monitors, application software, and interface capabilities are all related to specific products, not the product platform.

In an application software product, the platform is the architecture (such as mainframe, client/server, desktop) and interfaces (database drivers, operating system linkages, user interfaces). These determine how the resulting products can be used and the computer hardware that is required. Individual features and functions of the applications are related to the specific products.

A product platform can also be a core chemical compound and the process for producing a range of products from this compound. It could be a unique resin that produces high-temperature materials of varying strength based on the fibers used. In life sciences, a platform could be a base chemistry used in a range of immunodiagnostic tests, or it could be a delivery vehicle for a class of drugs.

FIGURE 3–1

Product Platform with Associated Products. Illustrates the relationship of the
product platform to resulting products based on it.

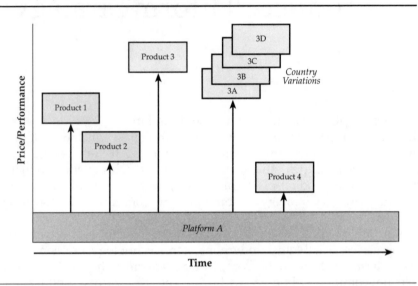

A product platform is the foundation for a number of related products, typically a product line. Figure 3–1 illustrates how new products
are built over time on a common platform. While all products are
unique in some way, they are related by the common characteristics of
the product platform.

Platform A was developed with a number of related products in
mind. Product 1 was the first product to utilize this platform, and it was
targeted at the middle of the market in terms of price/performance. It
was followed by Product 2 and Product 3, which implemented the platform at lower and higher price/performance levels respectively. Products 3A, 3B, 3C, and 3D were international variations of Product 3 that
incorporated country-specific modifications. Finally, Product 4 was
developed toward the end of the platform life-cycle. It was a low-cost
product developed to sustain the platform.

The decisions on the extent and sequencing of specific products are
made through product-line strategy. Here the focus is on the underlying platform.

Focusing product strategy at the platform level simplifies the product strategy process, enabling senior management to concentrate maximum attention on the most critical decisions. The strategy is simplified
because there are fewer platforms than products—typically 80 percent

to 90 percent less—and major platform decisions are only made every few years, not every few months. With this focus, senior management spends 90 percent of their time on the most critical 10 percent of the decisions that determine 90 percent of the success. A clear platform strategy leverages the resulting products, enabling them to be deployed rapidly and consistently.

Setting product strategy at the individual product level dilutes focus, distributing senior management attention across all products. It also diminishes the leverage gained from using a common platform as a foundation and can create confusion about individual products. For example, one company that set its product strategy at an individual product level developed ten different products that overlapped each other. The differences among the products confused its salespeople, as well as its customers. Even more importantly, the company could not keep all these products competitive. The cost of repetitively making similar improvements for each of the multiple products was simply prohibitive.

In spite of its importance, many companies tend to skip this foundation level of product strategy and go directly to product-line strategy, or skip that, too, and go directly to the development of specific products. Eventually, they look back and realize that they have developed a new platform as part of one of these products and say, "If only we'd thought of subsequent products before we completed the platform." Or even worse, they may forget to invest in developing a new platform before their current one becomes obsolete and say, "The market (or technology) changed on us."

For example, one computer company had difficulty separating platform strategy from product-line strategy. Its new product attempted to address the collective requirements of many vertical market segments instead of being built as a platform from which various configurations could be developed to address different vertical markets. As a result, there was just enough wrong with the product for each vertical market segment to reject it in favor of a competitive product that was better focused.

On the surface, skipping over platform strategy looks faster, easier, and less restrictive. The usual pattern is to develop a high-end product by incorporating new technology and numerous features. Then the company decides it needs more than one product, typically a lower-priced version. It tries to reduce the cost of the original product as best as possible, but runs into design constraints created by the original product design, and in some cases, may even need to make the products incompatible to achieve different goals.

A product platform strategy would have prevented these problems. Multiple products could have been developed from the same platform, each implementing different features and functions to focus on specific market segments and distribution channels.

Platform strategy was used to avoid these same problems in a consumer telephone products company. Various models of cordless phones were developed from the same base platform, which consisted of a few circuit boards that contained the common radio technology and software. The physical styling and extra features varied for each model based on the targeted distribution channel. Models developed for high-end channels, such as phone centers, contained many extra features and combinations of features, while models developed for low-end channels, such as Walmart, were basic products with a minimal number of extra features. This approach leveraged a single platform into multiple products, minimizing development and manufacturing costs.

A platform approach also encourages more of a long-term view of product strategy. For example, a medical products company developing a new biosensor product had the choice of using two alternative base chemistries. One was low risk but could only be used in a stand-alone product for the company's existing home-testing market. The alternative base chemistry was higher risk but could also serve as a platform to create devices for a series of other tests, thus opening the door for expansion into new markets. By taking a platform approach, the company created a longer-term opportunity that it would have otherwise neglected.

PRODUCT PLATFORMS

Before a company can develop a platform strategy, it first must clarify what its product platforms are. This is not always as easy as it initially seems. The need for clarification between platforms and products can be seen in the confusion between platform development and product development.

Platforms are defined by their most important underlying characteristics. For high-technology companies, the technology of a platform is its most important characteristic. Precisely defining where other elements are categorized is less important.

The Defining Technology

The key to a high-technology product platform is the technology that underlies it. Underlying technology establishes the performance characteristics of products based on a platform, provides their primary basis of differentiation, establishes the limits of their capabilities, and defines their relative cost. While several technologies may be necessary to create a successful platform, the *defining technology* is most critical.

The defining technology is also the key to understanding a product platform. Typically the defining technology of a platform differentiates the products that are based on that platform. The Macintosh platform, for example, is differentiated by its easy-to-use graphical interface. The Motorola 68000 microprocessor and the Mac's electronic architecture are an integral part of the Macintosh product platform, but they are supporting rather than defining technologies. Without its graphical operating system, the Macintosh platform would not have any significant distinguishing characteristics. It would still be a platform but would not have been very successful.

Advanced composite materials combine multiple materials such as fillers, resins, and reinforcing materials in order to achieve specific performance characteristics. The underlying platform of these composite products is the material that provides the critical characteristic. For example, DuPont's Kevlar 49 is a prepreg material (a reinforcement or carrier material that has been preimpregnated with a liquid resin) that provides composite materials with the characteristics of light weight and high tensile strength. It is combined with other materials for different composite applications, such as aircraft structural components and sports equipment. For example, the Kevlar 49 platform is combined with low shear strength polyester to form for bullet-proof armor products.

Failure to understand the defining technology of a platform dooms a platform strategy to failure. When Steve Jobs started Next Computer, he had the intention of producing a computer that he felt was clearly differentiated from others. However, Jobs failed to understand the defining technology of his product platform. Next's workstations—the Cube and the Nextstation—were sleek-looking boxes with advanced microelectronics technology and innovative disk storage. Yet these factors were not the defining technology of Next's workstations.

Experts estimate that fewer than 50,000 Next workstations were sold, and most of those were purchased because of Next's operating system.[1] Ironically, this operating system, NextStep, was acquired almost by accident. NextStep incorporated object-oriented programming, which significantly improved programmer productivity. It was based on software called Mach developed at Carnegie Mellon University. However, Jobs did not select this operating system because of this differentiation, but because it enabled other programmers to write applications software faster, thereby helping Next sell more workstations.

By early 1993, Next finally recognized its defining technology and began to sell an effectively differentiated product: its software. NextStep 486 ran on other computers, namely Intel 486-based systems, and was offered as an alternative to other operating systems. To implement this shift in its product strategy, Next Computer closed its manufacturing facility and eliminated more than half of its employees. For personal computers and workstations, the defining technology of the product platform is not the computer hardware; it is the operating system, which drives the microprocessor and interfaces with the user.

The defining technology is not always obvious. For example, the major product line of a medical products company was biological sample collection devices. These devices incorporated several technologies including chemical reagents, the design and shape of the device, the gas mixture within the device, and the manufacturing process to produce high-quality devices. However, the defining technology was the material used to make the device. The properties of this material determined the performance of the device, its cost, and its shelf life. The material also determined its susceptibility to breakage, which was a major factor due to the fear of infectious disease.

Platform Development

Platform development is distinctly different from product development. Unlike product development, the goal is not to directly develop a new product, but to create the pieces or elements that enable the development of subsequent products. This difference in goals leads to differences in investment criteria, planning, and actual development.

Investments in new platforms cannot be justified on the planned success of a single product, but rather need to be evaluated on the expected success of all the resulting products that will be based on that platform. Financial evaluation of new platform opportunities is done at a strategic level, using assumptions of the success of the resulting products. Some companies confuse platform development with development of the initial product and are surprised when this first product is not financially justified. They either justify it as strategic and ignore the financial evaluation, or they discard it, possibly missing long-term opportunities.

A platform development plan is different from a product development plan. It defines the common elements of a new platform and how they will be developed. A product platform is completed when these common elements are ready to be incorporated into the initial product. Platform development generally consists of three phases:

- *Platform Concept Evaluation.* This initial phase of platform development defines the objectives and scope of the platform. It includes an evaluation of the feasibility of the platform, comparing alternative platforms that would accomplish the same objective. A company may put several alternative platforms through this phase—either sequentially or in parallel—in order to select the best one. The decision to select a particular alternative and proceed with the next phase is the major decision of platform strategy.

- *Platform Planning.* Detailed platform planning, which takes place during this next phase, includes specification of the platform's scope and its elements. This is where the common elements of the platform are distinguished from the elements that are unique to individual products. The detailed plan for the subsequent platform development phase is also prepared at this time.

- *Platform Development.* The actual development of the platform elements takes place during this phase. When completed, these are transferred to the development project for the initial product.

Platform development is also different from technology development. In its broadest sense, technology is a skill or core competency. Technology development can then be defined as creating this competency. In some cases, this is a high-risk effort where progress is uncertain.

The goal of technology development is to bring a particular technology to the point where its application is feasible. Platform development begins with feasible technology and incorporates it into the elements that make up a product platform. Platform development can be accurately scheduled since there is a known amount of work, while technology development cannot always be scheduled. Technology development is not always necessary. In some high-technology industries, the emphasis is on the application or engineering of known technology. Even though the technology may be evolving, it is still known.

Platform development requires synchronization with product development and technology development. This synchronization is illustrated in Figure 3–2. At the completion of platform development, the common platform elements are transferred to the product development effort. Usually the evaluation and planning phases of the initial product development project are done in parallel with platform development. Technology development integrates with platform development by transferring the completed technology to the platform.

Platform Characteristics

Product platforms have characteristics that are different from individual products, and failure to understand these differences can cause strategic difficulties.

FIGURE 3–2

Synchronization of Platform Development. Product development and technology development are closely synchronized with platform development.

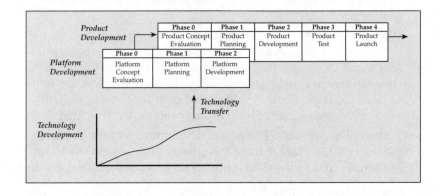

- *Product platform life-cycles define product generations.* New generations of products stem from new platforms, not individual products. The life-cycle of a platform usually ends when it is replaced by a new, more competitive platform, and a new platform usually introduces a new generation of products.

- *Product platforms can be extended.* The life of a platform can be extended through periodic improvements. Personal computers illustrate this characteristic by using increased microprocessor speed to improve performance.

- *Product platforms can create derivative platforms.* A derivative platform is one that is primarily based on an existing platform but is different enough to be managed as a separate platform. The Macintosh PowerBook is an example of a derivative platform.

- *Product platforms are essential, not incremental.* A decision to introduce a new product has incremental revenue impact. A decision not to introduce a new platform can take a company out of a particular market for an entire generation of products.

- *Platforms take significantly longer to develop.* A new platform can take four to ten times longer and cost proportionally more to develop than individual products that are based on an existing platform. This has obvious implications in planning and product strategy decisions.

These unique characteristics require that product platforms be managed differently than individual products. These are also why product-platform strategy plays a critical role within overall product strategy.

PURPOSES OF PRODUCT-PLATFORM STRATEGY

Product-platform strategy is the most critical of the three levels of product strategy because it serves several essential purposes:

1. *Focuses senior management on the most important decisions.* Decisions regarding new platforms are critical. They impact the success of all of the resulting products. They are also the most difficult decisions, since the timing of new platforms and the selection of technology require sufficient market and technical judgment.

Platform strategy leads senior management to focus on these important decisions instead of diluting attention across numerous products. It separates platform strategy decisions from individual product decisions, raising them in importance and attention. Some companies distinguish the level of authority between these. Platform strategy is the responsibility of senior management, while individual product decisions could be made by a lower level of management.

2. *Establishes the foundation for the resulting product line.* The product platform creates the opportunity for individual products. While the characteristics of the individual products vary, the underlying platform, particularly the defining technology, is the same. Within the Macintosh product line, for example, there are products with different hard-disk capacities, varying processor speeds, and alternative monitors (built-in/separate, monochrome/color, small/large), but the operating system is the same.

The characteristics of the product platform aim products toward a particular market, while specific products can then vary that aim toward segments of that market. For example, Polaroid's instant photography platform is aimed at people who want to see their pictures immediately. Specific camera products can then emphasize differences in cost, quality, or special functions. One version even produces identification badges.

3. *Provides the framework for long-term business strategy.* Product platforms are planned at an aggregate level, covering the long term. Individual products, on the other hand, are more detailed and short-term focused. By looking at a company's product platforms, one can see at a strategic level what it has done and where it is going.

Figure 3–3 shows Apple Computer's major product platforms over time. The Apple II platform, including the related IIe and IIc platforms, carried Apple for a very long time, longer than any other personal computer platform. The Apple III and Lisa platforms proved unsuccessful and were short-lived.

Fortunately for Apple, the Macintosh platform was a big winner, fueling Apple's growth for almost ten years, and Apple began to replace

FIGURE 3–3

Apple Computer's Product-Platform History. Shows the timing and relationship of
Apple's product platforms.

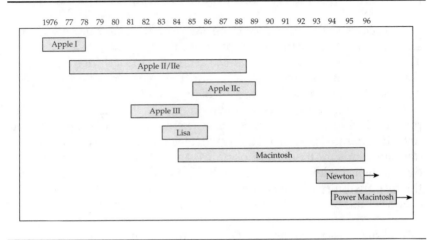

it in 1994 with a Power Macintosh platform. It also introduced the
Newton platform in 1993, aimed at the hand-held computing segment.

Apple did not introduce a new product platform for almost a decade.
While still successful, critics of this platform strategy believe that
Apple should have developed other platforms during this period, par-
ticularly given the highest level of R&D spending in the PC industry.

4. *Links a company's strategic vision with its product-line strategy.* The
product-platform strategy is the link between the strategic vision and
the product line. Without this link, product-line strategy or individual
product development tends to be scattered.

An advanced materials company was in the process of developing a
rugged panel technology to be used as the platform for aerospace structural applications. While the market potential was vast, the platform
strategy analysis showed an extremely long certification cycle as well
as more extensive market fragmentation than originally foreseen.
These market characteristics violated the company's strategic vision,
which had an emphasis on short-term, high-impact applications of material technology. As a result, the company proactively curtailed R&D
expenditures in this area and focused on other platform opportunities
more closely aligned with its strategic vision.

Platform strategy is developed to achieve the strategic vision. A
company can check to see if the platform strategy can be expected to
achieve its vision. If not, the platform strategy or the vision needs to
be revised.

5. *Provides specific direction for technology development.* Product-platform strategy provides more specific direction for technology development than strategic vision does. Most technology development is intended to improve an existing platform or create a new one. This is how defining technology is developed. The platform strategy guides these development efforts by identifying when new platforms are anticipated and what type of defining technology is needed.

Technology development is usually needed to support the platform strategy. New defining technology is usually necessary for upcoming product platforms. Without developing new defining technology, it is difficult for a company to differentiate itself. To be fully effective, product-platform strategy must be married to, and enabled by, core competencies.

A company in medical diagnostics determined that the advent of DNA-based diagnostics would soon render its immunodiagnostic product platform obsolete because of dramatically improved speed and accuracy. The product-platform strategy was to create a proprietary base chemistry to amplify the target DNA signature for identification. With a clear platform strategy, the company got a jump on development.

INGREDIENTS OF SUCCESSFUL PLATFORM STRATEGY

Many product-related problems can be traced to an incomplete product-platform strategy. A company may have missed or ignored critical ingredients of the strategy or may have made bad choices about some of its ingredients. Successful product-platform strategy incorporates all key ingredients including appropriate technology, clear differentiation, platform integration, life-cycle management, and sustainable competitive advantage.

Appropriate Technology

A company makes its choice of underlying technology when it defines a new product platform. Since this decision is frequently irreversible, technology choice in platform strategy is perhaps the most critical strategic decision that a high-technology company makes. The technology underlying a product platform defines the potential and limits of its performance and frames its cost structure. While the choice of underlying technology is sometimes obvious, more frequently it is a difficult decision.

The alternative architectures for supercomputing provide an example of the challenge in selecting the best underlying technology for a product platform. In 1993, there were three alternative supercomputing architectures: vector-based machines, massively-parallel-processor (MPP) systems, and workstation clusters. Each offered advantages and differing performance characteristics, but one would likely emerge as the most successful supercomputing platform.

Traditionally, supercomputing platforms were vector-based, using a small number of very fast custom-built processors. Writing software for this technology was reasonably straightforward, and as a result there was a large amount of application software available. In 1992, sales of supercomputers with vector-based platforms exceeded $1.3 billion, but this was declining. The underlying architecture of this technology was reaching its limits, and performance improvements were becoming more difficult. Cray Research, Cray Computer, Fujitsu, NEC, Hitachi, Convex, and IBM used this product platform.

Massively-parallel-processor platforms incorporate relatively inexpensive microprocessors—hundreds or even thousands—linked together in a coordinated system. This technology provides the advantage of scalability, the ability to increase or decrease performance by adding or subtracting microprocessors. It also benefits from the cost advantage of microprocessors made in extremely high volume for the personal computer market. The limitation of this technology is the difficulty of writing software to break a computing problem into hundreds of pieces so that each microprocessor handles a manageable piece. Intel, Thinking Machines, Kendall Square Research, nCube, MasPar and NCR Teradata used this technology for their product platforms in 1993. IBM and Cray Research were developing platforms using this technology in addition to their vector-based platforms.

Workstation clusters offered a third technology for supercomputing. With this technology, groups of workstations and servers create the computer power equivalent to a parallel-processor platform. This approach faced a similar, but even more difficult, challenge of segmenting and distributing computing tasks. Its advantage was lower cost and flexibility to be used outside of supercomputing. Traditional workstation companies such as Silicon Graphics, Hewlett-Packard, Convex, and Sun Microsystems competed in supercomputing using this technology, as did IBM and Cray Research.

The choice of a particular technology is the most critical ingredient of platform strategy. Some companies may evaluate or even partially develop multiple platforms before they choose one as the basis for a new product platform. However, when it is time to launch development of the new platform, they must make the strategic decision.

Clear Differentiation

Differentiation is implemented primarily through the product platform, not the individual products. The differentiation in a product platform provides the constant theme woven throughout the product line built upon it, with individual products providing variations on the theme.

A product platform could be based upon materials that have unique properties. For example, products made from the Kevlar 49 platform have some clearly differentiating characteristics. They are 20 percent to 35 percent lighter than traditional metal products. They have higher tensile strength, which provides the stiffness desired in skis, tennis rackets, and golf clubs. They have good fatigue resistance and vibration dampening, which are required in applications such as aviation products.

Apple used ease of use as the vector of differentiation for its Macintosh. Its operating system was developed specifically for this differentiation. The Macintosh hardware was designed for easy installation and was integrated with the operating system to make the total system easier to use. Apple also invested in peripheral products and communications software that were integrated to make the complete system easier.

It should not be surprising that some of the most successful products come from platforms that are clearly differentiated. The following are some examples:

- NEC designed its UltraLite Versa personal computer platform for versatility.
- Stratus and Tandem designed their computer platforms for fault tolerance.
- Digital Equipment designed its Alpha Workstation platform for superior price performance.
- Hewlett-Packard designed its OmniBook computer platform for portability (the lowest weight and longest battery life).
- Microsoft designed its Office 4.0 product for integration of common functions.

Platform Integration

Sometimes a company has multiple product platforms addressing the same general market. Each may use different underlying technology, target different market segments, and be at a different point in its lifecycle. The integration of these platforms with one another is an ingredient of platform strategy. Too many overlapping platforms can confuse the market and create inefficiencies in distribution and sales. Yet a single platform may leave market opportunities open to competitors.

Multiple similar platforms can retard development and hinder competitiveness. For example, one data communications company maintained two network management systems: the first on a powerful workstation platform; the other on a PC-based platform. Two platforms required twice the effort to update with new communications devices. This delayed, by 6 to 12 months, the release of new versions of each network management system as well as new communications devices. It would have been cheaper for the company to sell the more powerful workstation platform at the lower price, instead of investing in redundant development.

In addition to eroding economies of scale, too many overlapping platforms can confuse customers. IBM fell into this trap in mid-range computer systems when it had five separate and incompatible platforms: the System/3 platform for small business, the System/38 and System/36 platform, the 8100 platform for distributed processing, the Series/1 platform for transaction processing, and the 4300 platform for running mainframe software on a minicomputer.

Customers became confused and frustrated as IBM salespeople, contradicting each other, told them that different IBM platforms were their best solution. It was difficult for customers to use multiple platforms because application software was not compatible across them. For IBM, the cost of maintaining and enhancing five different platforms became a competitive disadvantage. By 1982, IBM realized that it needed to merge these into a single platform and launched the Fort Knox project—one new mid-range system platform that would be compatible with all five platforms. However, this was too difficult a problem to solve quickly. Even with four thousand people working on it for four years, the new platform proved to be too ambitious and was canceled.[2]

Overlapping platform life-cycles too closely can be expensive, while leaving gaps between platform generations can result in a precipitous drop in revenue. Timing is essential to platform integration.

Platform Life-Cycle Management

Product platforms go through life-cycles as technology changes and the basis of competition evolves. Platform life-cycles drive the major competitive changes in high-technology industries by introducing new product generations, forcing companies into dramatic changes in product strategy. It is the platform life-cycle that needs to be managed, not the individual product life-cycle.

Data General Corporation faced a platform life-cycle challenge in 1988 as its proprietary 32-bit ECLIPSE platform became less competitive. It had been a successful platform, providing computing cost advantages using Data General's proprietary architecture. Then the applications software business changed. Software developers moved

FIGURE 3-4

Data General Revenue. While AViiON revenue increased, other revenue declined faster.

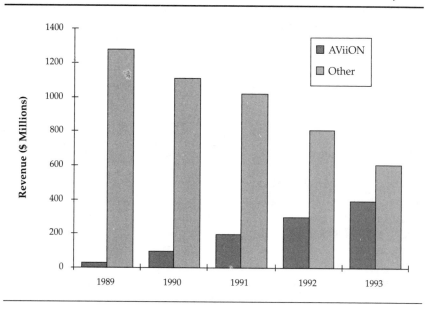

toward open, nonproprietary platforms, and the ECLIPSE platform started its decline.

In 1989, under the direction of its new CEO, Ron Skates, Data General initiated a strategic shift to a new platform, the AViiON, based on the Motorola 88000 RISC (reduced-instruction-set-computing) microprocessor and the UNIX operating system. This platform generated a wide range of workstation, server, and multi-user system products. Data General's strategy was to release products from the AViiON platform at a fast enough rate to offset the decline in the ECLIPSE platform.

AViiON revenue grew steadily, as can be seen in Figure 3–4. However, despite this growth, total Data General revenue declined during this period, as the ECLIPSE platform moved to the end of its life-cycle faster than AViiON grew. This is a classic case of a high-technology company racing to replace a dying platform with a new one. Data General eventually realized that it was not going to offset the decline in its ECLIPSE revenue fast enough and in 1992 launched another product platform aimed at a different market. The CLARiiON platform is an open data-storage system based on disk-array technology.

Companies frequently need to make strategic choices among platforms. Should they continue to invest in extending an existing platform or invest in developing an entirely new one? Resource limitations place restrictions on doing everything.

Pratt & Whitney faced this choice in its jet engine business. It planned on investing $2 billion in an all new engine, the Advanced Ducted Prop, intended for the Airbus A340. At the same time, however, its PW4084 engine for the Boeing 777 was reaching range limitations. The engine was effective at a 5,000 mile range, but to be effective at a future range of over 8,000 miles, it required a major redesign. The cost of that redesign would exceed $500 million. Pratt & Whitney could not afford to do both and had to choose which platform to support.[3]

Changing platforms is sometimes necessary because a product itself depends on another platform. For example, when the DOS operating system became the standard for personal computers, a new market was created for DOS applications. Companies such as Microsoft, Borland International, Lotus Development, Software Publishing, WordPerfect, and others were successful with DOS-based application products. However, with the advent of Windows 3.0 in 1990, the preferred operating system changed, and another totally new market was created: Windows-based applications.

This new market brought with it totally new criteria for success. It was not enough for products to simply run on Windows; they had to really take advantage of its graphical environment. However, once they did that, it was difficult to differentiate products based on user interface, or "look and feel," since these were now managed by the operating system. Less differentiation led to more price competition, and the increased importance of other differentiators such as integration with other applications.

Many of the leading DOS-based software companies failed to anticipate the change properly. They bet on IBM's OS/2 as the operating system to replace DOS, developing products based on it rather than Microsoft's Windows. As a result, WordPerfect, Lotus Development, Borland, and Symantec were late with Windows-based products. Microsoft, of course, placed the right strategic bet, as did Intuit with its Quicken financial software product.

Alan Ashton, the founder of WordPerfect, thought that its hold on word-processing customers was so strong that it did not need to rush a Windows version of its word-processing product to market. He later acknowledged that was a mistake. Along with Windows, Microsoft introduced a new version of its word-processing software, Word, that took advantage of these easier-to-use features. WordPerfect's sales declined as Microsoft took the market lead. By the time the WordPerfect product caught up in 1993, Microsoft changed its product platform again, this time by bundling separate applications into a single suite to create an integrated platform with a price slightly higher than separate applications. WordPerfect had to lower its prices to compete and then had to eliminate free customer support and lay off 1,000 employees to reduce loses.[4]

As an ingredient of their product strategy, high-technology companies need to clearly understand where each product platform is in its life-cycle. From this, they can identify the priority and timing for replacing their platforms.

Sustainable Competitive Advantage

A new product platform can be a success, but a proprietary or defensible platform makes that success more sustainable. In high-technology products, a sustainable advantage can only be achieved through technology. The most successful strategy for a new product platform is to achieve a competitive advantage based on proprietary or defensible technology. IBM's System/360 platform and Polaroid's instant photography platform are classic examples of this strategy.

The strategic trade-off to this advantage in many markets is the need for open and compatible products. Proprietary products may be sustainable, but they may also be at a competitive disadvantage.

The IBM PC and the Apple Macintosh demonstrate different strategies relative to sustainable advantage. IBM's first personal computer, launched in August 1981, was a big success. The IBM PC immediately became the market leader and initiated a shakeout in the personal computer industry. However, to get to market faster, IBM broke from its tradition and used outside suppliers for key components. The defining technology of the IBM PC platform was not IBM's. It was based on the Intel 8088/8086 microprocessor and the Microsoft-developed PC DOS operating system.

While the IBM PC was a very successful product platform, it did not give IBM a sustainable advantage. PC-clone manufacturers were able to acquire the underlying technology and reproduce the platform. As a direct result, IBM was forced into price competition much earlier and lost market share trying to maintain prices. An alternative strategy for a company with the resources of IBM could have been to acquire all rights to the defining technology, make the system open for software developers, and license the defining technology to a limited number of competitors.

Apple Computer pursued a very different strategy with its Macintosh by maintaining strict control of the defining technology, the Macintosh operating system. The Macintosh operating system permitted Apple to clearly differentiate its personal computer from all others. If Apple had lost proprietary control of its defining technology, then it probably would have had to share its market segment with many competitors.

The problem with Apple's sustainable advantage strategy was the exact opposite of IBM's; it held on too long, thinking that Microsoft would never catch up to the Mac's ease of use. It did not anticipate the continued dramatic increase in memory, allowing Windows to be successful. It also did not foresee the PC price wars that rapidly expanded the market, dwarfing Mac sales in the process. In desperation, it tried to sue for infringement by claiming that Windows copied the Mac's "look and feel," but it lost. If Apple would have licensed the Mac operating system, it could have become the dominant operating systems company instead of Microsoft.

Even innovative platforms can be difficult to sustain as competitors quickly follow a company's early success. This leads to rapid dispersion of new product platforms. Consumer electronics product platforms have been particularly vulnerable to this. Sony, for example, was successful with its 8mm compact camcorder based on a new platform that enabled hand-held video recording. However, this success was short-lived as competitors copied the platform. In 1991, Sony upgraded the 8mm platform with the Video Hi8 system, which offered hi-fi stereo sound and improved picture quality. Several products with new features, such as a color viewfinder and an active prism to compensate for accidental movement, were released from this new platform, helping to stimulate sales for a short time. In this market, platform lifecycles are very short, and sustainability of a platform advantage is almost impossible.

A key method for sustainability is patent protection with emphasis on broad rather than specific patents. A good example of effective use of broad patent protection is the success of Symbol Technologies, a manufacturer of bar code scanning devices used in retail stores for checkout and inventory tracking. Gerry Schwartz founded Symbol to patent the concept of a gun-type scanning device that combined a laser scanner with a trigger so the user could point the device at a bar code and "zap" it. This seemingly simple patent allowed Symbol to attain a virtual monopoly position for years, only allowing others to produce hand-held scanners by paying royalties.

Sustainability is a key element of any platform strategy. All opportunities such as proprietary technology, patents, or operational advantages should be considered as part of the strategy. All too often, high-technology companies make the fatal misjudgment regarding ownership of defining technologies and core competencies. Experience suggests that core competencies should never be outsourced. Where a sustainable advantage cannot be achieved in a platform, a shorter platform life-cycle should be planned.

PRODUCT-PLATFORM STRATEGY CASE STUDY: NCR'S DUNDEE ATM DIVISION

NCR's ATM (automated teller machine) division in Dundee, Scotland, illustrates a good example of product-platform strategy. When Jim Adamson—the dynamic VP of the NCR Dundee ATM business—took over in 1980, he realized that the current model 1780 product platform had severe quality problems. As he visited customers to resolve their complaints, he also began to realize that NCR had an exciting opportunity.

His strategic vision was becoming the world leader of the ATM business. World leadership would be achieved by offering a wide range of superior quality products that fit customers' key needs and by offering those products ahead of the competition.[5]

Jim Adamson's vision identified superior quality as the key differentiator. In the ATM business, this included superior reliability, simple maintenance, and low total ownership cost. Banks wanted their ATMs to be available to customers as much as possible. Units that were down with malfunctions cost them business and created ill will. They wanted to be able to repair their ATMs as infrequently and as easily as possible. Jim Adamson came to this vision after numerous customer visits.

Achieving this vision would require a new platform, one that would emphasize quality and reliability. However, there were also some immediately pressing problems of satisfying angry customers. The Dundee division decided to develop an interim platform that would be a step on the way to a new platform but that could be released sooner. It released the 5080 as a replacement for the 1780 in 1982. It incorporated an improved printer and cash dispenser.

Jim Adamson set a goal that to achieve his vision the new platform needed to be twice as reliable as the next best competitive product. This would be the platform's vector of differentiation. When that goal became feasible, he changed it to three times. This required a significantly new platform in addition to the improvements in the 5080. More reliable components were designed into the new platform. The overall design used replaceable modules that were easier to maintain. New computer software was written for the imbedded computer.

The new platform achieved its reliability target. The first product from this platform was the 5070, a full-function interior ATM, released in November of 1983 at ATM-5, an industry trade show. Seven months later, the 5081, a full-function through-the-wall ATM, was released from the same platform. This was followed by the 5084, cash-dispensing-only version in June of 1985. In 1986, the 5080 interim-platform product was replaced by the 5085, based on the new platform. Also in 1986, the new platform was used to release the 5088 (a drive-through-island version), 5571 (machine for inquiry and document printing), and 5572 (interactive video machine). In 1987, the 5070L, low-priced model, was released.

The new platform gave NCR significant competitive advantages. Higher reliability was a vector of differentiation highly valued by ATM customers. Competitors could not easily copy NCR Dundee's strategy since they also needed to develop entirely new platforms to compete on this basis. Meanwhile, NCR was continuing to release a multitude of products from its new platform. Competitors did not know whether to design new products from their old platforms to compete on variety or to stop to develop a new platform to compete on reliability.

Burroughs and Docutel withdrew from the ATM business, followed later by IBM and others. NCR captured the major share of the worldwide ATM market. By 1990, it was well on its way to developing its next new platform.

PLATFORM PLAN

The result of platform strategy is a platform plan. This shows the expected life-cycle of all current platforms and the anticipated schedule for new platforms. It shows where there may be serious gaps between platforms and when development of new platforms must begin. In addition, a platform plan forces companies to start the development of defining technologies in advance.

Figure 3–5 illustrates a platform plan that could apply for most high-technology platforms. It shows three different categories of product platforms. Each category illustrates a different platform strategy situation. The plan shows both current and planned platforms, with the dashed line distinguishing the past from the planned.

The high-performance systems platform E-Comp is approaching the peak of its life-cycle, and a platform extension is planned to lengthen its competitive life. The strategy is to replace E-Comp with a new high-performance platform, N/C-13, which uses an entirely different architecture. The extension of E-Comp is necessary since the technology for the new platform will not be available in time to prevent a gap between the two.

The mid-range systems platform, ESP, illustrates a derivative platform, the ESP-Port. This platform is similar to the ESP, but significantly different enough for the company to manage it as a distinctly different platform. It is also at an earlier stage in its life-cycle. The company has

FIGURE 3–5

Sample Product-Platform Plan. Illustrates the 5-year plan for multiple platforms.

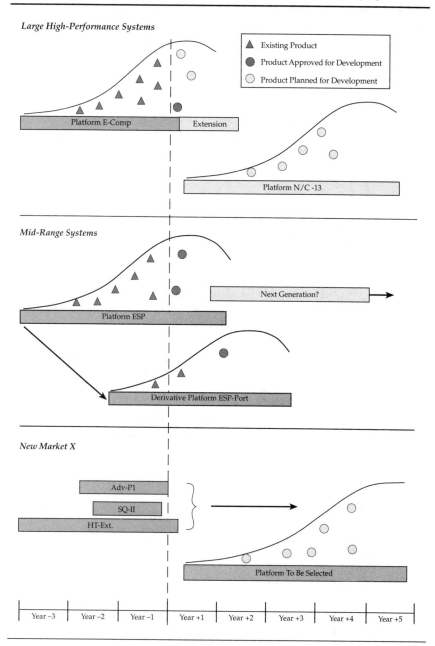

not yet decided on a next generation replacement to its mid-range systems platform. Through platform strategy, the company identified this as an open issue and initiated a project to address it. Since the next generation platform is not defined, and it is indicated by a question mark; the company plans to initiate development within a year.

The third segment of the platform plan shows the platform strategy for a new market opportunity. In this case, the company decided to enter this new market but is still unsure of the specific platform for its new products. There are three very different product platforms being researched and evaluated: the Adv-P1, the SQ-II, and the HT-Ext. As the plan illustrates, the company will select one of these in the next few months as the platform for the new market entry.

SUMMARY

Product platforms are the primary strategic unit of measure for product strategy, and, accordingly, this is where senior management should pay the most attention. Product platforms have unique characteristics and are defined, planned, and developed differently from individual products. In high-technology products, the defining technology of the platform is its most critical characteristic. Product-platform strategy serves several essential purposes that affect the resulting product line, long-term business strategy, and technology development.

Successful platform strategy must incorporate some essential ingredients. These include the choice of technology, the basis for differentiation, integration of other platforms, life-cycle management, and sustainability.

The result of product-platform strategy is typically expressed in the form of a product-platform plan. This plan guides the evolution of current product platforms and ensures that they are replenished.

NOTES

1. Alan Deutschman, "Steve Jobs' Next Big Gamble," *Fortune*, February 8, 1993.

2. Roy A. Bauer, Emilio Collar, and Victor Tang, *The Silverlake Project* (New York: Oxford University Press, 1992).

3. Howard Banks, "Desperately Seeking Partners," *Business Week*, November 22, 1993.

4. G. Pascal Zachary, "Consolidation Sweeps the Software Industry," *The Wall Street Journal*, March 23, 1994.

5. John P. Kotter, *A Force for Change* (New York: The Free Press, 1992).

Chapter Four

Product-Line Strategy

P roduct-line strategy addresses the third layer in the product strategy structure. It flows from the product-platform strategy to define the type and sequence of products that make up the line of products from that platform.

Product-line strategy is less critical than product-platform strategy. The defining technology has already been selected. The primary vector of differentiation has been decided. The general cost structure has been determined. A brilliant product-line strategy is unlikely to save an inept product-platform strategy.

Nonetheless, product-line strategy plays a crucial role in product strategy. A poorly implemented product-line strategy can restrict the success of any platform strategy. Without product-line strategy, companies fail to develop and release products in the proper sequence. They miss opportunities and out of frustration try to do everything at once, only to find that they do not have sufficient resources to do so.

Limited resources are a reality for all high-technology companies. All potential products in a product line cannot be developed simultaneously. So choices must be made. It is the product-line strategy that makes these choices and reflects them in the development plan for the product line.

Product-line strategy is a time-phased conditional plan for the sequence of developing products within a product line. There are several important elements in this definition. A product-line strategy determines the *sequence* in which products are developed and released. This sequence is *time-phased* throughout the life-cycle of the platform and the product line. Finally, it is *conditional*. It can change based on a better understanding of the market, competitive factors, or resource availability.

Many companies neglect to create any comprehensive product-line strategy. They develop the products in a product line sequentially; when one is complete, they then decide which one to develop next. They stop development when they have better things to do. By developing products in this manner, they lose the opportunity to implement a strategy that would improve their position in the market. Products may not cover the appropriate segments of the market, or they may be released in a less effective sequence.

A division of a major computer company developed a completely new product platform with some unique characteristics but failed to think beyond the first product based on this platform. As soon as it completed this first product, the company began working on its next product. Because the engineering group was excited about applying the latest version of the technology, it began developing a more powerful version of the product. After almost a year of development, the company realized that the more powerful version would only appeal to a very small segment of the market. The largest segment wanted a less expensive, less powerful version. Because it got sidetracked, the company lost out to competition that beat it to this segment.

PRODUCT LINES

A product line consists of multiple products released over time from a common platform. A product line is primarily a planning unit between the product platform and individual products; it is not actually developed or sold to customers.

Common Platform

A product line is built on a product platform and all products within the product line use that common platform. Each incorporates the elements of that platform and changes to those elements generally change all products within the product line. Some products in a product line may not use every element from the product platform, but they will generally not use alternative elements. The key is that they use the same defining technology that is the essence of the product platform.

For example, NCR's ATM (automated teller machine) product line described in the previous chapter used a common platform that was three times more reliable than competitive products. The product line included the 5070 full-function interior ATM, the 5081 full-function through-the-wall (used outside of a bank on the exterior wall) ATM, the 5084 cash-dispensing-only ATM, the 5088 drive-through-island ATM, the 5571 inquiry and printing machine, and eventually the 5070L—a lower-priced version of the 5070. Each of these products varied in size, shape, and mix of functions, but all used a common platform.

A product line can also expand to include other related products, such as accessories and supplies. These are not based on the same platform, but are usually incidental.

Multiple Products

A product line is an integrated set of products with a similar, but somewhat different, purpose. Each product varies from others in the product line by some characteristic such as the following:

- *Capacity.* The products in a product line may differ based on their capacity. Examples of capacity differences include disk drives (data storage), airplanes (number of passengers), switchboards (number of lines), and voice mail systems (number of messages).

- *Performance.* Performance differences may distinguish each product in a product line. Examples include microprocessors (processing speed), airplanes (speed and distance), data modems (data transmission speeds), and database software (response time).

- *Features.* Features can define product differences within a product line. Examples include cellular telephones (models with number recall, hands-free operation, etc.), personal computers (models with color monitors, different keyboards, etc.), and consumer electronics.

- *Packaging.* Packaging or configuration differences can also distinguish products. Examples include ATMs, (design for different currencies), personal computers (predefined configurations and options), and videoconferencing systems (predefined communications and display configurations).

- *Quality.* Quality differences do not mean that some products are poorly made while others are well made. In this sense, higher quality products are sold for a higher price. Examples include advanced materials (higher quality materials with fewer impurities are necessary for certain applications) and ruggardized computers (made to withstand field conditions for military use).

In some cases, the characteristic for distinguishing products in a product line is clear; however, in other cases there may be multiple choices and combinations. Deciding how to distinguish products in a product line and how many to have are ingredients of product-line strategy.

Besides the primary products in a product line, add-on products, product upgrades, and custom products may be part of a product line. Add-on products could simply be accessories such as ribbons and toner for printers, but they could also be more important. Add-on products in some high-technology markets can be similar to razor blades in the razor market where the real profit is made selling a continuing supply of blades, not the original razor. For example, medical diagnostic instruments require disposable reagents for each test. Usually, reagent revenue is where the company makes its money. The product-line strategy in this case is to sell or lease the instrument at an attractive price. An instrument placement is a guaranteed revenue stream because the reagent will only work with that instrument.

Add-on products are important in other high-technology industries as well. In personal computers, add-on products include additional computer memory, modems, additional disk drives, and so on. These may even be more profitable than the original product. In the pre-press industry, the major imagesetter manufacturers such as Agfa, Crosfield, and DuPont rely on sales of film products to support lower price offerings on their electronic products.

Product upgrades are a form of add-on product that is important to many high-technology products, particularly computer software. Product upgrades provide additional revenue from the existing customer base, getting them to upgrade by purchasing a new version of the product. Product upgrades can be critical to extending the life-cycle of many high-technology products. Once the market approaches saturation, upgrades become the primary source of continued revenue growth.

In the software market, some companies have implemented product-line strategies based entirely on future upgrade revenue. They sell the initial product at almost giveaway prices in order to have the opportunity to sell upgrade versions in the future to a large installed base.

Some product-line strategies revolve around providing customized products. Large high-priced products, such as commercial aircraft, are built to customer configuration. Some components, such as disk drives, are modified to fit the requirements of high-volume customers. Modern flexible manufacturing processes enable companies to sell products in customer-defined configurations that previously needed to be standard products. Even personal computers can be ordered from some companies, with customer-defined configurations for memory, software, and other options pre-installed.

Custom products can be the primary basis of the product-line strategy, or they can be an adjunct to it. IBM's Ambra product line, for example, offered "custom built" products. A customer could choose one of five system types (Slimline, Desktop, Minitower, EISA Desktop, or EISA tower), one of six microprocessors, numerous memory configurations, one of six hard disk alternatives, one of four monitors, numerous options, and pre-loaded software applications.

Sequence

Each product in a product line usually requires some development in addition to the original platform and previous products. In some cases, this may be significant (performance improvements in a microprocessor, for example), while in other cases it may be relatively simple (different configurations of personal computers). Since each product requires additional development, the sequence for the release of each product is critical.

Product-line mapping can analyze and plan the time-phased release of each product within the product line.[1] The decisions regarding the priority, sequence, and timing of product releases are important ingredients of product-line strategy.

PURPOSES OF PRODUCT-LINE STRATEGY

The purposes of product-line strategy are very different from those of vision or product-platform strategy. They tend to be more short term and constrained by the focus provided by the product platform. Product-line strategy serves four primary purposes:

1. *Defines product variations aimed at specific segments within a market.* While the product platform targets the market, the specific products within the product line target individual segments of the market. Each product within a product line is modified to appeal to customers in a particular segment. High-priced, high-performance products, for example, appeal to the segment of the market that will pay more for increased performance.

Product-line strategy tries to capture targeted segments. This requires identifying and understanding each major segment to define the necessary product variations. Companies who see and interpret the needs of customers in each segment can achieve an advantage.

2. *Schedules the rollout of products within a product line.* The schedule for introducing various products within a product line can provide some strategic advantage. Since competition takes place in specific market segments, a company can gain a temporary advantage by being the first to introduce a product targeted at a newly identified segment.

For high-technology products, the rollout of products in a product-line is typically completed in the first half of the product-line life-cycle. Since life-cycles tend to be short, it is rarely worthwhile to introduce a new product at the end of the life-cycle when a product may have only a one-year or two-year life. The exception to this is a product that is a "mid-life kicker," extending life of the product-line through increased performance.

3. *Provides guidance to the product development teams.* If development teams understand the product-line strategy, the rollout of the entire product line is usually quicker and better. By understanding the targeted market segments for each of the products in the product line, they can design the products to better fit those segments. Without a

product-line strategy, most product developers have a tendency to put everything in the first product, trying to cover all segments but making the product less attractive to any specific segment.

The development team can frequently implement designs that are flexible enough to make subsequent product variations easier to develop. For example, they can make the design more modular, anticipating changes to some modules for future product variations.

4. *Schedules the initiation of product development.* The product-line plan drives the product development schedule by backward scheduling individual products from their planned release date. This is typically an iterative process with the desired schedule matched to available development resources and then modified to meet constraints.

Without a product line plan to schedule development, a company lacks a trigger point to initiate the next product. Typically, it would start thinking about the next product after finishing the current one.

INGREDIENTS OF SUCCESSFUL PRODUCT-LINE STRATEGY

If a company develops a potentially successful product platform, what does it need to do to translate this into a successful product-line strategy? Generally, successful product-line strategy incorporates several essential ingredients, including market segment coverage, focus, time-phased schedule, and coordination.

Market Segment Coverage

Various products within a product line are intended to appeal to different market segments; otherwise, there would be no reason to have more than one product in a product line. The objective of each individual product is to have more appeal for a targeted segment of customers. Collectively, the products within a product line should cover the major segments of the market; the primary objective of product-line strategy is to achieve this coverage.

Dell Computer illustrated this in 1993 when it found itself under pricing pressure as IBM and Compaq retaliated against it with lower prices. Its strategic response borrowed a lesson in marketing from the auto companies, which targeted variations of the same basic chassis at different market segments. After conducting market research, including an analysis of its telephone order database, Dell redesigned its product line.

Dell organized its products around product families by configuring its computers differently. Each product family was aimed at a specific type of customer. Dell believed that it had four customer types, each of which could be considered a segment within the market[2,3]:

- The Dimension family was aimed at customers ("techno-to-go") who wanted a simple, affordable, home computer that was ready to use right out of the box. Maximum value and simplicity were the main focus. Prices ranged from the $1,299 486/25S to the $1,799 486/33.

- The Dimension XPS family included jazzed-up computers with fast graphics, enhanced video, built-in CD-ROM, and audio capabilities. It was targeted at sophisticated users ("techno-wizards") who buy "hot" components from computer magazines. This was a segment targeted successfully by Dell competitor Gateway 2000. This family of products maximized video performance. Configurations were priced from $2,498 for the XPS 450V to $2,999 for the XPS 466V.

- The OptiPlex family was an advanced set of computers aimed at high-end corporate buyers ("techno-criticals") who were interested in advanced features and enhanced productivity. It stressed maximum performance and upgradability. In September 1993, prices ranged from the 433S/L at $1,878 to the 433/MX at $2,548.

- The NetPlex family with built-in networking was aimed at price-sensitive corporate buyers who sought networking capabilities ("techno-teamers"), name brands, and reliability.

Using the same platform, but targeting different segments with each product family, Dell reduced the confusion of product proliferation while broadening its offerings. Sometimes a company neglects certain market segments in its product-line strategy. Until Dell introduced the Dimension XPS product family, it missed the high-performance graphics segment of the market.

The key to avoiding this mistake is an understanding of the market and how it is segmented. Market segments are groupings of customers with similar characteristics who choose a similar product or service. While there are many ways to segment a market, the key is to segment it in a manner that provides competitive advantage. For example, in the previous case, Gateway 2000 identified the segment of sophisticated users and targeted a product at that segment, while Dell initially missed that opportunity. Successful segmentation requires sufficient understanding of the market to identify segments with opportunities and knowledge of how to match product capabilities to each segment of the market.

Without a product-line strategy, individual products will emerge based on other criteria. For example, instead of targeting releases of a new product platform at clearly defined market segments, a company will design the initial product based on features that it believes are currently possible. The next product will be slated to contain additional features that will be possible at that time. These product decisions are made without consideration of the target segments that the product will address. The inevitable consequence is a range of products, none of which match a defined market segment.

Market segmentation is not a static analysis. Segmentation can change rapidly, particularly in high-technology markets. As new segments emerge, the product-line strategy needs to be modified, and new products may be necessary to address these newly emerging market segments. Inflexibility leads to failure when conditions change. Either the company will continue to march down a path that is no longer viable, or the entire plan will be discarded and the company will hop from one product to the next in an effort to "catch up."

This is what happened to a company that dominated its segment of the transaction terminal business. Unwilling to recognize that the market and technology were shifting, this company stuck to its initial product-line plan. The result: overpriced products leading to a slippage to the number three market position.

Variation of products within a product line is limited by the constraints of the product platform. The differentiation of the product platform is usually the primary way that a product appeals to a market segment. For example, a high-performance high-priced platform will appeal to the segment of the market willing to pay for that performance. Variations in performance and price can subdivide the market segment, but the appeal to other segments may be limited.

Fault-tolerant computer manufacturers Stratus and Tandem target products at companies willing to pay for this capability. From a market segment standpoint, these are companies with mission-critical transaction processing requirements, such as banks and airlines, as well as companies with process control requirements, such as utilities. Within this segmentation, Stratus and Tandem can offer products with a range of capacities and interface capabilities that subsegment the market.

Focus

In an effort to cover all market segments, a company may release too many products. Product proliferation is the result of a company's failure to focus on selected segments. It tries to be "all things to all people," and in the process it confuses customers.

Apple Computer suffered from product proliferation in early 1993.[4] It was selling the Macintosh product line using a variety of overlapping product families: Centris, Performa, Quadra, Classic, LC, PowerBook, Duo, and Workgroup. The PowerBook was clearly different from the others, except for the Duo, which was a combination notebook and desktop. At the low-end of the Mac product line were the Classic products, followed by the LC. The Performa products were renamed versions of other products. The Performa 200 was a renamed Classic II; the Performa 400 was a renamed LC II. The Performa 600 was an LC III with a CD-ROM. The only difference in this product line was that it was sold through mass-market retailers with different software and support.

The Centris was the middle of the product line, replacing the IIci and the IIsi. The IIvx remained in the product line as part of the Centris family but was not renamed. The Quadra family was the high-end of the product line. There was little difference between the 800 and the 950. The Quadra 700 was the low-end of the Quadra family and equivalent to some of the Centris products. The Workgroup 60, 80, and 95 models were a Centris 610, Quadra 800, and Quadra 950 with networking software.

Sound confusing? It was. This proliferation of products confused and frustrated many customers. It also increased Apple's inventories. Apple finally got the message and simplified its Macintosh product line around the Quadra for desktops, the PowerBook for notebook computers, and the Workgroup for servers.

Product proliferation can result from being overly customer focused. A manufacturer of equipment for the cable TV industry focused too much on its customers. Since the cable TV business is dominated by large customers, this company began all its development projects at the request of specific customers. When it completed the product, the company found that it had to be modified for other customers. As a result, the company experienced product proliferation.

The point of creating a product-line strategy is to comprehend the market and competition and to make the difficult decisions on which products to develop. In the absence of a product-line strategy, a company tends to become reactive instead of focused.

Time-Phased Schedule

Another essential ingredient of product-line strategy is the timing of individual products. Each potential product in the product line needs to be prioritized and sequenced since all versions cannot be released simultaneously.

For example, Intel released the 25-MHz DX product of its 486 product line first, directly addressing the middle of the market for midrange performance but also covering a little of the higher-range performance segment. The 33-MHz product met the needs the high-performance midrange segment better and helped in the server/multi-user segment. The 50-MHz product eventually provided better coverage of this segment. As part of its product-line strategy, Intel covered the key market segment first with some applicability in other segments.

Predictability of the timing for individual product releases is also a key aspect of timing. If the scheduled product releases cannot be accurately predicted, then the product-line strategy can be unreliable.

For example, one company created an overly optimistic product-line strategy. The initial product was targeted to have a rich feature set; however, the allotted development time was too short to allow all the features to be developed. Instead of prioritizing the features and matching them with required development resources, the initial product was based on whatever features were ready. Because there was not any reason behind the combination of features, the product did not address any specific market segments. The next product release was then rushed to market, and some of its planned features were not ready when product was launched. These leftover features became the next release. As a result, the timing of release did not follow the original product-line strategy, and the products did not match the needs of any market segments.

The product-line plan links to the development plan to match the product release schedule and the resources required. This enables a company to validate the schedule to the rough-cut estimate of required resources and to identify the start dates for all projects.

Coordination

Product-line strategy needs to coordinate similar product lines, particularly when there are multiple product lines from the same or similar platform.

Trying to serve a large broad market with a single platform can be a limiting product strategy. IBM, Apple, and Compaq tried this for awhile in the PC market. Each offered a premium-priced platform, competing on advanced technology and new features. Together these market leaders captured only 30 percent of the world market in 1992; the remainder of the market was divided by numerous companies selling PCs primarily on the basis of low price. Market shares like this are not characteristic of a relatively mature market. It became clear that the market leaders were focusing on a single product line, leaving the bulk of the market to be divided by competitors with a lower-priced product line.

IBM and Compaq saw the light in 1992, and each launched a new low-cost product line: IBM the PS/ValuePoint product line and Compaq the ProLinear product line. Their early success was dramatic, and by the end of 1993 they were on the way to capturing market share in the low-price segment of the PC market. One can only wonder how the PC market would be different if IBM or Compaq had launched a low-price product line three years earlier.

In some cases, it may be desirable to launch more than one product line based on the same or similar platform. Both are aimed at the same market, but they have characteristics that are meant to address different segments. Typically, each product line is distributed through a different channel, sells in a different price range, and carries a different brand name or product designation.

IBM implemented this strategy in its personal computer business, eventually offering four product lines in 1993. It targeted the high-performance non-IBM market segment with its Ambra product line. Although based on a similar product platform with minor variations, it was promoted as a different product line, sold by a separate company. Ambra Computer Corp. was a small (60 employees in August of 1993) "virtual corporation" owned by IBM, which marketed a product line of low-cost personal computers aimed at customers who buy PCs based on price. The strategy of this product line was to attack competitors such as Dell, Zeos, and Gateway 2000 with non-IBM brand-name computers. The Ambra product line was aimed at more sophisticated customers who buy for price through telephone ordering. They do not need technical support through retail stores.

Ambra was IBM's fourth personal computer product line. The IBM brand-name product line, selling the PS/2 and other products, was its traditional product line. PS/2 products carried premium prices and were positioned as premium products. They had a three-year on-site warranty, faster disk drive, better graphics, and higher quality components. In early 1993, there were 36 models in the PS/2 product line. The PS/1 product line contained 21 models and was targeted at the consumer market segment.

The ValuePoint product line consisted of 21 models of low-price computers sold through retail outlets and through IBM PC Direct. By early 1994, IBM concluded that there was little difference between the ValuePoint and PS/2 product lines, and the two were combined.

Using the same platform for multiple product lines is risky because the burden of differentiation between the product lines is placed more on feature differences and brand name rather than the underlying platform. This can be done, but implementation relies on discipline to separate features. Unless this creates a sufficient increase in volume, it simply dilutes resources. In the extreme case, one just cannibalizes the other. Typically, the lower-price product line cannibalizes the more expensive one.

One consumer electronics manufacturer fell into this strategic trap. The company had two product lines: one with premium prices and high margins sold through specialty dealers, and the other with lower prices and lower margins sold through high-volume outlets. Originally, each product line was based on a different platform, but the company slipped into using the same platform, differentiating the two product lines through features. Tempted by opportunities in the high-volume segment, it began to migrate features from the premium-priced product line. This left the brand name as the only differentiating factor between the premium and low-priced product lines, and eventually the entire market shifted to the low-priced products. Specialty dealers stopped selling the product. The resulting profit margins were too low to sustain its business, and the company was forced to downsize.

PRODUCT-LINE STRATEGY CASE STUDY: THE INTEL486 PRODUCT LINE

The best way to illustrate product-line strategy and visualize a product-line plan is through an actual example, and the Intel486 microprocessor provides an excellent one. Intel introduced the Intel486 DX microprocessor in 1989 as the first in a new family of 486 products based on a new platform intended to replace the 386 product line. It featured 1.2 million transistors on a computer chip and had twice the performance of the 386 product line. At the same time, it was 100 percent compatible with the previous generation of software developed for the 386.

Figure 4–1 illustrates the 486 product-line plan. It diagrams the introduction time frame and relative performance of each product. The table at the bottom shows how well the products cover various market segments. Fully shaded boxes indicate complete segment coverage, while the partially shaded boxes indicate partial segment coverage. Superimposed on the product plan is the 486 unit sales, showing the increase in sales as each market segment was better covered.

The 486 was among the most powerful and complex microprocessors developed at that time. It integrated many system-level functions, including a 32-bit integer processor unit with an instruction set and a variety of addressing modes. The 486 DX was available in 25-MHz and 33-MHz versions to serve the high-performance requirements of the midrange computing environment. The 50-MHz version of the 486 DX was introduced in June of 1991 for the large server and high-end workstation segments.

Intel introduced the 486 SX product in April of 1991 for the entry-level business computing segment. It used the same architecture, but was less complex, less powerful, and less expensive than the DX products. Technically, the SX had a lower bus band width (16 MB instead of

FIGURE 4–1

Intel486 Product Line Plan. *Illustrates an example of a product-line plan.*

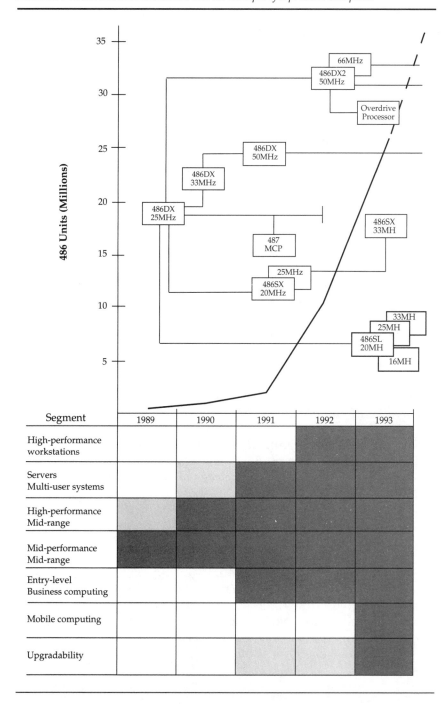

160 MB), had less memory addressability, and did not have an integrated math co-processor. The 486 SX replaced the high-end processor in the 386 product line, the 386 DX. The 25-MHz 486 SX had twice the processing power of the 33-MHz 386 DX.

Intel's strategy was to overlap the two product lines (386 and 486) by providing more power at a higher price with the 486 DX versions. This provided a continuing 386 market for almost two years. Then in 1991, it cannibalized the 386 market with the SX low-cost version of the 486 product line and ceded the 386 market to AMD and other competitors.

Intel also provided two 486 products that upgraded the performance of the SX processors, enabling customers to initially buy a lower-cost PC and then upgrade later on. The first was the 487 Math CoProcessor (MCP), which performed floating point mathematics. The second was the OverDrive Processor, which doubled the 486 SX internal speed using the DX2 "speed doubling" technology.

The Intel486 DX2 incorporated the "speed doubling" feature, which let the microprocessor run at 50-MHz while interfacing with the system at 25-MHz. Computers using this processor could be designed for high performance without the complex issues of high-speed design.

The last set of products in the 486 product line was the Intel486 SL, targeted specifically for the mobile computer segment. The features of this product were designed to reduce the power requirements and manage power at a system level.

Intel completed the rollout of the 486 product line over four years. By the time the rollout was complete, it covered all major segments of the microprocessor market. Intel's sales of 486 microprocessors increased to 27 million units in 1993 and an estimated 40 million units in 1994.

To accomplish this product-line rollout, Intel developed a product-line strategy detailing the products expected. Development of some of these products had to begin even before the initial 486 product was introduced. Fortunately for Intel, it understood the market from its 286 and 386 product-line experience, and could base its 486 product-line strategy on this experience.

The product-line plan in Figure 4–1 is historical, but the same format could be used as a plan for a new product line. It combines three elements. It defines the anticipated time-phased plan for the introduction of products within the product line. This plan is then matched to its coverage of the various market segments. Finally, it shows expected unit sales based on this plan. If additional products and coverage of market segments is important, then this is the best way to develop a sales forecast for a new product line.

LINKING PRODUCT-LINE PLANNING TO PRODUCT DEVELOPMENT

Once a product-line strategy is developed, the resulting product-line plan links to the product development schedule. This schedule shows when development is anticipated to begin for each product contained within the product-line plan.

This is an iterative process. When the development plan for the product line is prepared, it may reveal that there are too many projects scheduled at once or that there are insufficient resources available to complete the work required. The development schedule needs to be balanced to these constraints, which may force a change to the product-line plan. If this change is acceptable, it is made. If it is not acceptable, priorities need to be changed in order to implement the strategy. Unfortunately, many companies do not link the product-line plan to the development plan and do not do the necessary re-prioritization.

Figure 4–2 illustrates a six-year product development schedule for the Intel486 product line, starting in 1988.[5] It shows some interesting characteristics. The 486 DX was already under development at the beginning of 1988. Toward the end of its development, but before testing, two additional projects were scheduled. The first was the development for the SX version of the 486. The second was the faster 33-MHz version of the DX.

The number of projects and resources increased during 1990–1991 as the initial products began to generate revenue. In total, there were 14 product development projects planned, with some taking much more time and resources than others. At the peak of the development effort, there were five projects in process at the same time. By the end of 1991, resource requirements began to decline, and 60 percent fewer were required by the end of 1993 than were necessary at the beginning of 1988. The other resources were assigned to other product line developments, such as the Pentium.

Estimating the approximate schedule of project start dates enables management to schedule the appropriate event for initiating a new project, such as a Phase 0 review under a phase review process. This review would typically trigger the formal decision to start, cancel, refocus, or delay the specific project.

When development capacity and load is balanced, this scheduling approach is similar to establishing a train schedule. A development project will start and end as scheduled. The estimated time between the start date and complete date is based on known development cycle times for various complexity levels of new products. If a project is can-

FIGURE 4-2

Sample Product Development Schedule for the Intel486 Product Line. Illustrates the start date, development time, resource requirements, and completion date for the entire product line.

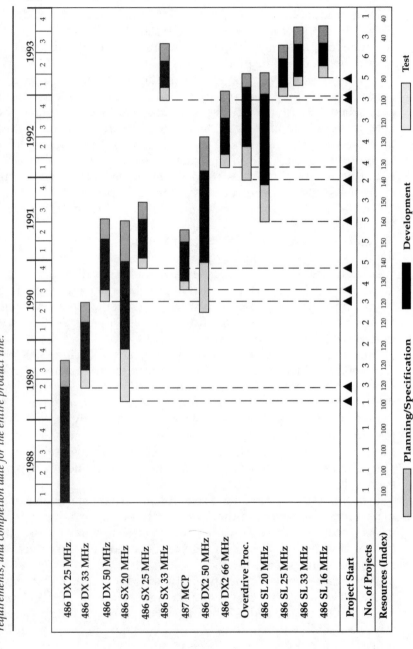

celed at the Phase 0 review, another product opportunity can enter the process to take its slot in the product-line plan. The time horizon of product-line plans is typically two to three times the longest development cycle time. This is long enough to provide visibility into the future and short enough to be realistic. This clearly articulated plan of future programs prevents one of the high-technology industry's cardinal sins: overcommitting scarce development resources.

SUMMARY

While product-line strategy does not have as significant a strategic impact as platform strategy, it is nevertheless critical to the overall success of any product strategy. Product-line strategy is a time-phased conditional plan for the sequence of developing products within a product line. It serves several important purposes. It defines product variations, schedules their release, and guides product development teams.

The primary objective of product-line strategy is to cover the market by penetrating the appropriate market segments. The major ingredients of successful product-line strategy include market segment coverage, focus, time-phased schedule, and coordination.

Product-line strategy results in a product-line plan that defines the sequence of products and the segments they cover. This plan is then used to prepare a development schedule for the product line that shows the project schedule for each product and estimates resource requirements. Product-line strategy, the product-line plan, and related development schedule are illustrated using the Intel486 product line as an example.

NOTES

1. For a discussion of product line mapping, see Steven C. Wheelwright and W. Earl Sasser, Jr. "The New Product Development Map," *Harvard Business Review,* May–June 1989. Also see example of product line mapping in Figure 4–1 in this chapter.

2. Scott McCartney, "Dell Programs New Products, Sales Strategy," *The Wall Street Journal,* August 2, 1993.

3. Pricing and other information provided by Dell in September 1993.

4. Phillip Robinson, "Centris, Performa, Quadra: All Apple Macs, Despite the Confusion," *Boston Globe,* April 20, 1993.

5. The schedule and implied cycle times in this schedule are illustrative only, and are not based on actual Intel schedules. The estimates and the sequencing are considered realistic, based on experience.

Chapter Five

Product Differentiation Strategy

R apidly advancing technology provides a rich set of opportunities for new products, product improvements, and innovative new product platforms. Each year, new products are increasingly faster, smaller, stronger, easier to use, and more effective. Competitive success of high-technology products, however, rests not only on their being improved, but on their being better than competitive products.

Most companies expect their new products to be better than those of their competitors (although some expect to get away with "good enough"). However, they may fail to appreciate the underlying strategy of what they are doing. They may not understand the concept of a product strategy based on differentiation; instead, they focus on the tactics of trying to design a better product. Then they are caught off guard when competitive products are more successful.

Products become better through competitive strategy. There are two primary types of competitive strategy: product differentiation strategy and price-based strategy.[1] Of these two, product differentiation strategy provides the source of competitive advantage for most high-technology products.

Differentiation is a way of distinguishing a product's value from competing products. It means more than being different. The Edsel automobile was different; however, the combination of features was not valued by the customer, and the car was one of the biggest failures in the history of the auto market. Differentiation is a strategic approach to advantageously positioning products as customers decide which product to choose. When successfully differentiated, a product can command a premium price because it provides higher added value.

Differentiation is a relative comparison. A product is differentiated only because it offers something that is not available in competitive products. Absent any competition—as is the case when a company creates a new market—differentiation can only be considered against imaginary competition. This is where second or subsequent companies to market may have an advantage. They can better position their products through differentiation against competitive products already in the market.

BASIC CONCEPTS OF DIFFERENTIATION

Successfully applying a differentiation strategy requires an understanding of the basic concepts of differentiation. There are four basic concepts underlying product differentiation strategy:

- Differentiation determines the relative position of competitive products and the overall level of differentiation in a market.
- Differentiation segments the market.
- Differentiation evolves throughout a market's life-cycle.
- Differentiation should be managed as vectors, not individual points.

Differentiation Positions a Product in the Market

Product differentiation combined with price defines the relative positioning of competitors in a marketplace. This concept is depicted in Figure 5–1, which illustrates a market with five competitors. Products A and B are the market leaders, but they are pursuing very different strategies. Product A is highly differentiated and sold at a premium price. It is much more successful than products C, D, and E because it offers much more for the same approximate price.

Product B is the price leader in the market. It is less differentiated than products C, D, and E, but successful because it is sold at a much lower price. Competition between products A and B is determined by customer preference. Some customers are willing to spend more for the advantages that Product A offers; others are not and will choose Product B. Products C, D, and E are in less-competitive positions in the market. Their success is based on unique appeal to certain segments or on imperfections in the market, and they need to reduce their price or increase differentiation to be more competitive.

An analysis like this provides a two-dimensional snapshot of a market, showing the relative positioning of competitors. Each product is more or less differentiated than others and can command a relative price reflecting the value of this differentiation. If the differentiation of a product is not valued by the market, then the price is usually reduced, or the product will die.

The goal of a product differentiation strategy is to continually move up or toward the upper right of this chart while capturing the largest market share. With most companies preferring to compete on this

FIGURE 5–1

Relative Differentiation. Competitive products are positioned by relative value of differentiation and relative price. Size represents market share. Differentiation strategy moves a product up in relative position.

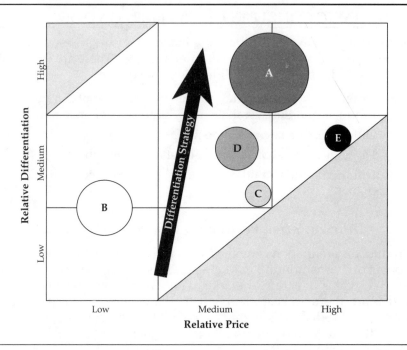

basis, average product requirements increase over time, and a company not continuously moving will drift to the bottom.

This snapshot analysis can also show whether the market is relatively differentiated or undifferentiated. In markets that are relatively undifferentiated, products are generally clustered together. Undifferentiated markets are commodity markets, and price becomes the primary basis of competition. Progressive snapshots of a market over time would show its evolution.

Differentiation Segments the Market

The success of differentiation varies by market segment as each segment values a particular vector of differentiation based on its own unique preferences. Market segmentation has two related, but different meanings. A population or group can be segmented by various characteristics. Examples are companies under $1 million, college-

FIGURE 5–2

Differentiation by Segment. Product A is much more differentiated in Segment 1, while Product E is much more differentiated in Segment 2.

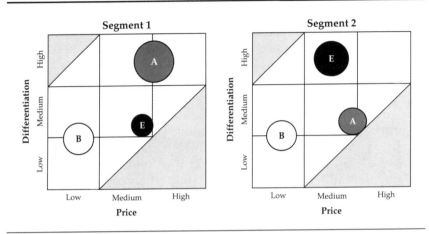

educated workers, businesses by industry type, people by age group, and so on. This is the traditional definition of market segmentation, but it only provides demographic information about the market. It does not establish the basis for competitive advantage.

The other meaning of market segmentation is based on the differentiation of competitive products. The market is segmented by various vectors of differentiation. Customers who prefer one vector of differentiation will choose products differentiated along that vector. In this view, the market is segmented not according to characteristics of the customers, but according to the vectors of differentiation selected by competitors.

In Figure 5–2, two different market segments are compared. Note that the price positioning of each product does not change, but the relative value of differentiation does change. The differentiation of product A is more valued in Segment 1, while the differentiation of E is more valued in Segment 2. Product B competes on price and does not have any significant differentiation.

Relating the two types of segmentation enables a company to effectively target prospective customers. This is crucial, since without this relationship a company cannot focus its marketing and sales efforts.

Differentiation can also be so significant that it creates new markets. That was the case with fault-tolerant computers. What began as a vector of differentiation grew to be an entirely new market with its own group of competitors.

Differentiation Evolves Throughout a Market's Life-Cycle

As a market evolves, so does the relative differentiation in that market. Understanding and predicting these evolutionary stages of differentiation is essential to competitive strategy.

Development.   In the initial stage of a new market, customers and competitors do not know which characteristics of a product are important differentiators. Initially, there may be a wide variety of different attributes perceived by companies entering the market as important, but customer acceptance of these varies. As customers begin to express their preferences for differentiation, they determine winners and losers. Products that win in this initial stage can begin to solidify their differentiation vectors, while others copy these attributes preferred by the market.

In the early days of the personal computer market, for example, nobody really understood what customers would value or establish as a standard. There were a wide range of operating systems, different microprocessors, various types of printers, bundled applications software, multiple configurations, and a variety of expansion capabilities. The market was confused.

The market for the next-generation product to replace audio-cassettes was also confused. Philips was pushing the digital compact cassette technology, which featured CD-quality sound and the ability to play standard audio cassettes. Sony was offering the mini-disk technology, which was the first recordable 2.5 inch optical disk for consumers. Each had varying support from record producers, and neither had emerged as the new standard by 1993. By the middle of 1993, Philips had sold fewer than 20,000 units in the United States, and Sony had only sold 40,000 units.[2] The market was confused by the differentiation and had not yet chosen what it preferred.

Early-stage markets are usually confused. Nobody is sure what is really important. Markets generally do not begin to grow until this confusion starts to diminish.

Growth.   In this stage, products become more clearly differentiated. Some are better for one use, while others are better for another use. Customers classify products into various categories, and market share starts to correlate to the relative importance of the vectors of differentiation.

When a particular vector of differentiation is less attractive to customers, the product is typically discounted or discontinued. Usually, a market shakeout begins in this stage. In some markets, a competitor can begin to take a commanding lead with a vector of differentiation that is not easily copied by others. In other markets, a successful vector of differentiation is more easily copied, and everyone incorporates the product attributes that customers prefer. As a result, minimum product requirements increase.

Maturity. As a market matures, it becomes relatively undifferentiated. Most products tend to be similar, and price becomes the primary basis for competition.

Electronic calculators, personal computers, printers, VCRs, compact disk players, and video cameras all matured into this stage. Application software, computer workstations, computer networks, high-definition television, and video-conferencing equipment will eventually move into this stage. Anticipating the evolution into this stage is critical to product strategy. In some cases, product strategy can even forestall maturity or initiate re-differentiation of the market.

Re-differentiated market. Sometimes a market can be re-differentiated after it reaches maturity by a company establishing new differentiation vectors that are important to customers. This shifts the basis of competition away from price and back to differentiation.

Even a very mature market can be re-differentiated by applying new technology. Take the $7 billion market for sports shoes and sneakers as an example. Through major investments in new technology, several competitors have been able to differentiate their products. Reebok introduced the Pump, Nike introduced Air, ASIC introduced gel, LA Gear introduced fiber-optic materials.

These companaies re-differentiated a mature market through new technologies, and in the process they were able to raise the price of their sneakers from $15 a pair to more than $100. They succeeded in growing the market (in revenue, if not units) and capturing more market share, while the share of market for companies without any unique differentiation declined significantly.

Differentiation Should be Managed as Vectors, Not Individual Points

Differentiation along a vector is much better than individual points of differentiation. An individual point implies that it alone is sufficient differentiation and that competitors will not catch up. There is either no need or no opportunity to go further with the same type of differentiation. The next step in differentiating a product can be entirely unrelated.

A vector, on the other hand, provides a direction for continuous differentiation in a specific direction. It says, "This is the direction that we are taking in differentiating our products, and we are going to stay ahead of competitors by doing it better and better." A vector of differentiation is not stagnant; it is a direction for continuous improvement.

Motorola, for example, differentiated its PowerPC from Intel's microprocessor based on performance. This was not simply leapfrogging performance; it was a sustainable vector of differentiation. The Intel X86/Pentium architecture was 15 years old, while the PowerPC architecture was just starting along its vector.

In another example, Network Systems Corporation, a data communications equipment producer, differentiated its products along the vector of "We can connect any computer to anything." It developed and applied excellent skills in high-performance internetworking as it continually moved along this vector.

Products can be differentiated in multiple directions, and vectors establish the direction for differentiation. Products differentiated by a single point have nowhere to go next. Products differentiated by multiple points in many directions generally do not get as far as those that go in a well-determined direction.

Figure 5–3 illustrates progressive improvement of a product along a particular vector of differentiation. Each new version (V1, V2, etc.) increases the differentiation and may increase the price that the product can command. The goal is continuous improvement along a particular vector. In reality, competition may limit the relative improvement, and in some cases progress along a vector may be necessary for the relative position to remain constant.

When competitive products in a market are differentiated along alternative vectors, customers select the vector they value most. Some products may "own" a particular vector of differentiation. They continue to make improvements along the vector, and no one can catch them. For example, the computer workstation market became very competitive, but one company was able to maintain consistently higher margins by "owning" a key differentiation vector. Silicon Graphics was the clear leader in workstations customized for graphics manipulation. This was a rapidly growing market segment with users ranging from three-dimensional scientific modeling to the lifelike animation used in Hollywood motion pictures. Silicon Graphics tailored its workstations' hardware and software to serve this market segment and, as a result, could not be matched by the producers of general purpose workstations.

In some cases, multiple competitive products may be differentiated along the same vector. Usually, the one that does it best will win.

FIGURE 5–3

Vector of Differentiation. Shows continuous improvement of a product with different versions (V1, V2, V3, V4) along a particular vector.

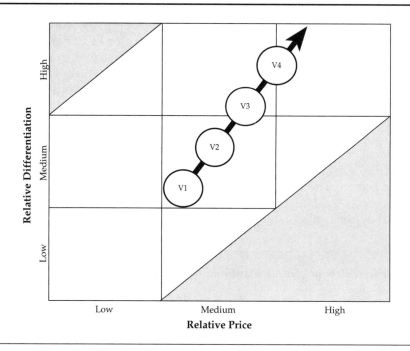

The strength of vectors also varies. Vectors have both angle and length. Vectors with a greater angle have higher relative differentiation. Longer vectors mean that continuing improvements can be made along the same vector for a reasonably long time.

DIFFERENTIATION STRATEGIES

High-technology products can be differentiated along many types of vectors, each of which represents a strategy for differentiating products. The experiences of high-technology companies lead to generic differentiation strategies that can serve as models.

Strategy: Differentiate products using unique features.

Many high-technology companies are drawn to differentiation based on product features, since advances in technology provide many opportunities for new and interesting features. This is generally the easiest differentiation to select but one of the most difficult to define as a continuing vector.

Differentiation can sometimes be achieved on the strength of a single feature. Sharp, for example, was able to differentiate itself in the very competitive camcorder market by replacing the conventional viewfinder on its ViewCam with a four-inch color LCD panel. Those taking movies could watch what they were filming in color, as if it was on a small TV. The competitive advantage of this feature was so successful that in Japan, Sharp increased its market share from 3 percent to 20 percent.[3]

Feature differentiation is most successful if the unique features can be grouped around a common theme or vector. NEC's UltraLite Versa personal computer grouped a number of related features under the vector of versatility. The monochrome screen could be replaced with a color screen. The screen could be flipped around to show presentations, or it could be used as a pen-based tablet. There are also a number of options, all of which relate to versatility.

Generic Product Differentiation Strategies

- Differentiate products using unique features.
- Differentiate products based on increased customer benefits.
- Differentiate products based on improved productivity.
- Differentiate products based on protecting the customer's investment.
- Differentiate products by lowering the cost of product failure.
- Differentiate products with high performance.
- Differentiate products based on unique fundamental capabilities.
- Differentiate products through design.
- Differentiate products as total solutions.
- Differentiate products based on total cost of ownership to the customer.
- Differentiate products based on brand name or service.

A vector of related features can be used to achieve various types of differentiation. In 1972, for example, Hewlett-Packard (HP) introduced one of its most successful products ever—the HP-35 hand-held scientific calculator—using new features as its differentiation. The HP-35 had several unique but related features: 17 arithmetic, trigonometric, and logarithmic functions; the capability for data storage; and 10-digit accuracy. These features significantly differentiated it from other calculators, enabling HP to target engineers as a very specific market segment. At the start of development, HP estimated sales of 10,000 units in the first year. It sold over 100,000.[4]

Eventually, competition caught up with HP's vector of differentiation. Today there are many calculators with these features, all at 10 percent of the original price of the HP-35.

Microsoft Word for Windows 6.0 provides another example of a vector of differentiation that groups related features. In this case, the features are grouped around the vector of improving the process of writing. They include automatically correcting misspelled words as they are typed, automatically reformatting documents to make them look better, listing most commonly used fonts at the top of the font menu, enabling a user to "drag" text from one document to another, and permitting a user to undo the past 100 changes.

Feature differentiation can also be used to address a specific segment of the market. Lotus Development released a new product called Improv in February of 1993 that was targeted at the so-called "power users" of spreadsheet software. It was differentiated from the Lotus 1-2-3 product by its flexibility and use of plain English commands instead of variables in formulas. For example, a cell could be defined as "Sales-1993" instead of "C12." As part of its product-line strategy, Lotus chose to introduce Improv as a totally new product rather than as an upgrade or new version of 1-2-3. The strategy was aimed at increasing revenue by targeting the product at a different segment of the market.

The Hewlett-Packard PC also introduced a feature that attracted the interest of a particular segment of the market. Its "coffee break" button enabled the user to clear the screen without turning off the computer. The company believed that this feature alone was responsible for the sale of 75,000 units to bankers, insurance companies, and financial concerns.[5]

Although attractive, differentiation based on features can be a limited strategy. As in the case of the HP-35 and the Sharp ViewCam, competition can copy features, neutralizing any competitive advantage. Eventually, the impact of more and more features diminishes, as customers have enough. Japanese consumer electronic companies saw this with VCRs as they struggled to find new features with enough value to maintain prices. When the feature war ends, the baseline product incorporates all important features, and there is little basis for any differentiation.

Strategy: Differentiate products based on increased customer benefits.

All differentiation should increase the benefit to the customer in some way; however, when a product is differentiated in a way that directly benefits customers, they will prefer it even at a significantly higher price. The challenge of differentiation based on unique benefits goes beyond achieving the benefits. It requires clearly quantifying and communicating them. For example, in the medical device and pharmaceutical industries, health care reform sharply focused buying behavior on "measurable patient outcomes," rather than simply the commonly perceived goal of cost reduction. In these industries, the story related below is becoming commonplace.

In 1992, Genentech Inc., one of the world's first biotechnology companies, tried to differentiate its blood-clot buster, TPA (sold as Activase), which was priced at $2,200 per dose, from a competitive product, streptokinase, which was priced at $200 per dose. Of the 900,000 people who suffer heart attacks in the United States each year, only about 20 percent received thrombolytic drugs like these, and TPA was used in only half of those cases. Genentech had a significant opportunity to increase both its share of the market and overall use, but only if it could clearly differentiate the benefits of TPA.

In order to statistically prove the performance difference, Genentech funded a $55 million 41,000 patient study by the Cleveland Clinic. Genentech's objective in this study was to show that heart attack victims' survival rates were higher with TPA, which would induce cardiologists to administer TPA despite the higher costs.[6]

The study results showed that TPA compared to streptokinase saved one additional life in every 100—a death rate one month after heart attack of 6.3 percent compared to 7.3 percent. Genentech's differentiation was clearly stated by G. Kirk Raab, its president, "If everyone used TPA, we could save six lives a day in the United States, or 2,000 people per year. It used to be that doctors had to find a reason to use TPA; now they're going to have to find a reason not to use TPA."[7]

The competitive response claimed that other studies did not show any significant difference. Genentech obviously anticipated this, which is why it invested $55 million and studied 41,000 patients.

Cost benefit is a critical metric in judging the value of differentiation. In this case, the benefit is one life per 100, and the cost is an additional $2,000 per treatment. Or put another way, an additional $200,000 saves one life.

Genentech could have instead chosen a strategy of lowering the price of TPA to achieve proximity to streptokinase. In 1992, Genentech sold approximately $180 million of TPA. Cutting the price in half would have cost it $90 million at the same volume. It would need to sell at least twice as much to offset this price cut, while still having a significantly higher price of $1,100 compared to $200 per dose for competitive products. Even though lowering the price to meet competition is a normal tactical response, Genentech considered alternative strategies before acting. If it met the $200 per dose price, it would need to sell at least ten times as many doses of TPA to break even—more than the total size of the market.

With the strategy it chose, even a slight increase in TPA market share would more than pay for $55 million invested in proving this differentiation, and a significant increase was possible given the market characteristics. This strategy was sound for Genentech given its position in the market. The major risk was that after $55 million, the study could have showed no significant performance difference. That could have been the end of TPA, at least $2,200 per dose TPA.

Within three months, the market share of TPA increased from 50 percent to 66 percent. Streptokinase dropped from 50 percent to 33 percent.

Strategy: Differentiate products based on improved productivity.

Increased productivity is frequently claimed as a benefit of differentiation. The customer can get more done with this product than with other competitive products. In high-technology products, differentiation based on increased productivity can be achieved in many ways.

For example, the Macintosh user-friendly interface enabled people to learn how to use the computer more quickly, leading to less frustration. This difference translated into more productivity, which is usually why the customer purchases a computer in the first place. Although user-friendly advantages are difficult to quantify, they do provide an understandable difference. Apple promoted this advantage in its commercials, which compared frustrated business people trying to use a competitive product (the IBM PC with the DOS operating system) to someone easily using a Macintosh.

Increased productivity was the benefit of Lotus 1-2-3 Release 4's workgroup capability vector of differentiation. It allowed multiple users to work together on common spreadsheets, significantly increasing productivity. A workgroup could distribute and manage 1-2-3 data using Lotus Notes. This was a powerful vector for Lotus because it offered continued differentiation of similar features along the vector, and it used Lotus' proprietary Notes technology.

Strategy: Differentiate products based on protecting the customer's investment.

Since advances in technology create change, a product can claim a competitive advantage by differentiating itself to protect a customer's existing investment. This avoids or reduces the loss incurred by upgrading to an improved product.

This was the primary differentiation advantage of the extremely successful IBM System/360 product line in the 1970s. It provided a compatible family of computers, enabling customers to upgrade to more powerful computer hardware without losing their investment in software or peripherals.

Digital Equipment's "one company, one architecture" strategy in the 1980s successfully differentiated the VAX computer family from other competitors by providing a range of compatible products. Companies that wanted a common set of products using the same operating system chose Digital VAX computers over IBM and others. To these companies, the savings in software, development, and operating costs outweighed any other factor.

Strategy: Differentiate products by lowering the cost of product failure.

The cost of a product's failure can be significant to some users. The direct cost of repair or maintenance is obvious. This drove the differentiation advantage for Japanese cars in the 1980s. With some products, there is also a significant indirect cost of product failure when the product is not available because of repair or maintenance. Computer systems are the obvious example.

When Bill Foster founded Stratus computer in the early 1980s, he intended to build a computer company based entirely on a strategy of product differentiation. This differentiation, or as Bill Foster likes to call it, the "Stratus Difference," is continuous availability. He believed that it would "retain the Stratus Difference by concentrating on hardware and software designs that achieve continuous availability." This differentiation enabled Stratus to grow to almost $500 million in 1992 and, more importantly, because of this difference Stratus continued to increase profitability during 1990–1992, while most other computer companies were losing money.

The value to customers of this differentiation is measured by avoiding the cost of system downtime. Stratus estimated the cost of downtime as follows.[8]

- The average direct revenue loss is $78,000 per hour.
- The loss per incident, including revenue and productivity losses, is $330,000.
- Some companies lose $500,000 per hour of downtime.

Because of these savings, Stratus computers could be priced at a premium compared to non-fault-tolerant computers.

Strategy: Differentiate products with high performance.

Performance advantages are also a popular vector for differentiating high-technology products, since advances in technology usually improve performance. Performance differentiation can be achieved in many dimensions: speed, power, and capacity, as well as others.

Digital Equipment used performance as the vector of differentiation in its Alpha AXP Workstations (DEC 3000 product line), which incorporated its new Alpha microprocessor. As Figure 5–4 shows, Digital positioned its DEC 3000 workstations as the best in price/performance (using a computational performance measure called Spec92), comparing performance to competitive products. Digital claimed price/performance advantage for the DEC 3000 at all major price points, proving the differentiation of the AXP platform, not just a single model in the product line. Digital's comparison showed how competitors Sun, HP, and IBM all clustered together at a lower price/performance level.

Performance differentiation can also be achieved on other factors. For example, Hewlett-Packard used battery life and size to effectively differentiate its OmniBook computer. The OmniBook is a DOS/Windows-compatible notebook computer weighing less than three pounds. Most importantly, it can run for up to six hours on four ordinary AA alkaline batteries—far longer on much less power than other notebook computers. This clearly differentiated the OmniBook in an increasingly crowded market. New technology was the key to this differentiation. The OmniBook used "flash cards" (technically called PCMCIA cards) instead of disk drives. These are semiconductor chips sealed in a card to store data, saving space and power over normal disk drives with spinning magnetic platters and moving read/write heads. The OmniBook had four slots for such cards, one for Microsoft Windows and DOS operating systems. Other applications are built in or added through additional cards.

FIGURE 5–4

Performance Differentiation for Digital's AXP Workstations. Shows the AXP (DEC 3000) performance differentiation. (Source: Digital Equipment, Computerworld, June 28, 1993, pp. 82–83.)

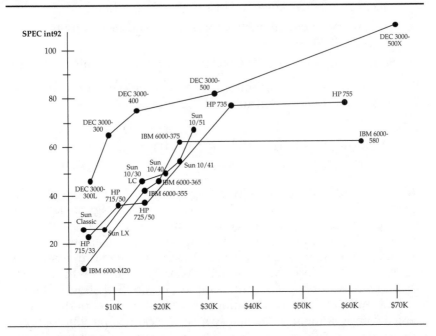

By using this design approach, HP was able to differentiate the OmniBook without sacrificing other characteristics, such as the keyboard and screen, which it believed were critical to users. By using new technology to differentiate the OmniBook, HP achieved an advantage over competitors that did not yet have a core competency in that technology.

Performance can also be used to position a product into a new segment in the market. This is what Convex Computer did in 1984 when it positioned its products between Cray and Digital Computer based on performance. It created the "minisupercomputer" market by offering a product with a price/performance ratio in between Cray's $5 million to $15 million supercomputers and Digital's $300,000 to $750,000 minicomputers.[9]

Strategy: Differentiate products based on unique fundamental capabilities.

Differentiation based on unique fundamental capabilities can be one of the most successful vectors of differentiation. It can usually be continuously improved, and sometimes it can be sustained for a very long time.

Polaroid cameras are clearly differentiated based on a unique fundamental capability: They instantly develop pictures within the camera itself. This is a unique capability that no other camera can match. It is a capability that is protected by patents that are vigorously defended by Polaroid.

While other camera manufacturers were fighting fiercely for survival, Polaroid was able to stand on the sidelines and watch the battle, protected by its unique differentiation. In high-technology markets, however, even a unique capability can be attacked. The spread of one-hour film developing diminished the value of Polaroid's instant cameras and forced it to lower prices. Video cameras then provided another competitive alternative.

Strategy: Differentiate products through design.

Even high-technology products can be differentiated successfully using product design. This is especially appropriate to high-technology products aimed at new users where the design differentiation promotes ease of use.

The Apple Macintosh PowerBook was differentiated from other notebook computers because of its unique design features as well as the Macintosh user-interface. The first Macintosh portable was a failure. It weighed 17 pounds and underperformed most other portables on the market. While different, the basis of differentiation was not advantageous, and even the Macintosh user-interface could not save it. Potential customers either stayed with Macintosh desktops or went with IBM-compatible portables.

Determined to learn from its mistakes, Apple wanted its next try, the PowerBook, to have advantageous differentiation as a notebook computer, not only as a smaller Macintosh. The entire Power-Book development team studied how potential customers used notebook computers. They discovered that people did not really want small computers; they wanted mobile computers. Size was just one aspect.[10]

The PowerBook was designed with two unique advantages: the TrackBall pointer and the palm rest in the front of the keyboard. These made the PowerBook more comfortable to use and therefore more user-friendly, supporting the overall ease-of-use differentiation vector for the Macintosh family of computers. In the first year, Apple sold more than $1 billion worth of PowerBooks (440,000).

However, by the second year, competition began to catch Apple on this vector of differentiation. Sales growth began to slow to an estimated 580,000 PowerBooks in 1993.[11] Apple did not continue introducing improvements along this vector until 1994 when it introduced a new version of the PowerBook.

Strategy: Differentiate products as total solutions.

Total solutions offer customers significant savings in the costs of using products. Total-solution differentiation is achieved in electronic systems by bundling software and hardware or by offering a range of compatible products.

IBM's AS/400 generated an estimated $14 billion revenue in 1991. If it were an independent company, the AS/400 division would have been the world's second-largest computer company. While the AS/400 offered significant price-performance advantages, its most significant differentiation was that it provided customers a total solution, eliminating the need for systems integration. The AS/400 included virtually everything that was needed: hardware, operating system, database software, and support. This made it not only cheaper for customers to use, but also easier for independent software vendors to develop application products.

"Open systems" can also provide total systems differentiation, but in a very different way. Sun Microsystems built its success on the differentiation provided by open systems. As a result, the company grew from start-up to more than $3.5 billion in 11 years. Ironically, a company may stumble into a successful product differentiation strategy based on other factors. In Sun's case, lack of sufficient financial resources was much more of a factor than strategy in its decision to publish the specifications for its SPARC microprocessors architecture in 1986.[12]

Integration is a frequent theme of a total solution vector of differentiation. Microsoft used integration to deliver a total solution when it launched Microsoft Office 4.0, a bundled and integrated set of application software products (spreadsheet, word processor, presentation maker, and database). This example also illustrates how a vector of differentiation evolves.

Microsoft's first step toward a total integrated solution was offering related applications that had the same type of interface (touch and feel), reducing user learning time. The next step was bundling these together at a more affordable price. Substantial integration came next. Microsoft Office 4.0 provided a common integration framework called Object Linking and Embedding (OLE). This gave Microsoft a significant lead over competitors that were still cobbling together applications with different software frameworks. Microsoft's framework enabled users to take a document-centric view of their work, erasing boundaries among applications. This was a fresh vector that Microsoft could use to maintain its lead over competition by continued enhancements.

Strategy: Differentiate products based on total cost of ownership to the customer.

The selling price of the product is only one aspect of the total cost to the customer. Over the ownership life-cycle, costs such as routine maintenance, service and repair, lost revenue due to downtime, cost of consumables and residual value can amount to significantly more than the initial purchase price, especially for high-value, relatively long-lived products.

NCR, with its range of highly reliable and easily serviceable automated teller machines (ATMs), prepared tables showing competitive machines. The tables took into account all cost factors and demonstrated the savings that would result over the life of the product.

This strategy relies on relatively sophisticated customers who are not easily seduced by a lower list price. It is particularly effective in the high-value capital purchase markets where products are expected to have a long life.

Strategy: Differentiate products based on brand name or service.

Coca-Cola can differentiate itself on brand name. L. L. Bean can differentiate itself on service. Over the long term, high-technology products must be differentiated on product characteristics, not just on brand name or service. Inadequate products from brand name companies have traditionally failed.

A company can delude itself into believing that differentiation based on reputation and service is sufficient. Often, this is a convenient differentiation of last resort but should be challenged and recognized as a last resort. The following case illustrates how companies come to rely on this type of differentiation.

Senior management asked the product development team leader how the product he proposed would differentiate itself in the market. The product was a next-generation datacommunications switch with features different from the company's existing products. Compared to competitive products recently introduced, it was competitive, but not unique.

The team leader went through the comparison of the new product to others on the market and showed that it was competitive, having all the same capabilities as those products.

"But how is this product different?" he was asked again.

After thinking for a moment he responded, "Our reputation for service and support is highly respected by our customers."

"Some of the new competitors in the market are highly respected multibillion dollar companies," one of the executives pointed out.

"But they are new to the market," the team leader responded.

Senior management bought this argument as sufficient differentiation, and the company invested $20 million to develop the product. It was unsuccessful in the market.

Service and support can be supporting vectors of differentiation. IBM used a three-year on-site warranty to differentiate its PS/2 product line from its ValuePoint product line. The increased warranty combined with other differences such as a faster hard drive, better graphics, and higher quality components presented a premium image. However, the purpose of this differentiation was mostly to distinguish the two product lines, not to provide the sole competitive differentiation.

RISKS OF A DIFFERENTIATION STRATEGY

Like other strategies, differentiation strategies contain risks. Companies frequently encounter these risks by chance, even though they are able to anticipate them.

Insufficient Proximity to Price

A differentiated product must maintain price proximity to products without that differentiation. This means that a customer faced with two alternatives will pay $X more for the product with the differentiation advantage. At much more than $X, the customer would decide to purchase the lower-price product and forego the advantages offered by the differentiation. The value of X varies among customers, but these values tend to be distributed so as to make rough approximations possible. A couple of examples illustrate this.

In the first few years after it released its personal computer, IBM was able to differentiate its computer against other IBM compatibles by the extent of compatibility with application software and peripherals. Only IBM's PCs were truly compatible; others were mostly compatible. However, this difference was significant to customers who found that a particular software package or printer would not work with the IBM compatible. Customers were willing to pay $1,000 to $2,000 more for the assurance that the computer they bought would work with all IBM PC software and peripherals. IBM could charge this premium for its PCs and still maintain sufficient proximity to IBM compatibles. As the IBM compatibles became truly compatible, the value of this differentiation changed, and IBM lost price proximity. Lower-priced compatible manufacturers captured the major share of the PC market.

IBM misinterpreted its initial success in the market. It thought that its differentiation advantage was based on reputation and service. Over time, the IBM name alone was not a significant differentiator, and service became less of a differentiator. One PC customer put it this way, "I can buy three compatible PCs for the price of two IBM PCs, so service is not important."

Industry standardization and common components eliminated most vectors of differentiation, turning the PC market abruptly into a commodity business, with price being the primary competitive factor. In a highly differentiated market, price proximity can be maintained even with a significant price difference. When the value of differentiation is virtually eliminated, it becomes a commodity market.

The market places a value on any new vector of differentiation. Price proximity is equal to that value. If the price difference is higher, the product will not attract as many customers. Sega of America introduced the Sega Genesis 16-bit video game player in 1989 to compete with Nintendo, which had almost 90 percent of the market. Genesis was more advanced than Nintendo's 8-bit game player, but at twice the price ($199 versus $100), it was not very successful. The price differential was greater than the value placed on it by the market. It did not have price proximity.

In 1990, Sega reduced the price of Genesis by 25 percent to $149 and bundled in one of its most popular games. This brought its price within proximity, and its vector of differentiation was a success. Sega's market share skyrocketed to almost 50 percent in 1993 from 7 percent in 1990, while Nintendo's dropped from almost 90 percent to 50 percent. Sega's U.S. sales increased from $80 million to more than $1 billion.[13]

Misunderstanding What the Customer Prefers

Successful differentiation requires advantages that customers value. Misjudge what the customer values, and the resulting product will most likely fail.

For example, the IBM PCjr was very different from the IBM PC and other personal computers. It had scaled-down characteristics that IBM thought were important to the targeted home-computer market. These included smaller keys, infrared connection of the keyboard to computer, limited operating system, and so on.

IBM found out the hard way that this differentiation was not of much value to targeted customers. The product was a monumental failure despite tens of millions of dollars spent on advertising and promotion. The features may have been different. They may have even been features that some customers liked, but they were not features that most customers preferred.

A misunderstanding of what customers prefer leads to a smaller market share since there are few customers attracted to this vector of differentiation.

Too High a Cost for Differentiation

Differentiation can be costly. Each additional capability or feature can add to the cost of the product. Differentiation can go beyond the point of diminishing returns, and eventually the cost of differentiation exceeds its value.

The Apple Lisa computer suffered this fate. It introduced some new and valuable features, namely the user-friendly interface that has been so successful in the Macintosh products. However, at a list price of $10,000 (down from the $13,500 initially considered), it was priced beyond its value. The Lisa example also provides an additional lesson in the cost of differentiation for high-technology products. As a technology evolves, its cost decreases. Technology that was too expensive in the Lisa was cost effective in the Macintosh. In between, there was a decline in the cost of the technology—memory chips, processors, and disk drives—needed to implement that vector of differentiation.

A company making electronic instruments also fell into this trap. It developed a new product based on customer input that incorporated every feature that its customers said they would like to have. The company thought that it developed the perfect product; its new instrument did everything that any competitive product did, all at once, plus more. It totaled the cost for making the instrument, added a 50 percent gross margin, and set the selling price. However, in the end, few customers were willing to pay that much for this perfect product. Each preferred to buy instruments that had the feature set that they preferred and did not want to spend more for the additional features that were of little importance to them.

Not all differentiation is costly. Inexpensive differentiation can provide an exciting product strategy. For example, Whistler Electronics introduced a clear differentiator into its product at almost no cost. The company made radar detectors for automobiles, which at the time was a very competitive market. In order to differentiate itself from competitors, Whistler developed "pulse protection" that immediately signaled the driver that police radar ahead was using pulse detection (radar that is shot from a hand gun in pulses instead of operating continuously). It implemented this feature entirely in the software of the product, requiring no additional cost except for a label put on the box promoting "pulse protection." Whistler was able to price these products at a premium and take away significant market share from competitors.

The cost of differentiation varies by company. The economies of scale, shared costs, and technology can all be different. The same differentiation vector can be more expensive to one competitor than to another. This can make a vector of differentiation successful for one competitor and too costly for another.

Too Much Differentiation

Some companies incorrectly think that a differentiation strategy means adding more and more features. Typical of this is the "checklist syndrome" where product designers believe they need to add every feature included on competitive products. They visualize customers as using a checklist to tick off features, making purchase decisions by adding up the number of features included. So they design the product to include everything.

In reality, most customers do not make decisions this way (although publications use this approach to rate competitive products). Customers decide based on the features that are most important to them. The results of too much differentiation is a price that is too high (as was seen in the electronic instrument example), customers that are confused, and lack of distinction in the market.

For example, advances in electronics and software made VCRs a formidable challenge to the average person. At this point simplification became a differentiator. Some manufacturers brought out de-featured machines that had remote control pads with only eight or so buttons. These machines could tune themselves to the local TV stations, thus eliminating the daunting setup requirement. This is an example of technology going beyond the point of value to the customer, leaving the market open to re-segmentation.

Market Subsegments

In some cases, differentiation can create a market segment that is large enough to become a significant market of its own. A new vector of differentiation can then subsegment this market.

Tandem and Stratus differentiated their products along the vector of fault tolerance, creating a large, successful market segment. However, as standard operating systems such as UNIX became an important vector of differentiation in the general computer industry, they also became more important in that market segment. New competitors as well as Tandem and Stratus began to subdifferentiate the fault-tolerant market segment by introducing UNIX-based network servers. These were differentiated from Hewlett-Packard, SUN, IBM, and DEC servers by fault tolerance and permanent availability.

The problem of subdifferentiation also affected Raytheon's Patriot defensive missile. The original intent of the Patriot missile when it was developed in the late 1960s was for it to work on a range of threats including aircraft, ballistic missiles such as Iraqi Scud missiles, and low-flying cruise missiles. It used a fragmentation warhead to explode near the incoming threats, crippling them with fast-moving fragments.

While still effective against these threats, it was not considered by many military officials to be as effective against a specific subsegment of this "anti-missile" market. This new subsegment is modern ballistic missiles carrying "high-penalty" warheads such as chemical or biological agents. In these cases, the hit-to-kill approach of the Erint missile made by Loral was considered superior. The Erint missile carried no warhead but destroyed enemy missiles by hitting them at high speeds. This approach would vaporize any chemical agents; whereas, the Patriot missile would permit a higher percentage of those agents to reach the ground. Raytheon's vector of differentiation proved to be less important in this new subsegment of the market.[14]

Emerging Technology that Changes the Vector of Differentiation

New technology, or sometimes continuing advances of the same technology, can reduce or eliminate a vector of differentiation as rapidly as it was created. In some cases, it can eliminate an entire market segment in the process.

For example, desktop-publishing systems became feasible when print-shop-quality printers such as the Apple Laser Writer and publishing software such as Aldus PageMaker created a system under $10,000. This differentiation took a segment of the market away from large electronic publishing systems, since desktop publishing software enabled text and graphics to be combined.

Technology eventually enabled this capability to be included in many word processors as well as operating systems such as Windows, reducing the differentiation in products such as PageMaker.

Failure to Build Perception of Differentiation

Differentiated products position themselves uniquely in the minds of potential customers. Differentiating a product in fact but not in perception does not place the advantages of the differentiation in the minds of potential customers.

Failure to build perception can be caused in several ways. It can happen when a company does not recognize how its product is being valued by its customers. For example, when Cullinet first introduced its report writer software, it differentiated the product based on flexibility. After a while, it noticed that most of its customers were using it for auditing EDP systems. So Cullinet renamed the product EDP Auditor, charged more, and its sales took off. Cullinet succeeded in building the perception to match its differentiation. Similarly, in the previous sport shoe example, Reebok, Nike, and the others clearly built the perception of their differentiation, possibly even more than the actual differentiation itself.

Failure to build the perception of differentiation can also be a failure of marketing. One software company developed spreadsheet software in the early 1980s that was clearly differentiated based on its virtual capacity, which was a major advantage to many users who were frustrated by the limited capacity of spreadsheet applications at that time. Unfortunately, the company was unable to reach the segment of the market where this differentiation was important, and the product was unsuccessful.

A company can also fail itself to perceive the differentiation of its product, and promote the wrong vector of differentiation. This was the case with the Next Computer example discussed earlier, where Next promoted the design and electronics of its workstations as the vector of differentiation instead of its unique operating system.

Differentiation Not Sustained

Differentiation is very difficult to sustain. While this may seem obvious, many companies are surprised or unprepared when their vector of differentiation runs out of gas and no longer provides sufficient competitive advantage.

Apple Computer ran into this problem when it was unable to sustain the differentiation of its Macintosh computers. For many years, the Macintosh was able to justify a higher price for its superior user interface that made its computers easier to operate. Apple's difference was primarily in its software, not its hardware. Compared to an IBM PC with a DOS operating system, the Macintosh was clearly worth more. Price proximity was maintained at a higher price of $500 to $750.

When Microsoft introduced Windows 3.0 for the IBM PC in May 1990, this differentiation began to diminish. Gradually, Windows became more stable and ran more application software packages that used its features. The Macintosh differentiation shrunk, and maintain-

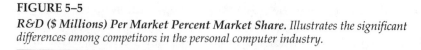

FIGURE 5–5

R&D ($ Millions) Per Market Percent Market Share. Illustrates the significant differences among competitors in the personal computer industry.

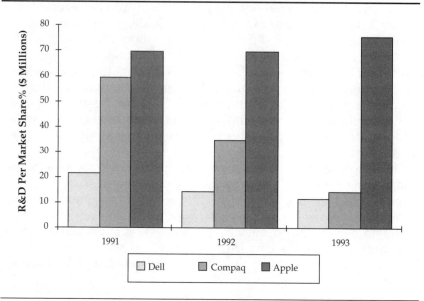

ing price proximity meant closing the pricing gap. By June of 1992, Apple's price difference was down to $200 and declining.

Obviously, Apple would have preferred to continue moving along its vector of differentiation and justify its premium price, but it could not. It had to compete more on price. Apple also found that it was spending more on R&D and not getting a competitive return for its investment. As Figure 5–5 shows, Apple was spending approximately $70 million for each percentage of market share in 1991, and Compaq was spending $60 million. However, Dell was spending only $20 million. Compaq changed its strategy to compete more on price and reduced R&D spending to approximately $15 million per market share percentage. Apple was left with a much higher development investment without the differentiation to justify it.

Sustainability is a major consideration in selecting the vector of differentiation. If the vector is successful, a company would like to stay on that vector as long as possible and distance itself from competitors. When a vector is not sustainable, a company needs to anticipate what it will do when competition catches up.

Sustainability comes from establishing barriers to entry. These delay the time it takes for competitors to catch up and erode the basis of differentiation. Barriers can be established in several ways.

Technological advantage.   When a company can pursue a vector of differentiation that uses its technical core competencies, it can establish a competitive advantage. To copy the basis of differentiation, competitors need to catch up technically by improving their core competencies. In some cases, they pay a cost penalty because they do not own the technology themselves. In other cases, they need to invest heavily to acquire the technology.

Motorola capitalized on its semiconductor technology when it differentiated its MicroTac portable telephone on size and weight. It continually pursued this vector of size and weight differentiation, introducing even better models as competitors were able to match it.

Sharp's introduction of the color LCD in its ViewCam utilized its underlying technological strength in LCDs. Many of its competitors did not have this technology, so it took some of them a little while to catch up.

Possessing or cultivating technical core competencies is only important insofar as they are applied to achieve a vector of differentiation in actual products. This is sometimes overlooked, and companies invest in a technical competencies then let them go to waste by not applying them to differentiate their products. Xerox's Palo Alto Research Center (PARC), for example, was infamous for developing groundbreaking technology that was not capitalized on by Xerox. One famous example was PARC's invention of the graphical user-interface for computers that Steve Jobs used to create the Macintosh.

Patent protection.   Patent protection, when available, is the ideal sustaining vector of differentiation because it "locks out" the competition. The challenge is to select the appropriate patent strategy in terms of breadth and completeness.

Patents should be as broad as possible to erect the widest barrier against competition. Many companies initiate the patent application process too late in product development or apply patents on detailed design elements that often do not provide sufficient protection. Patents that are too broad can also fail in court as evidenced by Apple's unsuccessful defense of the Macintosh's "look and feel" emulated by Microsoft and HP. An outstanding example of correct breadth is Polaroid's patents on instant photography, which allowed it to "own" this significant differentiation vector.

Completeness is also critical to full patent protection. An animal health biotechnology firm developed a new, general-purpose antibiotic for livestock. Their patent specified mammalian treatment at a low-dosage level. Unfortunately, this did not cover high-dosage-level applications and excluded the largest animal health market segment— poultry! Not covered by the patent, this application was in the public domain and available to any other drug company.

   Rapidly advancing vector.   Another way to sustain a competitive advantage is to move along the vector of differentiation so fast that competitors cannot catch up. This is the implied strategy when a company does not think about how it will sustain its differentiation. For years, Sony managed to maintain high margins in the cutthroat "Walkman" business by staying a step ahead of their copycat Japanese competitors. From the basic Walkman platform, Sony stayed ahead by continued miniaturization and by subsegmenting the market with products such as the waterproof "Sports Walkman."

SUMMARY

Product differentiation is the primary strategy to achieve a competitive advantage in high-technology products. Successful differentiation strategy comes from vectors, not individual points. These vectors provide the direction for continuously extending the basis of differentiation.

   Vectors of differentiation determine the relative position of products in the market, segment the market, and evolve throughout a market life-cycle. Selecting the differentiation strategy is one of the most critical product strategy decisions that a company makes. A strong differentiation strategy will drive the market to choose a product over competitive ones. It will also enable a product to be priced at a premium, as long as it maintains proximity to less differentiated products sold at a lower price.

   Generic differentiation strategies can be successful models for high-technology companies. They illustrate examples of success and failure. Failure in many cases stems from the risks of differentiation.

NOTES

1. This classification was introduced by Michael F. Porter in his three generic competitive strategies. The application of differentiation, particularly the concept of differentiation vectors, expands on this. See Porter, *Competitive Strategy: Techniques for Analyzing Industries and Competitors* (New York: The Free Press, 1980), and Porter, *Competitive Advantage: Creating and Sustaining Superior Performance* (New York: The Free Press, 1985).

2. Patrick M. Reilly, "Sony's Digital Audio Format Pulls Ahead of Philip's, But Both Still Have Far to Go," *The Wall Street Journal,* August 6, 1993.

3. Gale Eisenstadt, "Unidentical Twins," *Forbes,* July 5, 1993.

4. Charles L. Leath, "40 Years of Chronicling Technical Achievement," *Hewlett-Packard Journal,* October 1989.

5. Jim Carlton, "Hewlett-Packard, After Missteps in PCs, Hits Its Stride," *The Wall Street Journal,* January 1994.

6. Marilyn Chase, *The Wall Street Journal,* April 29, 1993, p. 1.

7. Marilyn Chase, *The Wall Street Journal,* May 3, 1993, p. B1.

8. Stratus Computer, Inc., 1992 Annual Report.

9. Regis McKenna, "Marketing Is Everything," *Harvard Business Review,* January–February 1991.

10. "Annual Design Awards," *Business Week,* June 7, 1993.

11. James Daly, "Can PowerBook Regain Its Cutting Edge?" *Computerworld,* November 15, 1993.

12. Mark Stahlman, "The Failure of IBM," *Upside,* March 1993.

13. Nikhil Hutheesing, "Games Companies Play," *Forbes,* October 25, 1993.

14. Aaron Zitner, "Rival Haunts Patriot Missile," *Boston Globe,* March 25, 1994.

Chapter Six

Price-Based Strategy

P rice is a competitive factor in all high-technology markets, and it is an element of strategy—whether explicit or implicit—for all high-technology products. Eventually, the success or failure of many products depends on their price strategy. Yet, despite its importance, price strategy is often neglected in many high-technology companies. It becomes a financial computation instead of a strategic consideration. Marketing managers and product developers will sometimes spend only a few days, or sometimes only a few hours, working on the pricing strategy of a new product. They do not estimate how customers will value the product, project how price will evolve in the market, try to understand how competitors will price products, or consider alternative strategies. In short, they fail to think about price strategically.

Price can be used as either an offensive strategy or a defensive strategy. As an offensive strategy, a company may choose to compete based on price. It distinguishes its products as a better value to customers by increasing the price difference from other products and causing competitive products to lose price proximity. As a defensive strategy, price can be used to fend off competitors that use price as an offensive strategy. Even companies that lead with a strategy of product differentiation need a secondary pricing strategy.

Price strategy for high-technology products is very different than it is for other products. High-technology products have short life-cycles. This causes a rapidly shifting price strategy. High-technology products tend to be innovative and have a high added value, giving them a wide latitude in pricing. They could be priced based on the value they add to customers or based on cost. Until the market begins to unfold, there may be no price framework to follow.

The underlying cost structure of high-technology products is also unique. Profit margins are generally high because development costs are significant, and some cost elements decrease rapidly during the product life-cycle.

Appropriate price strategy varies by product, competitive pricing, and stage within the life-cycle of a market. Products with distinctive vectors of differentiation can sustain a higher price. Market share leaders can introduce a lower price because they have scale advantages, particularly in products where there are high fixed-cost requirements, such as R&D or capital. Aggressive pricing by competitors such as market share leaders can force lower-than-desired pricing. Price strategy also changes during the life-cycle of a market, typically getting more aggressive in later stages.[1]

High-technology products are more susceptible to price wars. High-fixed-cost, high-margin businesses are ripe for price wars, particularly when there is excess capacity in the industry. A company needs to anticipate how competitors will react to price reductions in order to outmaneuver them. Successful price strategy for high-technology products requires an understanding of customer perceptions and an anticipation of competitor strategies.

Competitors in a market have different cost structures, and eventually these differences provide a source of competitive advantage, whether price is used as an offensive or a defensive strategy. The sources for cost advantage provide the foundation to support price strategy. Without a cost advantage, a company competing based on price is really just cutting its profit.

BASIC CONCEPTS OF PRICE-BASED STRATEGY

Effective price-based strategy in high-technology products involves applying some basic underlying concepts:

- Price determines the relative position of competitive products in the market.
- Prices can decline rapidly throughout a product's life-cycle.
- Lower prices increase market penetration.

Price Positions a Product in the Market

Relative price combined with relative differentiation positions a product in the market. Figure 6–1 illustrates this positioning. Product B is the price leader in the market. It also has a lower relative differentiation than the others. Products C, D, and E compete in the middle of the market; they are not competitive on price or differentiation. Product A competes based on its higher differentiation and is priced higher than B. The objective of offensive price-based strategies is to move a product to the left of this chart, while preserving a sufficient profit and increasing market share.

The relative positioning of products actually varies by segment within the market. Each segment places its own value on the differen-

FIGURE 6–1

Price Positioning in a Market. Products are positioned relative to each other on price and differentiation. Size represents approximate market share. Price strategy moves a product to the left.

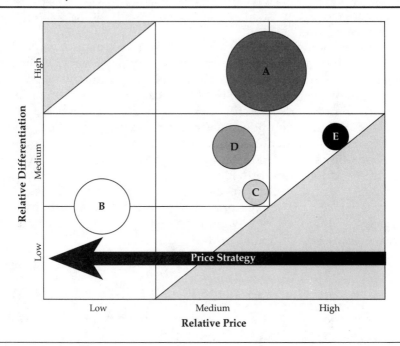

tiation among products, making positioning relative by segment. For example, if product E were a multimedia PC, it would be positioned much higher on the differentiation axis for the multimedia segment of the market.

Prices Decline Throughout the Stages of a Market's Evolution

As the life-cycle of a high-technology market evolves, competitive characteristics of the market also change. As was discussed in the previous chapter, differentiation changes throughout the life-cycle. Price also changes. Unit price can decline significantly during the evolution of a market, and generally this decline can be anticipated. Perhaps the exact timing or amount of decrease cannot be accurately projected, but the general trend can be estimated.

Development.   In its initial stage, a market is still developing, and all products are generally at their highest price. Costs are also initially high. Differentiation is not established, and a pricing framework is not yet set. Since the products are new, they can be value priced according to the benefit they provide the customer. Competition has not yet set in. Everyone—customers as well as competitors—is groping to understand the price framework within this new market.

Growth.   In this second stage, a new market begins to define itself. Customers select their preferences. They place a higher value on some vectors of differentiation than on others. Competitors also begin to define how they intend to compete. Vectors of differentiation are established, and price reductions are used to compensate for products with differentiation that is not valued sufficiently by customers.

This stage provides the first signs of how pricing will be structured in the market. Competitors who expect to compete aggressively on price begin to make those strategies apparent, although it may be difficult to distinguish them from companies compensating for noncompetitive products.

High-technology product prices generally decline during the growth stage. Competitors with weak differentiation continue to use price reductions to compensate. Price-based competitors introduce lower-priced products to establish their position. At the same time, customers are better able to evaluate alternatives than they were in the development stage.

In 1993, the personal computer industry was in its growth stage, and prices had been rapidly declining for two years. The price of a Macintosh IIvx, for example, dropped almost 50 percent, from $2,595 in October 1992 to $1,369 in June 1993. During that same period, the price of a Compaq DeskPro 4/25 fell almost 25 percent, from $1,742 to $1,355 and a Zenith Z-station 425Sh plunged more than 50 percent, from $3,083 to $1,419.[2]

Price-based competitors captured almost two-thirds of the market. That was until the more established companies reduced their prices to be more competitive. Then competitive advantage shifted. In one year from 1992 to 1993, the top five PC vendors increased their share of the American market from 36.9 percent to 48.8 percent.[3] The decline in PC prices also accelerated the growth of the market from 11.8 million PCs in 1992 in the United States to 13.8 million in 1993, with all of this growth going to the top five companies.

Maturity.   Price competition accelerates as a market moves from the growth to the maturity stage. Competitors are able to imitate the successful vectors of differentiation, and with products less differentiated, price becomes more important as a competitive advantage.

Loss of market share in the mature market stage has different implications than it does in the growth stage. In the mature stage, losing market share causes a decline in sales, not just slower growth. Competitors who have already made investments in capacity and inventory are hit with losses as sales decline. They react aggressively, usually by cutting prices.

FIGURE 6–2

Price and Volume of Calculator Market. Shows the direct relationship between declining price and increasing volume.

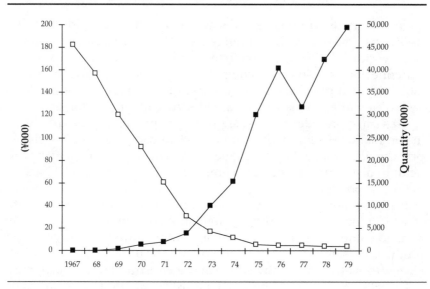

Costs are also lower in the maturity stage. Initial investments in developing the product platform have been recovered. The costs of developing the market are lower. The defining technology underlying the product platform has typically matured, and the manufacturing costs have been lowered through experience and volume.

    Decline.   Market declines are usually messy. Some competitors exit the market, but they do not usually do this gracefully. They typically dump their excess inventory at "fire sale" prices.

Those companies that remain in the market usually have reduced margins. By this point there is little to differentiate competitive products. As a result, there is less justification for a high-margin, high-price strategy.

Lower Prices Increase Market Penetration

High-technology markets are very elastic; lower prices drive higher volumes. This was true for calculators, VCRs, televisions, telephones, personal computers, computer networks, application software, and medical drugs. As prices decline, products become affordable to more customers willing to try them for the first time.

Figure 6–2 dramatically illustrates this relationship in the calculator market during the 1970s. At a price of ¥180,000 (approximately $750) in 1967, the calculator market was very small—only 63,000 were sold. They were used in critical applications or shared among work groups.

By 1976, their price declined to ¥4,800 (approximately $21), and production volume increased to more than 40 million.

Price reductions increase volume, but only up to a point. When the price becomes so low that it no longer matters, or when the market becomes saturated, price reductions have little or no impact on volume. This happened in the calculator market where they eventually cost less than $10 and were even given away free with magazine subscriptions.

OFFENSIVE PRICING STRATEGIES

Pricing strategies can be classified as primarily offensive or primarily defensive. Offensive strategies are used when a company intends to compete with price as the principal competitive weapon.

Strategy: Establish price leadership as basis for competing.

Price leadership[5] is the primary price-based competitive strategy. Customers buy the product because it is the least expensive (cheapest). This strategy is particularly effective in a mature market when the price

---

Generic Price-Based Strategies

Offensive

- Establish price leadership as basis for competing.

- Use penetration pricing to increase market.

- Use "experience-curve" pricing to discourage competition.

- Compete based on price-performance.

- Use promotional discounting to accelerate purchases.

Defensive

- Adapt prices to maintain highest competitive price.

- Use price to segment market.

- Use skim pricing to maximize profit.

- Use value-based pricing to maximize profit.

- Redirect sales within a product line with bait-and-switch pricing.

leader can narrow the differentiation between its products and those of higher-priced competitors.

For example, in the microprocessor market, Intel competes on performance using its market-standard architecture. A nonstandard (not Intel compatible) microprocessor cannot be successful at any price since it will not run standard software. However, a compatible microprocessor can compete very successfully as a lower-priced alternative. Companies such as Advanced Micro Devices (AMD) and Cyrix Corporation grabbed 80 percent of the 386 microprocessor market in 1993 by using a price-leadership strategy for a compatible product.[6]

Intel's strategy was to avoid price competition, staying ahead of its competitors by introducing more advanced products. It abandoned the 386 market in favor of the faster 486 microprocessor market. The objective of AMD and Cyrix was to take sales away from Intel, not to increase the size of the market.

However, Intel's competitors were getting better at their price-leadership strategy by reducing the lead that Intel had in the market. In 1993, Texas Instruments introduced a low-power 486 clone for the notebook segment to be sold at less than half the price of Intel's product. Cyrix planned to introduce a clone of Intel's newer Pentium microprocessor.

Strategy: Use penetration pricing to increase market.

As was seen earlier in the calculator example in Figure 6–1, lowering the price increases the size of the market. This is another price-based offensive strategy: Rapidly decrease the price to increase the size of the market. It is both a growth strategy and a competitive strategy.

In a penetration pricing strategy, price is set far below the economic value of the product to encourage more customers to purchase the product. This accelerates the natural evolution of a market, growing it at a much faster rate. It may also take much of the profit margin out of the market, so lower profit can be the cost of accelerating a market's evolution.

Penetration pricing is a variation of the price-leadership strategy. It is similar in that it is a compete-based-on-price strategy, but it is different in that its primary intent is not to take away today's customers from competitors. Its objective is to increase market share while growing the market. Competitors' sales may not decline.

The IBM-clone manufacturers competed on price using a penetration strategy. They increased the size of the market by making personal computers more affordable to many people. Meanwhile, personal computer sales at Apple and IBM continued to increase.

The extreme penetration price strategy is to give the product away for free. This is what Computer Associates did with its Simply

Money accounting product. It offered the product free to customers willing to pay the $6.95 for postage and handling. The objective of its strategy was to penetrate the market to create a stronger position and then use this position to generate upgrade revenue. Computer Associates followed the same strategy on its Simply Tax tax planning software.

Eventually a penetration strategy runs out of gas. The market becomes penetrated to the point where growth inevitably slows. A penetration strategy then shifts to a price-leadership strategy, and competitors become more aggressive. Losing market share in a growing market is one thing. (It is not really painful.) Losing sales in a flat market is another. (That is painful.) This usually precipitates a price war.

Strategy: Use experience-curve pricing to discourage competition.

Experience-curve pricing is a strategy for setting prices lower than cost in anticipation of cost reductions based on the experience-curve benefits. The key to this is that cost benefits are achieved at a predictable rate. For example, unit costs can decline at 20 percent to 30 percent each time accumulated experience doubles.[7]

It is a strategy that has been successfully employed in industries such as digital watches, calculators, specialty chemicals, and semiconductors. Experience-curve pricing was a particularly popular strategy back in the 1970s. For example, in 1976 when Gillette Company entered the market for digital watches, most observers expected that it would not be long before the big marketer would take a significant market share. But in early 1977, Gillette announced that it was pulling out of the market because of "the continual erosion of the retail price structure and because the watches failed to produce the profit levels it was seeking."[8]

Several companies had preceded Gillette in dropping out of the market, and more followed. Experience-curve pricing was the reason for this shakeout. Gillette was selling its digital watches in the $40 to $75 price range; Texas Instruments (TI) priced its watches in the $40 to $50 range; and Litronix was the price leader with a low price of $39.95. However, TI surprised everyone by introducing a $20 watch, cutting the retail price by more than half in a dramatic bid to force others out of the market and block new entries.[9]

TI implemented an experience-curve pricing strategy. This strategy worked and many competitors including Gillette and Litronix were forced out of the market. TI was beginning to achieve a cost advantage through its experience curve and projected even more reductions in the future based on increasing volume. It set its prices to make money in the future based on these anticipated reductions.

FIGURE 6–3

Normal versus Experience-Curve Pricing. Illustrates the differences in experience-curve pricing. The cost curve is the same, but the pricing steps are significantly different.

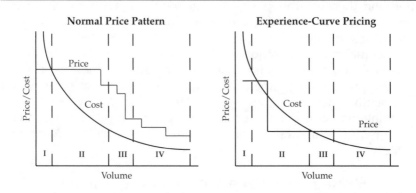

Figure 6–3 illustrates an experience-curve pricing strategy. The two charts have the same reduction in product cost based on the experience curve. In the first chart, introductory prices are held throughout most of the first two stages of the product's life-cycle. This permits margins (the difference between price and cost) to increase in stage II. During stage III, a shakeout occurs and prices decline repeatedly. By stage IV, prices become more stable with declines less frequent.

By contrast, the experience-curve pricing strategy is entirely different. The expected eventual price is implemented early in stage II, creating a loss through most of that stage. This price can then be maintained because most competitors have been forced out of the market. This forces the shakeout much earlier, in stage II instead of stage III. It may also compress stage II because of increased penetration.

Experience-curve pricing is a preemptive strategy. Some may even call it predatory. It is an aggressive strategy that prices products below cost, in hopes of forcing those already in the market to exit, while keeping others out of the market.

Strategy: Compete based on price performance.

Price-based competitive positioning does not mean just lowest price. In high-technology products, a competitive strategy based on price performance combines the performance vector of a differentiation strategy with a price-based strategy. The goal is to offer the lowest cost per unit of performance.

Too many companies confuse three competitive strategies that are really very different. Competing based on price leadership was discussed previously. The strategy is to offer the lowest price without an emphasis on performance difference. The low-end PC market is an example. Performance does not matter, as long as it is sufficient.

Competing based on performance emphasizes performance without much regard to price. Cray computers are an example. If customers need that level of computing performance, they pay more. A customer cannot buy several lower-priced computers to do the same job (although this is changing).

Competing based on price-performance combines elements of performance differentiation and price-based competition into a single strategy: to be the leader in price performance. Digital Equipment used this strategy in its Alpha-based workstations. In 1993, it claimed an edge in price-performance over IBM, Hewlett-Packard, and Sun Microsystems, and used independent audited comparisons to back up its claims. Compared to IBM's $70,000 high-end workstation, for example, Digital's system has equal performance at $36,000.[10]

Competing based on price-performance usually requires some inherent cost advantage, usually in the design of the product, and preferably in the defining technology. In Digital's case, it used the advanced Alpha microprocessor, which performed the same functions in a single chip that required an eight-chip set in IBM's workstations.

Strategy: Use promotional discounting to accelerate purchases.

Discount-based promotions are becoming more popular with high-technology products, especially higher-volume products and those sold to mass markets. The objective behind promotional discounting is to lower a product's price without diminishing its perceived value. This encourages people to buy now rather than defer their purchases (since the value is higher and the discount is only temporary).

Companies selling application software products use promotional discounting strategies to successfully accelerate sales and gain temporary competitive advantages. There is another advantage also. Once customers purchase a software product, they are likely customers for regular upgrades, creating an ongoing revenue stream. Upgrades frequently have lower selling expenses and can be more profitable.

The economics of computer software makes this type of pricing strategy particularly attractive. The per-unit cost of application software products is very low. It is only the material costs of disks and a manual as well as some reproduction costs. The original development costs are the most significant cost element. These are amortized over the volume sold, so the higher the volume, the lower the per-unit share. After-sales support is another variable cost, but this service is increasingly priced separately.

There are a variety of promotional discounting pricing strategies. The following are two examples.

Competitive upgrades.   The competitive upgrade promotion is aimed at prompting customers to switch from a competitive product. For example, in 1993 Microsoft Word for Windows version 6.0 sold for $320, but the price was reduced to $135 as an upgrade from either an earlier version of Word or a competitive product (WordPerfect or AmiPro). A customer needed to turn in the master disk or title page of the user manual in order to get the 58 percent discount.

In order to gain enough market share to become competitive, Borland introduced Quattro Pro 5.0 with a competitive discount that reduced the price from $99 to $35. The work-group version was introduced at a competitive upgrade discount, reducing the price from $495 to $99. Borland believed that strong sales from this promotion would offset lower margins and put it into second place in the market. It expected to sell 500,000 units during the five-month promotion period.

Even if competitive upgrades are discounted so deeply that there is little or no profit, the potential value of future upgrade revenue is high.

Bundles and packages.   These are groupings of related products that are sold together at a discounted price. The objective is to attract the customer to buy more for a slightly higher price, similar to the "buy one and get a second for $1" retail pricing strategy. It is a particularly effective strategy when the incremental cost of the bundle or package is very low. Again, application software (combined with other software products or computer equipment) is particularly successful with this strategy because of its low unit cost.

Microsoft Office for Windows version 4.0 was sold in 1993 as a bundle for $505 ($305 as a competitive upgrade). It contained four applications: Word, Excel, PowerPoint, and Mail. Purchased separately, they would have cost three times as much. Lotus SmartSuite included five applications for $484.

DEFENSIVE PRICING STRATEGIES

Some pricing strategies are more appropriately categorized as defensive. They are secondary to a differentiation-based strategy, often supporting the implementation of that strategy.

Strategy: Adapt prices to maintain highest competitive price.

With an adaptive pricing strategy, a company wants to maintain as high a price as possible. It is reluctant to lower its price and reduce its profit margin. Only when competitors lower their prices to the point where the company loses market share, will it adapt by lowering its price. Adaptive pricing is one of the most popular defensive price strategies for high-technology products. However, in most cases, it is the default of no price strategy. When a company does not have any price strategy for a product and simply reacts to competitive changes in price, it follows adaptive pricing strategy.

A company following this strategy implicitly believes that more aggressive pricing is not to its advantage. Offensive pricing strategies have been discarded. IBM and Apple followed this strategy for their personal computers. They maintained higher prices—justified initially by significant vectors of differentiation—until low-price competitors captured the major share of the market. Then they adapted by lowering prices and margins.

Imagine what would have happened if IBM had pursued a penetration pricing strategy instead. It might have had a market share two to three times greater in 1992, increasing revenue by more than $10 billion. Or, even better, what if Apple had followed a penetration pricing strategy instead of a maintain-the-margin adaptive price strategy? The Macintosh could be the standard for personal computers, and Apple could be several times larger! Examples like these suggest that companies should pay more attention to pricing strategy. Adaptive pricing is appropriate in many cases, but should not always be used by default.

Strategy: Use price to segment market.

Price strategy can be used to segment the market. This is done by pricing a highly differentiated product at a premium price. When the differentiation is highly valued by specific segments of the market, the product will be most successful in these segments.

Computers with fault-tolerant capabilities, for example, are priced much higher than comparable computers without this capability. This higher price helps to segment the market. If there was not any significant price difference, then most customers would prefer fault-tolerant computers. At the higher price, fault-tolerant computers are attractive to companies with mission-critical applications where downtime is very expensive. Airline reservation systems, bank ATM networks, utility control systems, and so on, are examples of mission-critical applications in that segment of the market.

Pricing can also be used to position products competitively in different channels of distribution. For example, drug companies charge more for prescription drugs sold through pharmacies than through HMOs (health maintenance organizations).

Strategy: Use skim pricing to maximize profit.

Skim pricing is intended to "skim the cream" off the top of the market by offering a premium-priced product that only a limited portion of the customer base will pay for. It is a high-price low-volume strategy, frequently employed by companies that can only supply a small volume of a highly differentiated product. While this is an effective strategy for prestige products like designer clothes and fancy cars, it does not always work as intended with high-technology products.

Apple attempted this strategy with the Lisa computer by pricing it at $10,000, twice as much as other desktop computers. They intended to skim the market, selling as much as they could produce at higher margins. The high price was justified based on its high development costs and unique differentiation.

What happened instead was that the pricing strategy segmented the market. Those who wanted to buy a computer to prepare graphics and do presentations found the value of the Lisa worth the higher price. Others did not. Even executives who could afford the higher price for the additional ease of use did not buy the Lisa, because it lacked compatibility with the other computers in their company and buying the premium priced Lisa for everyone was too expensive.

Strategy: Use value-based pricing to maximize profit.

A value-based pricing strategy is intended to maximize profit margins by setting prices at higher levels than is justified by product costs. High-technology products typically have a high value since they use advanced technology to solve critical problems or displace other costs.

CAT scanners, for example, provide extremely high value and were value priced when they were introduced. Value pricing is usually only possible when there are no competitors or when a product is significantly differentiated based on value.

Polaroid could value-price its instant camera because there was no competition. It was protected by patents. As seen in an earlier example, Genentech was able to value price TPA at $2,200 per dose against $200 streptokinase because its value was higher—it saved one more life per hundred.

A value-based price strategy is most effective in the early stages of a market. Once competition begins to set in, it becomes less tenable.

Strategy: Redirect sales within a product line with bait-and-switch pricing.

Bait-and-switch strategies are typical of appliances, automobiles, and clothing, but they are not confined only to these products. High-technology companies have also learned to use this strategy, although it has not yet taken on the negative aura that it has in other industries.

Companies that compete in markets with increasing price competition generally need to offer a low-priced product in their product line. The bait-and-switch strategy draws attention to the product line using the low price, but then tempts customers to purchase a higher-priced product with more features or capacity.

The laser-printer market provides an example of the bait-and-switch strategy. Increasing price competition and advancing technology drove prices from $4,000 to less than $1,000 in only a few years. To be competitive, companies needed a "dirt cheap" product, but hoped to sell more fully featured products where the profit margins were higher.

Hewlett-Packard offered the LaserJet 4L, a low-cost version of its popular LaserJet 4, for $849 in 1993. The L-version printed 300 dots per inch (dpi), compared to 600 and offered no upgrade options. The $1,279 4ML model, however, offered upgradability, more memory, the ability to network, PostScript capability, and Macintosh/PC compatibility.[11]

Competitors followed a similar strategy. Texas Instrument's micro-Writer was priced at $729, but the $999 model included additional features. For $1,299 there was a model with more fonts, which had the capabilities needed by most users. Similarly, Epson's ActionLaser 1000 was priced at $799 and had options for upgrading to higher-priced models.

Bait and switch is usually a product-line pricing strategy. The purpose of the low-priced product is to draw customer interest, and then get the customer to upgrade by purchasing a higher-priced product within the same product line.

RISKS OF OFFENSIVE PRICING STRATEGIES

Just as there were risks in differentiation strategies, there are also risks in strategies that are based on price as the primary offensive strategy. Of these risks, three are most significant.

Price Leadership not Sustained

A market generally has room for only one price leader. Customers who are primarily influenced on price will buy from the competitor with the lowest price—and only one company can have the lowest price.

When a company embarks on price leadership as its primary competitive strategy, it is committing to maintaining the lowest price to be successful. If a competitor follows with a lower price, the company must respond by undercutting the competitor's price. Otherwise, it will not attract the segment of the market that buys based on price, and it has little else to offer (or it would compete on some other basis).

This risk is different than the risk of differentiation since there are varied vectors of differentiation but only one vector of price leadership. Competing on a vector of differentiation that is not as strong as others can still achieve limited success based on customers in segments that prefer that particular vector. However, competing on the primary basis of being the second lowest price can only be successful if customers do not know the competitor's price or if the competitor is out of stock.

Aggressive Pricing Precipitates Price War

Aggressive pricing like price leadership, penetration pricing, experience-curve pricing, or promotional discounting, can precipitate a price war. Other companies may not be passive to attempts to steal market share through price reductions. They may respond by lowering their prices or possibly retaliate with even lower prices. When this happens, a price war erupts. Generally, all competitors lose in a price war—some just lose less than others.

Price wars were precipitated in the hard-disk-drive industry in 1993. The transition from the growth to the maturity stage happened quickly in this $24 billion industry. Coming off their most profitable year in the previous five, disk-drive companies began slashing prices by over 30 percent (more than triple the usual rate of price decline) during the first six months of 1993.[12]

The disk-drive industry at that time had many characteristics that made it ripe for a price war. Competitors rapidly expanded production to meet their individual sales growth expectations, which in total exceeded industry demand. A slight reduction in the rate of growth triggered an exaggerated reaction, and market share shifts, common in this stage, caused a particularly acute problem for some of the Asian disk-drive manufacturers. As a result, they began to sell their excess drives at bargain prices to distributors.

At the same time, technology shifts moved customer interest to higher-capacity drives. This increased inventories of lower-capacity drives and precipitated fire-sale prices to move them before their value dropped even further. This scenario is reasonably typical of high-technology products during the maturity stage. This is what leads to industry consolidation.

Aggressive Pricing Not Supported by Cost Advantage

A price leadership strategy is really a cost leadership strategy.[13] A company that tries to achieve price leadership without a competitive cost advantage will make less money than its competitors. While this may be acceptable for a time—particularly if there is a price umbrella in the industry where other competitors are making "excess" profit—it is not sustainable over the long term.

For a while, this was the case in the personal computer industry. The market leaders such as IBM, Compaq, and Apple created a price umbrella for their competitors to compete on price, even though the cost structure of these competitors was higher than the market leaders'. These low-priced competitors accepted making a lower profit. This made sense after all since a low profit was better than not being in the business at all.

Eventually, the market leaders realized that their profit margins were too large for the high-volume market that this was becoming. When they lowered their prices to more competitive levels, they forced the low-priced competitors to accept an even lower profit; in fact they began to lose money.

Any aggressive price strategy needs to be supported by an equally aggressive cost strategy. The company must understand its cost position relative to competitors and exploit all sources of cost advantage.

Even when a cost advantage is attained, it is not always possible to maintain it. Competitors can improve their cost advantages by copying improvements or by exploiting other sources of cost advantage. Changes in technology can also shift the sources of cost advantage. This happened in the computer industry when technology shifted to standard microprocessors, eliminating the cost advantage by companies that had their own semiconductor manufacturing facilities.

SOURCES OF COST ADVANTAGE

A price strategy—whether offensive or defensive—must be implemented through cost management; otherwise, declining prices will simply bring declining profits. Companies pursuing an offensive price strategy must exploit all sources of cost advantage in order to be successful. Companies with a defensive price strategy need to keep costs under control. The sources of cost advantage vary by product and company, but the following are usually most important:

- Low-cost design advantages come through design-to-cost techniques.
- Manufacturing process advantages use efficiencies in the manufacturing process.
- Experience-curve advantages are based on the continuous improvement of costs, quality, and performance as volume increases.
- Supply-chain cost advantages leverage efficiencies in the supply chain.
- Technology-based cost advantages come from superiority in a defining technology.
- Development process cost advantages are derived from having a more efficient product development process.
- Global scale advantages are achieved when very large international companies integrate their global operations.

Low-Cost Design Advantages

The cost structure of a product is determined at the time a product specification is completed. For many high-technology products, by the time the specification is completed, 80 to 90 percent of the product's life-cycle costs are locked in, leaving only 10 to 20 percent of the cost to be managed after the product is released.

Traditional design approaches do not sufficiently integrate cost objectives into the design of a product. The traditional approach to product design is illustrated on the left side of Figure 6–4.[14] It emphasizes designing to the product specification, which describes its functionality, performance characteristics, operating parameters, tolerances, and so on. Product cost is then estimated based on the completed design, and gross margin is computed by subtracting this cost from the estimated price that the product can support. If the resulting margin is less than anticipated, the company must go back and redesign the product or proceed with lower margins, hoping to reduce costs in the future. Periodic future cost reductions are not planned in the initial design, and therefore are decoupled from the process. Under this approach, product cost is a consequence of product design, not a requirement.

FIGURE 6-4

Design to Cost versus Traditional Design Approaches. *The design-to-cost approach uses price/cost as an initial design constraint.*

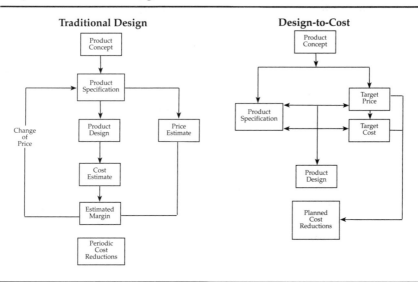

When product cost is of strategic importance, it is better to use a design-to-cost approach, similar to that illustrated on the right-hand side of Figure 6–4. In this approach, low cost is established as a product requirement of equal importance to other critical requirements. In the product specification step, the low-cost requirement is evaluated against other requirements. This is an iterative process. Each requirement or feature has a different cost that needs to be compared to its value. The target price and cost are linked by the required gross margin, while the price that can be charged depends on the product specification. The product's design is a result of this iterative process, not the product cost as in the traditional approach. Also, unlike the traditional approach, future cost reductions are planned from the beginning.

A new test tube for medical applications made this trade-off in its design. The test tubes were very price sensitive because of budget constraints in research laboratories, but the company wanted to introduce an improved tube using advanced plastics to replace glass. This would differentiate the product based on safety, but the additional cost would result in a price that was too high. A solution was eventually found in the design by replacing the costly stopper at the end of the tube with a cheaper one. The new test tube could be sold at the same price but appeal to those research labs where safety was more important than the quality of the stopper.

Establishing target cost as a requirement also encourages creativity early in the design process. Hewlett-Packard (HP) did this in the design of its DeskJet printer. To meet the needs of international markets, 2,240 symbols representing 18 different character sets were necessary. Implementing this would have required 9-bit characters and one megabyte of ROM (read-only memory), but this would have been too expensive for the market. To solve this dilemma, HP mapped the commonalty between all of the characters required. Next, it broke this character map into 256 elements. Finally, it developed software to reconstruct a specific character from these elements. The resulting ROM requirement was reduced to 30K bytes.[15]

A design-to-cost approach is necessary for a product that competes based on price. Price and the resulting cost target become a primary design requirement. It can also be a helpful approach for products using a defensive price strategy to make them less vulnerable to cost-based competitors.

Manufacturing Process Advantages

The usual source of cost advantages is the manufacturing process. Manufacturing cost advantages can be derived in several ways. Economies of scale are achieved through volume. These can be particularly significant when there is a high fixed-cost content in the total product cost. Highly automated manufacturing, as opposed to labor intensive processes, are typical of those that have a relatively high fixed-cost content. When volume is higher, fixed costs are leveraged over many more units, reducing the cost per unit.

Historically, volume has been a popular basis for cost advantage, but it has lately been overlooked. For example, the cost of electronics manufacturing is more sensitive to volume than most people think. This is measured in Figure 6–5, where the cost per component insertion is compared at two volume levels. The resulting cost advantage to the high-volume manufacturer is significant. Economies of scale are why most companies competing on the basis of price need high volumes. They cannot afford to concede this cost advantage to others with higher prices.

The manufacturing process itself can also be a source of cost advantage. This was demonstrated clearly by Japanese manufacturers in the 1970s and early 1980s, when they introduced JIT (just-in-time) and TQM (total-quality management) manufacturing techniques. These techniques significantly reduced cost and increased quality simultaneously. As a result, these manufacturers were able to compete with a strategy of lower price combined with higher quality differentiation.

FIGURE 6–5

Printed Circuit Board Cost Per Placement.[16] *Illustrates the cost difference at high and low production volume.*

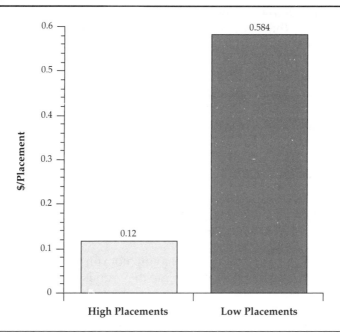

This product strategy, enabled by manufacturing process advantages, became the dominant strategy. It changed the competitive balance of many industries, including automotive, consumer electronics, machine tools, and portions of the semiconductor industry.

Vertical integration can sometimes provide a manufacturing cost advantage. If a company manufactures most of the basic materials, semiconductors, or components, it gets these at a lower cost. However, vertical integration can reduce flexibility as technology changes. It can be a cost advantage today and a disadvantage tomorrow. Internal suppliers must be competitive with external suppliers. If not, then what was a cost advantage can become a disadvantage.

Manufacturing process advantages can also come from creative changes. One of the most unusual examples of ways to reduce manufacturing costs is provided by Genzyme Transgenics, which is moving its manufacturing from sterile labs to farm animals in order to reduce production costs of drugs like tissue plasma activator (TPA).

The cost savings could be significant. Using cell cultures in a lab, scientists can get 2 to 20 milligrams of TPA protein per liter of cell culture at a cost of $20 to $50 per liter. By contrast, milk-producing goats can produce 10 to 40 grams of the proteins in a liter of milk at a cost of 50 cents per liter.[17]

The approach to building this "manufacturing process" is not simple. Goat DNA that produces proteins in milk is spliced with the human DNA that makes the desired protein, such as TPA. This is then injected into a just-fertilized egg removed from a normal goat. The egg is then transferred to a female goat, and in some cases the result is a baby goat that carries the desired protein. When mated with another goat, it produces milk with the desired protein. This can then be purified to produce TPA.

Experience-Curve Advantages

Experience-curve advantages are derived from the cumulative effect of increased experience. This effect has been proven based on the increase in efficiency when a task is performed repeatedly. It is a common effect applicable to almost any task.

People who begin jogging after having not run for many years find that their elapsed time the second time they run is faster than the first. The fourth is faster than the second, and the eighth is faster than the fourth. In fact, the percentage improvement may be the same at each of these intervals. This is the experience-curve theory. Each time the number of repetitions doubles, the process improves by a specific percentage.

The experience curve is especially important to high-technology products because of the rapid cost descent at early volume levels. Remember that improvements come when the cumulative experience doubles, and cumulative experience happens rapidly in the early stages of a new market. The cumulative volume for personal computers doubled frequently during the first five years of the market. In comparison, the production of something like light bulbs may now take 40 to 50 years before the cumulative production volume and experience doubles.

Figure 6–6 illustrates the experience-curve cost advantage on the digital watch example discussed earlier. TI achieved a significant cost advantage over Gillette through experience-curve advantages. At its cumulative volume of 3 million units, TI's cost was 50 percent lower than Gillette's at 250,000 units.

Supply-Chain Cost Advantages

Increasingly, high-technology companies need to look beyond manufacturing to achieve cost advantages. Other cost elements in the supply chain can frequently become a source of cost advantage.

FIGURE 6–6

Experience Cost Curve. TI's position on the experience curve gave them a 44 percent cost advantage.

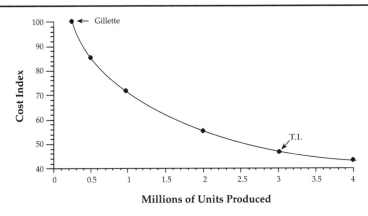

The supply chain includes the cost of acquiring materials, manufacturing, inventory, order management, distribution, invoicing, and warranty. These are illustrated in Figure 6–7. It also illustrates the cumulative cost advantage that can be achieved throughout the supply chain. For example, it costs some companies 2¢ to acquire $1 of components, while it costs most others an average of 7¢. (The 2¢ is referred to as the "best practice" cost and represents the best 20 percent of the companies, while the 7¢ is the average.) By the end of the supply chain, the accumulated difference between the best practice low-cost company and the average is $1.21 for each dollar of material cost compared to $1.59, a difference of 31 percent.

Assuming two companies with these supply-chain cost differences, one could be as profitable as the other while maintaining a 25 percent lower price. Clearly, companies competing based on price need to achieve competitive advantages in their entire supply chain.

Gateway 2000 based its initial strategy for PCs on a low-cost structure throughout its supply chain. This began with its location at the intersection of Iowa, Nebraska, and South Dakota, and extended to its mail-order distribution. Gateway's product strategy was clear: low-cost, no-frills computers sold through mail order. Its cost structure was one of the lowest in the industry. These combined to enable Gateway to grow to $1.1 billion in 1992 and maintain a 10 percent profit while being a low-cost provider.[19]

Leading communications companies such as Cisco and Wellfleet Communications have kept pace with an explosive market by managing, but not owning, their complete supply chain. This has allowed

FIGURE 6–7

PC Supply Chain Costs.[18] *Illustrates the cumulative cost advantage that can be attained by a "best practice" supply chain process. The higher numbers are average costs, while the lower numbers are best-practice costs. The % indicates the relative cumulative cost advantage.*

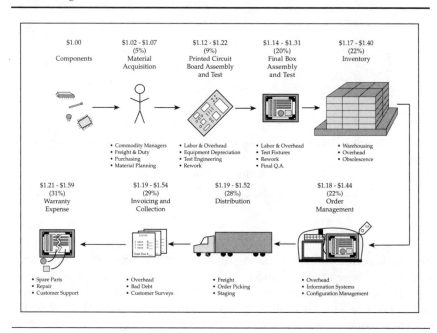

them to insulate themselves from viciously rapid technology advances and simultaneously gain a substantial cost advantage on their competition. This innovative approach of not physically touching its product at any time in its sourcing, building, or distribution has enabled Wellfleet to claim the distinction as the fastest growing company in America for both 1992 and 1993.

Technology Advantages

Technology can also be a source of cost advantage, particularly if a company has an advantage in the critical technology of a product. This is an advantage not easily met by competitors.

Motorola's PowerPC microprocessor, for example, utilizes RISC (reduced instruction-set computing) technology that gives it an advantage over the competitive Pentium microprocessor from Intel. RISC technology enables Motorola to pack more processing power into fewer transistors, resulting in a computer chip that is half the size (120 square millimeters versus 262). Motorola can manufacture twice as many microprocessors in the same time and space as Intel, giving it a significant cost advantage. Comparing the two microprocessors of equal processing power, Motorola could initially sell the PowerPC 601 at $450 compared the Intel Pentium at $965.

Cost advantages through technology are typically used as a defensive price strategy. Technology leaders usually are not low-cost competitors since they invest heavily in technology and product development to position their product using a differentiation strategy. They make it very expensive for a competitor to copy their differentiation.

Price/performance advantages (which is a hybrid price and differentiation strategy) are almost always achieved through technology. Digital Equipment's strategy of price/performance leadership with its Alpha workstations is based on the unique technology of its Alpha microprocessor.

Technology can also provide a source of cost advantage within a particular market segment. For example, Motorola introduced lightweight portable cellular telephones based on its microelectronics technology. This created a new market segment for lightweight telephones and, because competitors did not have the same technology, Motorola enjoyed the advantage of having the lowest cost in this segment for some time. This lead was so significant that Motorola was delayed permission to sell into the Japanese market in order to give Japanese competition time to catch up.

Development Process Advantages

Development cost can be one of the most significant cost elements in high-technology products. In some products, such as computer software and biotechnology drugs, the allocated development cost per unit exceeds the cost of goods sold. In many other products, the allocated cost per unit may exceed other controllable costs, such as labor and overhead.

Many companies are now beginning to discover that product development productivity can be improved, and the resulting cost differences can be significant. Pittiglio Rabin Todd & McGrath in working with over 75 companies to improve product development found a 30 percent average improvement in development productivity (with an associated 40 to 60 percent reduction in development time).

This improvement came from several sources. Improving time to market reduced new product development cost since most of the costs are run-rate based. Developing a product in one year instead of two required fewer man-years of development resources. Another source of improvement was a reduction in wasted development. In 1992, electronic systems companies wasted an average 18 percent of their development on products that never came to market. Individual performance, however, ranged from 3.5 percent for the "best-in-class" companies to others at 40 percent or more.[20]

The amount of R&D investment can also provide a source of cost advantage. Gateway 2000, for example, supports its low-cost, low-price strategy by investing almost nothing in R&D. Compare this to Apple Computer, which invested 8.5 percent of sales in R&D. As long as Apple was able to sustain a significant vector of differentiation, this additional cost was worthwhile. However, when the Macintosh lost its differentiation, high R&D spending became a cost disadvantage. If Apple's investments had paid off by creating new products to absorb this high investment, it would not have been a problem.

Global-Scale Advantages

In the 1990s a new form of scale advantage is being achieved by large multinational companies as they integrate far-flung operations into a tightly integrated and flexible process. By doing this, they are able to increase the leverage due to their size, while simultaneously improving their flexibility.

This new scale advantage comes from increased integration both across and within all functions. When companies globalize their product development process, they are able to offer a single product to all world markets at the same time, while designing the flexibility to manufacture it wherever the cost is the lowest. They attain a significant cost advantage by leveraging development and lowering manufacturing cost.

The globally integrated company may supply its component plants with raw materials from a single source; standardize its manufacturing process in British, Taiwanese, and American final assembly plants; and enter customer orders into a worldwide order-fulfillment system. Products can be assembled in and distributed from the most convenient site. The globally integrated company links all product developers, demand analysts, and production planners from all facilities through a worldwide network to coordinate and balance all activities.

Those large companies that successfully link their global resources are evolving into stronger, more responsive operations, better able to cut costs and serve a worldwide customer base. This new manufacturing scale advantage will provide a source of cost advantage that cannot be achieved by smaller single-country competitors.[21]

CASE STUDY: COMPAQ'S SHIFT
TO A PRICE-BASED STRATEGY

As discussed in the previous chapter, to be successful a differentiation strategy needs to maintain prices in reasonable proximity to the price of those competing primarily with an offensive price strategy. Reasonable proximity equates to the value of the differentiation. When this reasonable proximity is reduced—as is often the case in maturing markets—even companies with previously differentiated products need to shift their product strategy toward more competitive pricing. Compaq Computer's 1992 shift in product strategy is a case in point.

Compaq Computer was started in 1981 to develop and market a portable personal computer. The portable IBM-compatible computer was successfully differentiated based on its smaller size, which enabled it to be carried from location to location. Compaq's revenues reached $100 million in its first year.

Later, Compaq offered desktop systems as well. Its product strategy shifted to differentiation based on higher performance using its ability to quickly develop products with leading-edge technology. In September of 1986, Compaq got a jump on competitors by releasing the industry's first 80386-based personal computer, beating IBM to market by several months. Compaq also developed some unique components and worked closely with key suppliers such as Conner Peripherals to introduce smaller form-factor disk drives. Primarily as a result of this strategy, revenue increased in 1988 by 69 percent to $2 billion, followed by a 40 percent increase in 1989.

In 1989, Compaq was a $2.9 billion company, and it competed on high performance and leading-edge technology. It followed a skimming price strategy. Michael Swavely, President of North American operations said, "We never positioned ourselves based on price. We sell a better product not a cheaper product."[22] All this began to change in 1990.

Penetration price strategy by clone competitors such as AST, Dell, and Northgate drove personal computer prices lower and lower as the market grew rapidly. The price difference between Compaq's PCs and low-priced clones exceeded 30 percent at a time when these lower-priced products were catching up in technology and performance. Revenue and profits were rising at these price leaders, but Compaq was beginning to have problems.

Compaq lost proximity with its differentiation. The differentiation Compaq offered was not worth a 30 percent higher price to many PC customers. By mid-1991, Compaq lost market share, and its revenue began to drop. It had its first ever loss and initiated a layoff of 1,700 employees.

To some extent, Compaq's faulty product strategy was based on IBM's. It positioned its products primarily against IBM's, ignoring other competitors. Compaq's PCs were more innovative than IBM's and were sold at the same price. Together, they created a price umbrella in which lower-priced PCs flourished.

In October 1991, the Compaq board of directors decided that a low-priced product strategy was required despite recommendations by CEO and co-founder Rod Canion to continue a differentiation-based strategy. They ousted Canion and made Eckhard Pfeiffer the new CEO. The next day, Pfeiffer launched new efforts to develop lower-priced PCs. He believed that a new PC design was needed because it was "far more difficult for a design engineer to achieve a 10% cost reduction than a 40% or 50% reduction, because no matter how hard you look at a problem, doing things the way they have always been done blocks your view of doing something fundamentally different."[23]

Compaq's new product strategy was to close the price gap in order to compete directly with lower-priced competitors. Pfeiffer supported this strategy with initiatives to shorten product development cycle-times and reduce manufacturing, materials, and overhead costs.

In the summer of 1992, Compaq launched its ProLinea line of cut-rate PCs, and in less than a year these new lower-priced PCs closed the gap in price to less than 15 percent—within a reasonable proximity. Sales in the third quarter of 1992 jumped 50 percent to more than $1 billion. Its share of the U.S. PC market increased from 3.5 percent to 5.1 percent.

A lower-priced product strategy requires a lower cost structure. This means lower development costs, lower materials costs, lower manufacturing costs, and a lower profit margin. Compaq's low-priced ProLinea PCs and Contura notebooks had fewer features. Compaq reduced component and material costs by forcing suppliers to compete more aggressively. Manufacturing was streamlined, and capacity utilization was increased. Lower profit margins were offset by higher volumes.

Eckhard Pfeiffer believed that winning at a price-leadership strategy would depend on manufacturing efficiencies and economies of scale: "Only the most efficient manufacturers will be able to continue ongoing price reduction while achieving acceptable profitability. As we move into volume production, cost for every process comes down significantly." In 1993, as volume doubled from 1.5 million to 3 million computers, total manufacturing costs fell almost $10 million.[24]

In implementing its new price-based strategy, Compaq changed the way it considered pricing in the design of its products. It identified price as a key to customer satisfaction. Compaq cut its prices dramatically in 1991 and 1992. Like many companies, the product price had been previously determined by computing the product cost after it was designed and then multiplying that to achieve the appropriate profit margin. With the new emphasis on price in its product strategy, price became the starting point instead of the ending point. Product development engineers started with the target selling price and then computed the cost budget that they had to work with.

Compaq's new product strategy was to challenge competitors on price and then up the ante with more features, a broader product line, and better services, such as a three-year warranty. In March of 1993, Compaq initiated another price cut, forcing IBM and Dell to follow. Compaq had reduced its cost structure below that of IBM and even Dell so that it had more profit margin to play with. At the same time, Compaq initiated direct-response selling for the first time, getting it into a new low-cost channel of distribution.

Compaq's shift to a price-based offensive strategy was very appropriate for that stage of the PC market. With this strategy, Compaq went from being a company in trouble to the most successful PC company in 1993. Revenues grew to more than $6.5 billion, and it captured 10 percent of the market.

SUMMARY

Price strategy is unique in high-technology products. Price-based strategy determines the relative position of products in a market, and prices decline rapidly throughout a product's life-cycle. Lower prices can increase market penetration, especially with new, innovative products.

Price can be used as an offensive strategy; examples include price leadership, penetration pricing, experience-curve pricing, competing based on price-performance, and promotional discounting. It can also be a defensive strategy; examples include adaptive pricing, segmentation-based pricing, skim pricing, volume-based pricing, and bait-and-switch pricing.

Price strategy can be risky. It needs to be supported by cost advantages such as low-cost design, manufacturing efficiencies, supply-chain efficiencies, technology differences, and development cost efficiencies.

A case study on Compaq Computer illustrates price-based strategy in action. Compaq shifted from a defensive price strategy to an offensive one in reaction to competitors' penetration pricing.

NOTES

1. For a comprehensive review of pricing, see Thomas T. Nagle, *The Strategy and Tactics of Pricing* (Englewood, NJ: Prentice Hall, 1987).

2. William J. Cook, "Computer Chaos," *U.S. News & World Report*, July 26, 1993.

3. Jim Carlton, "Popularity of Some Computers Means Buyers Must Wait," *The Wall Street Journal*, October 21, 1993.

4. Gene Gregory, "Japanese Electronics Technology: Enterprise and Innovation," *Japan Times*, (Tokyo), pp. 96–97.

5. Price leadership is sometimes used to describe the product in a market that establishes the price structure. While frequently this is also the lowest-priced product, it is not necessarily so. Price leadership is used here as the lowest-priced complete product.

6. Catherine Arnst and Peter Burows, "Showdown in Silicon Valley," *Business Week*, November 1, 1993.

7. Bruce D. Henderson, *Henderson On Corporate Strategy*, (Cambridge MA: Abt Books, 1979), p. 106.

8. "Why Gillette Stopped Its Digital Watches," *Business Week*, January 31, 1977, pp. 37–38.

9. "Litronix Cuts Out of Consumer Products," *Business Week*, February 28, 1977, pp. 32–33.

10. *The Wall Street Journal*, October 12, 1993.

11. Phillip Robinson, "Falling Laser-Printer Prices Can Put Them in Schools and Home Offices," *Boston Globe*, July 27, 1993.

12. Robert D. Hof, "Blood on the Tracks," *Business Week*, July 12, 1993.

13. In fact, Michael E. Porter refers to this strategy as a Cost Leadership Strategy. See *Competitive Strategy: Techniques for Analyzing Industries and Competitors* (New York: The Free Press, 1990). The term *price strategy* is used here to emphasize that there can be a difference, but that there is a risk in not linking price and cost.

14. Based on Michel Robert, *Strategy Pure & Simple* (New York: McGraw-Hill, 1993). It references *Fortune*, December 9, 1991.

15. Donna J. May, et al., "Data to Dots in the HP DeskJet Printer," *Hewlett-Packard Journal*, October 1988.

16. Pittiglio Rabin Todd & McGrath, PCBA (Product Circuit Board Assembly) Benchmarking Study, 1992.

17. Ronald Rosenberg, "Down on the Farm," *Boston Globe*, July 20, 1993.

18. Pittiglio Rabin Todd & McGrath, Supply Chain Benchmarking, 1993.

19. Jim Impoco, "Milking the Market," *U.S. News & World Report*, July 26, 1993.

20. Pittiglio Rabin Todd & McGrath, Product Development Benchmarking, 1993.

21. For more information, see Michael E. McGrath and Richard W. Hoole, "Manufacturing's New Economies of Scale," *Harvard Business Review*, May–June 1992.

22. Rick Whiting, *Electronic Business*, October 30, 1989.

23. Eckhard Pfeiffer, "The Compaq Turnaround," *Audacity*, Spring 1993.

24. Stephanie Losee, "How Compaq Keeps the Magic Going," *Fortune*, February 21, 1994.

Chapter Seven

Time-Based
Product Strategy

T ime is becoming an increasingly important competitive factor in product strategy, particularly in high-technology products where the underlying technology advances rapidly, and the markets change quickly. Companies using time-based strategy successfully are able to get a jump on their competitors. They can even achieve advantages to help them stay ahead. However, being first does not guarantee success. Companies that move prematurely can stumble and fall, enabling competitors to walk over them on the way to success.

Time-based product strategy makes the difference between these successes and failures. It is usually a supporting strategy to a primary competitive strategy of differentiation or price leadership, enabling a company to be the first to market with the chosen differentiation or price advantage. Without a primary strategy, a company is merely first with something.

There are two different types of time-based advantages that are frequently confused. One is derived from being first to market; the other comes from being the fastest to market. Being first is the usual focus of time-based competitive strategy. It is a glamorous strategy. Many of the legendary successes, such as Xerox, Polaroid, Kodak, DuPont, Corning, and so on, are companies that were first to create a market. The first company to introduce a new technology is typically hailed as the innovator, and companies preempted by competitors are usually frustrated by being too late.

Time-based competitive strategy can also come from being a follower, but it is important to distinguish between intentionally being a follower and simply being late or slow. Slow or late-reacting companies are less competitive. They are not followers by intention. They are followers because they do not have the competencies to be leaders. Time-based follower strategies are different. The term "fast follower" will be used to emphasize the difference between the slow company and the company that stands by, poised to jump into a market when the timing is right.

There is no notable time-based strategy for the slower or late-reacting company. It is unlikely that a company will be successful in a market where competitors are using time-based strategies to defeat it. Short of a dramatic innovation that is protected by patents, the slow company cannot rely on other competitive strategies to compensate. Any early successes would be generally matched and then improved by the faster competitor. A company with a time-based disadvantage can only be successful if its competitors do not use time-based strategy against it.

No matter what time-based strategy a company chooses to follow, it must have a competitive product development process. Without this, time-based strategy is not feasible. Even if it does not plan to use a time-based strategy, a company should recognize that it may need to defend itself against faster competitors that are using time-based strategy against it.

BASIC CONCEPTS OF TIME-BASED STRATEGY

The primary concepts of time-based strategy come from understanding the two competitive advantages it provides:

- Being the first to market with a new product, feature, or improvement.
- Being faster than competitors.

Though related, they are very different, and the difference is frequently overlooked in a company's haste to move quickly. In some cases, this leads a company to select the wrong time-based strategy.

Advantages Derived from Being First to Market

A company can be first to market even though it is slower than competitors. It just needs to start sooner. Even if its development process takes longer, it can achieve the first-to-market advantage by identifying opportunities before its competitors. Beating the competition by being first to market has several advantages.

1. *The first-to-market company can capture a market share advantage.* Whether introducing a new product platform, a more advanced product, or a new feature, the first to market can capture additional market share by being first. Customers cannot buy a similar product from anyone else, so there is no competition. The first company to market has a temporary monopoly.

In addition to a stronger initial position in the market, there are other advantages as well. A company's reputation can be enhanced by being seen as more innovative. If the advantage is significant enough, a company can preempt competitors or establish barriers to entry. Competitors may see a follower strategy as less attractive since someone has already established an advantage in the market.

In 1977, Larry Ellison cofounded Oracle Systems to develop relational database software. His inspiration came from reading an IBM research paper that described the concept of a relational database. Ironically, Oracle beat IBM to market by three years. It then modified its product to run on computers from a number of other manufacturers. By 1993, Oracle's revenue rose to more than $1.5 billion, and it had 34 percent of the market, compared to IBM's 26 percent.[1]

In another example, Sega introduced its Genesis 16-bit video game player ahead of market leader Nintendo. After a slow reception because the game player was overpriced, Sega was able to increase its market share from 7 percent to 50 percent at the expense of Nintendo, which eventually came out with a 16-bit player. But because Sega was first with the new technology, it displaced Nintendo. Nintendo said that its goal was "to be best, not first." Bing Gordon of Electronic Arts believed that this was a mistake for Nintendo. "In technology the trick is to get in there first. Don't get killed, don't over invest, learn quickly and come out with a new generation of technology."[2]

First-to-market advantages can be particularly successful when a company targets niche markets. Raychem Corporation, for example, makes sophisticated materials products such as irradiated plastics and specialty connectors. Its chairman, Paul Cook, estimated that the company introduced 200,000 products in its first 25 years. Raychem's idea of a great product was one with a 90 percent operating margin, and a 100 percent market share in a $10 million niche.[3]

2. *The first-to-market company gets earlier experience.* Being first enables a company to get earlier experience with customers, technology, suppliers, and channels of distribution. The company can then use this experience to refine the product to stay ahead of competition.

There is nothing like having an actual product in customers' hands to help a company understand what customers really want. Being first to market provides the opportunity to get this experience before competitors. Competitors, of course, can also get much of this information by interviewing customers, working with the same suppliers, or doing research. The information they get is usually not as accurate or detailed, but it is a lot cheaper. Ironically, some companies fail to follow up a first-to-market strategy with a process to capture this experience. Their competitors study it more thoroughly and actually learn more.

The company that first develops a product based on new technology has a head start in refining the technology and its application to the product. Xerox (Haloid at the time) introduced its first commercial xerographic copier in 1949. Initially, the product was not very successful, and most customers returned it because it was too complicated and took several minutes to make a copy. Its only successful application was in making paper masters for offset printing.

Competitors such as 3M, American Photocopy, and Kodak followed Xerox into the market over the next three years. They were not successful either. However, Xerox kept refining and improving its product. Finally, it released the Xerox 914 in 1959. The 914 proved to be the successful product that launched Xerox. It was easy to use and made excellent copies for 5¢ each. Xerox used its early experience to better understand the market and refine the technology. Competitors such as 3M and Kodak were not able to catch up.

The same advantage of early experience can be gained with channels of distribution, manufacturing processes, and suppliers. The key in all of these advantages is *applying* this early experience. The experience itself does not constitute the advantage.

3. *The first-to-market company can influence the definition of standards.* The first to market has a better opportunity to influence product standards. Informally, customers may make the first product to market the de facto standard. For example, in 1956 IBM introduced FORTRAN, one of the first high-level programming languages, using mathematical notation for machine-independent programming. This language became widely accepted as the standard for early mathematical and scientific programming.

Formally, standards groups may use the first product to shape the approved standard. Being first does not necessarily provide control of standards; it just provides an advantage. However, being first also reduces flexibility to change to new standards since the first to market has already committed to a particular approach.[4]

Sony, using its Betamax format, had first-to-market advantages with an 18-month head start in the home VCR market. Competitors JVC and Matsushita followed, but introduced a different and incompatible format: VHS. Betamax offered superior picture and audio quality, while VHS was less expensive and had a longer recording time. The longer recording time turned out to be a major competitive advantage, and Sony lost the battle even though it was first to market.

VHS-based competitors had more time to understand the market before they finalized their designs. When VCR technology was first introduced, nobody was sure whether customers would use it for prerecorded tapes, recording TV programs, or home movies. As customers showed a preference toward recording TV programs, playing time became the more important differentiation between the two standards.

Advantages Derived from Being the Fastest to Develop New Products

A company that is faster than its competition can be first to market even if it starts later. A last-to-start/first-to-finish strategy can be very effective. In most cases, the advantages of being the fastest are more significant than those of being the first.

1. *The fast product developer is nearer in time to the eventual market.* This is an often overlooked advantage of faster time to market. The ability to predict what will be important in a market declines with time. The further out in time, the more difficult the prediction, since the evolution of technology affects product differentiation, and customer expectations change. New competitive products change relative advantage, and competitive prices also change over time.

When a company starts developing a new product, it must predict what the market conditions will be at the time the product will be released. It forecasts market size and price levels. It anticipates competitive products that will be on the market. It estimates the vectors of differentiation that will be preferred by customers. It predicts the impact of technology—its own and that of competitors.

These predictions are easier for a company with a faster product development process since it does not need to forecast as far into the future as its competitors. Figure 7–1 illustrates this concept. The curve shows how accuracy declines over time. As with most predictions, such as the weather, accuracy drops at a faster rate as the length of the prediction period increases.

Two companies, A and B, are both bringing new products to market at the same time, but A's time to market (TTM) is only 18 months, while B's is 36 months. When B started development, it needed to predict market conditions 36 months into the future. Company A started development 18 months later and only had to predict 18 months in advance. Company A is likely to be more accurate.

2. *The fast product developer can get ahead and stay ahead.* By continually staying ahead of its competitors, a company can eventually drive competitors out of the market. The source of this advantage is the speed of the product development process.

Figure 7–2 demonstrates this competitive advantage. Competitor A has a 33 percent advantage in TTM because it has a superior product development process. Assume both companies start development of a first-generation product at the same time. Company A's TTM advantage enables it to bring its product to market a year ahead of Competitor B. Then it starts developing the second generation.

Competitor A releases its second-generation product, while Competitor B's product is still early in the life-cycle of its first generation.

FIGURE 7–1

Accuracy of Predicting Eventual Market Decreases over Time. Competitor A has
the advantage of developing a product that better fits the market.

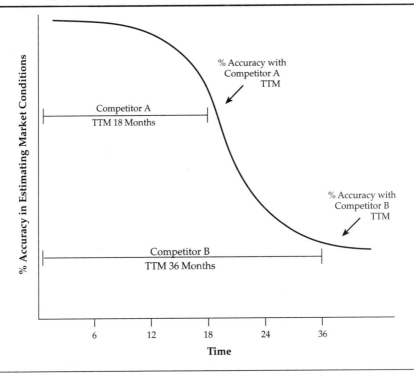

Competitor B is forced to bring out its second-generation product
prematurely. In spite of this, Competitor A introduces its third-
generation product at the same time. In order to be competitive,
Competitor B starts development of its own third-generation product.
However, before it is even finished, Competitor A introduces its
fourth-generation product. End of competition. Competitor B with-
draws from the market.

3. *The fast product developer can use newer technology.* When a company has a shorter development cycle, it can use more advanced technology in its products. Assume that Competitor A has an 18-month
time to market and Competitor B has a 36-month time to market. If both
companies introduced competitive products in 1997, then Competitor
A could use technology available in mid-1995 to design its products,
while Competitor B would need to use 1994 technology.

The advantages of using new technology can vary from none to critical, depending on the differences in the technology used in the two

FIGURE 7–2

Faster Product Development Enables a Competitor to Gain an Advantage.
Competitor A can get a generation ahead of Competitor B.

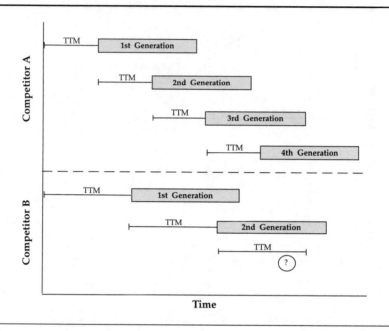

products. In practice, if there is a significant technology advantage, the slower competitor would cancel its product before completion and go back to redesign a more advanced version. However, it may not know if its disadvantage was the result of starting later than its competitor or having an inherent disadvantage in time to market. If it started later, it may be able to catch up, but if it has an inherent disadvantage in time to market, it has no chance.

Sun Microsystems achieved this time advantage in the mid-1980s. It introduced new product platforms every two to three years, more than doubling performance each time. Its major competitor, Apollo, introduced new platforms every four to five years. Eventually, Apollo was unable to keep up with Sun's technology advantage. The two companies followed different development strategies that enabled the differences in development cycles. Sun designed its products with extensive use of off-the-shelf components, including its UNIX operating system. This strategy made its design and manufacturing very flexible. Apollo followed a proprietary strategy. Its Aegis operating system was more powerful than UNIX, but this also caused Apollo to be slower to introduce new technology.

TIME-BASED STRATEGIES

These competitive advantages—first-to-market and fastest—are created through time-based strategies. The strategies themselves are a little different. First-to-market strategies can be pursued even if a company is not the fastest, although the fastest company has the advantage of waiting longer before it acts. There are four specific variations of the first-to-market strategies.

Fast-follower strategies are more successfully executed by companies with TTM advantages. There are two primary fast-follower strategies.

Generic Time-Based Strategies

First-to-market strategies

· Be the first to upgrade products with new technology.

· Respond rapidly to market changes.

· Introduce continuous product innovation.

· Be the first to create a new market.

Fast-follower strategies

· Wait until a new market is clarified before entering it.

· Reverse-engineer successful competitive products.

First-to-Market Strategies

"The early bird catches the worm." This saying embodies first-to-market strategies that are intended to achieve the first-to-market advantages discussed earlier. The four specific strategies vary. Two of them—technology upgrade and market change response—are more responsive. The other two are more innovative.

Strategy: Be the first to upgrade products with new technology.

This is almost always a winning strategy when the market is well understood and the new technology is desired by many customers. The product incorporating the new technology will have a clear differentiation advantage over competing products.

Compaq executed this strategy in September 1986 when it got a jump on IBM by using the faster Intel 386 microprocessor. Compaq's market share increased dramatically as it took sales away from IBM and other competitors that were still using 286 technology. The strategy was clear in this case. There was no confusion about new standards or unproven features. It was a matter of offering better performance for a higher price in a market where continued performance improvements were not only expected, but eagerly anticipated.

The first to market with the new technology wins. How much it wins depends on how long it takes everyone else to catch up. Eli Lilly was first to market with a new technology applied for antidepressant drugs in January 1988. Prozac captured a significant share of the market, and revenues grew to $1.2 billion by 1993. Prozac, which enhances the action of serotonin, a chemical transmitter of messages between nerve cells and the brain, had the market to itself for nearly four years. Pfizer introduced Zoloft in 1992 and SmithKline Beecham introduced Paxil at the beginning of 1993. For these four years, Prozac competed only with older drugs that sold for pennies compared to the $1.75 per pill that it was able to command. Additionally, its early presence in the market gave it a significant lead over the other two drugs. In 1993, Prozac's sales were almost twice as much as those of Zoloft and Paxil combined.[5]

This can also be a risky strategy if the market is not well understood, and the new technology is not clearly anticipated by customers. For example, Philips was the first to market with a new multimedia technology called CD-i, which provided an interactive compact disk for use in entertainment, education, publishing, and training. Philips invested an estimated $1 billion in developing the technology platform along with the related products and software.[6] To be successful with this new technology, Philips needed to establish it as a standard, either by achieving a significant market penetration on its own or by licensing it to others. This was a high-potential, but high-risk, strategy for Philips. In the first two years, it sold approximately 300,000 units using this technology, too few to declare it a success at that time.

Strategy: Respond rapidly to market changes.

When there is a significant change in the market, the competitor able to respond first can get a significant advantage. The change could be a shift in customer preference to a specific vector of differentiation. It could be mandated by law, such as the phase-out of CFCs, or it could be due to the natural evolution of the market. In any case, those companies that respond rapidly can capture the advantage. Those that respond slowly may be left behind.

This was illustrated in the applications software market in 1990 when Microsoft introduced Windows 3.0, and it became the operating system preferred by most PC users. Some software companies moved quickly and converted their applications to the Windows operating system. Microsoft was obviously one of them, but so was Intuit with its Quicken financial software application. These companies that responded quickly achieved an enormous competitive advantage as Windows-based applications were greatly preferred over DOS-based applications. Others such as Lotus and WordPerfect suffered by being slow to respond.

There is also danger in being the first to respond to a change in the market. IBM launched a "clone-killer" strategy in 1987 with its PS/2, incorporating its proprietary Micro Channel architecture. IBM thought that these new capabilities would attract customers and could be used to establish a defense against competitors manufacturing IBM clones. Customers were not attracted to this change. IBM read the market wrong and paid a price. This mistake combined with several others caused it to lose 20 percent market share by the end of the decade, which translated to almost $10 billion in lost revenue.[7]

Strategy: Introduce continuous product innovation.

With this time-based strategy, a company tries to get ahead of its competitors along a vector of differentiation, and then jump out ahead again as soon as they react. It places competitors in the position of continuously reacting and playing catch-up, and eventually it can accumulate a decisive advantage.

This was the strategy followed by Mitsubishi in residential air conditioners where previously an American company had led the market.[8] In 1980, Mitsubishi introduced a product using integrated circuits to control the heat-pump cycle, increasing energy efficiency. The following year, it modified the product with two improvements that enabled simpler installation, thereby bypassing HVAC dealers in the distribution channel. These modifications were "quick-connect" freon lines and the use of a microprocessor to simplify wiring. In 1982, Mitsubishi introduced a new version with a high-efficiency rotary compressor and modified electronics that increased energy efficiency. Electronic cycle control was improved in 1983 by adding sensors, and energy efficiency was increased still further. The next step in increasing energy efficiency was to include an inverter in 1984 to manage the electric motor speed over a wide range of variability.

In 1985, it introduced shape-memory alloys to automatically adjust to the most efficient circulation pattern. Meanwhile, the slower

American competitor was only beginning to introduce electronics in 1986. Mitsubishi upgraded its air conditioners with optic sensors to adjust for day and night conditions, and introduced a remote control. Learning circuitry was added in 1988, adapting each product to local environmental conditions and initiating defrosting. In 1989, electronic air purifiers were added as an option.

The slower American competitor did not have a chance. It was so many years behind Mitsubishi, it could not possibly catch up. It conceded defeat and started to source its advanced air conditioners, heat pumps, and components from Mitsubishi and other Japanese companies. Mitsubishi's strategy incorporated small improvements instead of putting them all together into a single release of a new product. It can be a successful strategy, but must be clearly established as the product strategy right from the beginning.

Strategy: Be the first to create a new market.

The innovative company that creates a new market can achieve significant first-to-market advantages. Xerox created the market for plain-paper copying with its application of xerography and, as a result, built a very successful business. Sony created the "Walkman" market and used first-to-market advantages to continue to lead this new market. Alexander Graham Bell invented the telephone in 1875, and his company, AT&T, grew until it constituted a regulated monopoly. Intel created the market for the microprocessor and continued to stay ahead of competitors.

Creating a new market often involves pioneering technology. Pioneering technology is usually at the beginning of the technology lifecycle and significantly improves during its early stages. The first company to focus on a new technology also has the lead in improving that technology.

Corning, for example, made fiber-optic technology feasible with its breakthrough in 1970. Corning scientists Robert Maurer, Donald Keck, and Peter Schultz developed an optical fiber that retained more than one percent of the light transmitted per kilometer. Optical fiber was first installed commercially in 1976, and since then Corning has continued to improve the technology. It made an early long-term commitment to invest in the manufacturing processes necessary to mass produce high-quality fiber. Corning continued to improve fiber optic technology, reducing the transmission loss by nearly 100 times. After more than 20 years of consistently improving fiber optic technology, Corning was well positioned to take advantage of it as the basis for the communications highways of the future.[9]

If a company creates a market, then by definition, it is the first to market. However, to be successful it needs to consistently build upon these first-to-market advantages.

A company has the opportunity to create a new market when it has new technology or sees a new market evolving. It can choose to wait by putting the technology "on the shelf" for future rapid deployment, or it can introduce it immediately. A decision to delay is taken by the market leader for one of two reasons. First, it may not want to cannibalize its existing products until the last possible moment, waiting until competitive moves force it to deploy the new technology. Second, it may want to let other companies enter this unknown market first, observe their shortcomings, then introduce a better product. To be successful using this method, the company must have excellent market and competitive sensing capabilities, so it can pounce as soon as market conditions are appropriate.

IBM actually developed reduced-instruction-set computing (RISC) but did not want to immediately cannibalize its existing complex-instruction-set computing (CISC) product lines. It delayed bringing out competitive workstation products and using RISC. It also delayed introducing RISC technology in microprocessors until the PowerPC in 1994.

Selecting the strategy of creating a new market is only possible if a company has the opportunity. It can then decide to act on the opportunity and be first to market, or wait until others act first and then implement a fast-follower strategy.

Fast-Follower Strategies

Being a fast follower is not the same as being slow. Fast-follower strategies can be very successful. The objective is to wait until the market is sufficiently clear before entering. Reverse engineering is a related strategy. With this, the company not only waits, but it copies the successful product.

Strategy: Wait until a new market is clarified before entering it.

New markets are exciting. They have few competitors and offer the possibility of rapid growth. It is not clear how they will be structured, how customers will use the new products, or what competitive factors will be most important.

Fast-follower strategies can be particularly successful in new markets that are created by advances in technology where nobody really knows how customers will eventually use the product or what they will prefer. The first company to market may fail because it misguesses what the market wants. Others standing on the sidelines can watch and then move into the market when it is clearer.

For example, when microwave ovens were first introduced, early manufacturers, such as Litton, saw them as a replacement for the conventional kitchen stove. This idea did not sell well. However, when microwaves were repositioned as a secondary method of cooking and their size was reduced, the success was enormous. Unfortunately, it was the later entrants, Japanese and Korean companies, that benefited from Litton's experience.[10]

New markets, particularly high-technology markets, must be educated. This is an expensive process, the cost of which is usually born by the first company to market. Competitors who cannot or do not want to educate initial customers will let someone else do it first. For example, in the market for on-line home data services competitors let Prodigy Services (a joint venture of IBM and Sears) educate the market. Prodigy aggressively went after the home market in 1984, and by 1993 it had two million users, but it also had cumulative losses of about $1 billion and was still not making money.[11] Prodigy needed to educate initial customers in this mass market about why they needed the service and how to use it. Substantial investment was required for advertising and support. Many early customers did not even know why they needed a modem to connect their computer to the telephone line. Competitors let Prodigy make this early investment in developing the market, and then entered the market when customers were better educated.

Market segmentation, pricing, and the vectors of differentiation valued by customers are also unknown in a new market. Using the Prodigy example, competitors CompuServe and America Online positioned themselves in more profitable segments of the market and fine-tuned their pricing. CompuServe focused on the business user and charged a premium for must-have data. America Online focused on more experienced home users. Both were very profitable in 1993, while Prodigy continued to lose money.

Sometimes a fast follower can actually develop a product and put it on the shelf until the timing is right. One communications company did this by developing an ISDN (Integrated Services Digital Network) product in the late 1980s, but not releasing it until the company saw what competition was doing. At the appropriate time, it announced the product with better price/performance than the competition. By that time, it had also developed the capability to deliver multiple releases of new ISDN products every six months.

Strategy: Reverse-engineer successful competitive products.

Reverse engineering is the process of designing a product by copying the function of a successful competitive product. It is different from directly copying the product itself, since the emphasis is on copying function, not the specific design. Reverse engineering significantly reduces development cost and eases market entry since there is already a comparable product that is already successful in the market.

For example, PC-clone manufacturers reverse engineered the IBM PC to create a product that was functionally similar. They avoided significant investments in technology and reduced market risk because they copied a product that was already accepted by customers. Amdahl used a similar process it called "better engineering" when it consolidated IBM's logic design to achieve higher performance at lower cost.

Cyrix reverse engineered Intel's 486 microprocessor by looking at how the 486 processed software and then developing its own architecture. Its microprocessors were compatible with Intel's since it followed identical software interface protocols. Cyrix also claimed that its CX 486 microprocessors were faster and more efficient than Intel's.

RISKS OF TIME-BASED STRATEGY

While time-based strategy can provide significant competitive advantage, it also presents significant risks. Too many companies blindly proceed with these strategies, assuming there is no downside. They believe that first is always better. Then they discover the cost of failure. The primary risks of time-based strategy fall into three categories: premature market entry, compressed product life-cycles, and inferior product development processes

Premature Market Entry

"Pioneers get arrows in their backs." This old saying is apropos to product strategy. The company that pioneers the application of a new technology or creates a new market is not necessarily the one that will be most successful. Sony had this experience in VCRs with the failure of its Betamax standard.

One of the more famous examples of this occurred with the innovation of the CAT (Computer Assisted Tomographic) scanner, which was invented by Britain's EMI Ltd. EMI was originally a record company that became successful marketing Beatles records. It used some of its profits to diversify into electronics. As part of this diversification, one of its engineers, Godfrey Housefield, invented the CAT scanner from the inspiration of a neighbor surgeon who complained about not being able to "see" brain tumors.

EMI became an instant sensation, outdoing traditional suppliers of X-ray equipment, such as General Electric, Siemens, and Philips. However, the CAT scanner was easy to improve technically since it was early in its technology cycle, and EMI did not have the technical resources to keep up with competitors. Nor did it have the marketing and support resources needed to be competitive. While Housefield received a Nobel prize and knighthood, EMI exited the business in 1979.[12]

Japanese electronics companies have successfully used first-to-market strategies to secure dominant positions in most major consumer electronics markets: home VCRs, video cameras, Walkmen, compact disk players, digital tape players, and so on. In many of these efforts, they skillfully used government support and consortia to strengthen the development and initial entry.

This was also the strategy they used in creating the market for HDTV (high-definition television), but their initial efforts failed. The Japanese consumer electronic companies, its Ministry of Post and Telecommunication, and its public broadcasting network (NHK) formed a triad for nearly 30 years to develop Hi-Vision. NHK invested ¥19 billion ($100 million). Their product platform used analog technology, but the United States and EEC waited until more advanced digital technology was feasible. Even in Japan, they sold only 15,000 Hi-Vision televisions per year.[13]

Companies need to ask themselves this question: Is it better to be first in this market or to let others do the initial pioneering, watch their experience closely, and then respond quickly? They need to make a conscious strategic choice between a first-to-market and a fast-follower strategy.

Compressed Product Life-Cycle

Time-based product strategies can shorten product life-cycles as major competitors aggressively battle to be the first to introduce the latest incremental improvement in technology and the newest features. This happened in consumer electronics products during the late 1980s where the life-cycle of new products was reduced in many cases to as low as several months. The cumulative effects of this were lower profit margins due to price reductions on the inventory of products that were replaced, inadequate returns on the investments in new product development from products having only a six- to nine-month life, and customer confusion about the proliferation of new products with negligible differences.

Time-based strategy, like other strategies, needs to be thoroughly thought through before it is implemented. The company should be confident that this is likely to be a winning strategy, and should identify the potential outcomes of its actions, including the expected competitor response. This response should include competitive escalations that may lead to deterioration of the entire market through factors such as compressed product life-cycles. The final judgment is made with this consideration in mind.

Inferior Product Development Processes

Companies that try to implement time-based product strategy without a superior product development process are setting themselves up to fail. They set an objective of being first to market or fastest to respond, but are incapable of achieving this objective or staying in the game if competitors follow. As a result, they create an opportunity for competitors that have a superior process and can move faster.

To avoid this mistake, a company needs to benchmark its product development process against the industry. If it is among the best, it has the option of time-based strategy. If it is among the worst, it is better not to precipitate time-based competition.

THE KEY TO IMPLEMENTING TIME-BASED PRODUCT STRATEGY: A SUPERIOR PRODUCT DEVELOPMENT PROCESS

Any time-based strategy—whether first-to-market or fast-follower—requires a competitive advantage in product development. A company with a product development process superior to its competitors can successfully execute a time-based strategy. It needs to have a product development process with several minimum performance characteristics:

- Its time to market must be at least as fast as that of its competitors.
- It must be capable of quickly reacting to new technology and changes in the market.
- Its product-development process needs to be integrated with its product-strategy process.

What makes time-based strategy most interesting is that there are significant time-to-market differences among companies, and these differences can be used to achieve competitive advantage. Figure 7–3 illustrates these differences quite dramatically. Based on a 1993 study

FIGURE 7–3

Time-to-Market Advantages and Trends. The best-in-class (BIC) companies have a 50% advantage in time to market. Reduced time to market is expected for all companies.

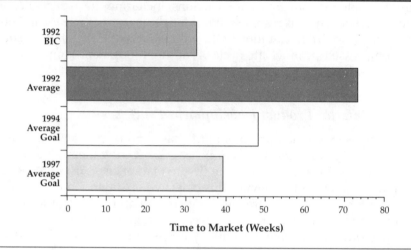

of similar products in 45 electronic-systems companies, it shows that the best-in-class (BIC) companies (those in the top 20 percent) have an advantage of more than 50 percent in time to market.[14] These companies have the opportunity to implement first-to-market or fast-follower strategies better than their competitors.

The results of a time-to-market difference of this magnitude can be dramatic. These companies could control their markets in the next five to ten years if they implement their strategies correctly.

As the figure shows, the average time to market is also expected to improve significantly (by almost 33 percent from 1992 to 1994, with continuing improvement by 1997. Many companies recognize the strategic implications of time to market and have begun implementing major improvements.[15]

SUMMARY

Time-based product strategy is a supporting strategy. It stems from two types of advantages: those derived from being first to market and those derived from being the fastest. While related, these are very different advantages. The first to market can capture a market share advantage, get earlier experience, and influence the definition of standards. The faster developer can make more accurate predictions, stay ahead of competition, and use newer technology.

These advantages lead to two types of time-based strategy: first-to-market strategies and fast-follower strategies. Time-based strategies are not without risk, and these risks need to be clearly understood before a strategy is selected. No matter what the time-based strategy, the key is the time required to develop a new product, and this depends on the effectiveness of the product development process.

NOTES

1. Alan Deutchman, "The Next Big Info Tech Battle," *Fortune,* November 29, 1993.

2. Nikhil Hutheesing, "Games People Play," *Forbes,* October 25, 1993.

3. Thomas Peters, "The Mythology of Innovation, or a Skunkworks Tale Part II," *Readings in the Management of Innovation,* ed. Michael L. Tushman and William L. Moore (New York: Ballinger Publishing, 1988), p. 143.

4. For a comprehensive discussion of standards, see H. Landis Gabel, *Competitive Strategies for Product Standards* (London: McGraw-Hill, 1991).

5. Milt Freudenheim, "The Drug Makers Are Listening to Prozac," *The New York Times,* January 9, 1994.

6. Merrill Lynch estimate, November 10, 1993.

7. Paul Carroll, *Big Blues: The Unmaking of IBM* (New York: Crown, 1993), p. 150.

8. George Stalk, Jr., and Thomas M. Hout, *Competing Against Time* (New York: The Free Press, 1990), pp. 112–114.

9. Information provided by Corning.

10. Thomas S. Robertson, "How to Reduce Market Penetration Cycle Times," *Sloan Management Review,* Fall 1993.

11. Nikhil Hutheesing, "The First Shall Be Last," *Forbes,* October 25, 1993.

12. Richard Foster, *Innovation—The Attacker's Advantage* (New York: Summit Books, 1986), pp. 193–194.

13. Takeshi Matsuzaka, "HDTV Shift Stuns Industry," *Nikkei Weekly,* February 28, 1994.

14. Pittiglio Rabin Todd & McGrath, Product Development Benchmarking, 1993.

15. For additional insights into improving the product development process, see Michael E. McGrath, Michael T. Anthony, and Amram Shapiro, *Product Development Success Through Product and Cycle-time Excellence,* (Stoneham MA: Butterworth-Heinemann, 1992).

Chapter Eight

Global Product Strategy

S elling products in foreign countries provided a source of growth and additional revenue for high-technology companies during the 1970s. With limited modifications, they were able to successfully export products to selected foreign markets. Competing was not the primary goal; incremental revenue was a sufficient achievement. In some cases, foreign markets even presented companies with the opportunity to sell older products that were no longer competitive in their home markets.

During the 1980s, global competition intensified, and by the 1990s, high-technology companies needed to compete globally to be successful. Any one national market, even the American or Japanese market, became too small a portion of the total worldwide market. Concentrating on one market made a company vulnerable to global competitors. The primary reasons for this is that the cost of developing a high-technology product is so great that spreading it across many worldwide markets provides significant economic advantage.

There are many reasons why products vary among countries. National languages, preferences, and uses vary. Technical standards and certification requirements differ. From country to country, market segmentation can be different. Finally, protectionism and nationalism can influence product preferences.

Yet, customers throughout the world are expecting products, particularly high-technology products, that meet global standards. They are increasingly reluctant to pay more for products that are less advanced but customized to local preferences.

Theodore Levitt used this trend to distinguish between multinational and global corporations.

> The multinational corporation knows a lot about a great many countries, and continually adapts itself to their supposed differences. The global corporation knows one great thing about all countries, and lures them to its custom by capitalizing on the one great thing they all have in common. The global corporation looks to the nations of the world not for how they are different but for how they are alike. While it recognizes the presumed need to be globally competitive as well as nationally responsive, it constantly seeks in every way to standardize everything into a common global mode.[1]

154

As worldwide product requirements become more common, or the advantages of commonalty are preferred to local alternatives, the opportunity for global product strategy increases. The advantages of a global strategy can be significant, but it needs to be implemented with an understanding of the reasons behind the international product differences. In addition, global product strategy is part of a broader global strategy. Its interdependence with other elements of the global strategy is so significant that the relationship must be understood before global product strategy can be formulated.

BASIC CONCEPTS OF GLOBAL PRODUCT STRATEGY

The strategy surrounding whether and how to globalize products is based on a few critical underlying concepts:

- Global products can have an enormous economic advantage.
- The reasons for international differences in high-technology products are diverse.
- Global product strategy is only one element of an overall global strategy.

The first of these three concepts provides the primary motivation for a global product strategy. The other two concepts help to shape formulation and integration of global product strategy within a broader context.

Economic Advantage of Global Products

The economic advantages of global products can be so great that global products may eventually dominate most products from national competitors. With sales in multiple worldwide markets, global products attain a much higher level of revenue, which can be used to fund even more advanced product development, and provide the global competitor a much higher return on product development investments.

The best way to illustrate the significance of this advantage is through an example. The product being illustrated is electronic instrumentation for medical diagnostics that is sold in four countries: America, Japan, United Kingdom, and Italy. The analysis summarized in Figure 8–1 shows the market size in each of the four markets. The market in each country has an indigenous (domestic) competitor (A-1, J-1, U-1, I-1) with approximately 40 percent share of the market. This is a typical market share for the leading national competitor. In the

FIGURE 8–1

Economic Analysis of Global Competition. *Shows the significance of the advantage achieved by a global product.*

Country Market ($M)	United States $800	Japan $500	U.K. $300	Italy $100	Total $1,700
A-1					
Market Share	30%				14%
Revenue ($M)	$240				$240
R&D ($M)	$10				$10
ROI	140%				140%
J-1					
Market Share		40%			12%
Revenue ($M)		$200			$200
R&D ($M)		$10			$10
ROI		100%			100%
U-1					
Market Share			40%		7%
Revenue ($M)			$120		$120
R&D ($M)			$10		$10
ROI			20%		20%
I-1					
Market Share				40%	2%
Revenue ($M)				$40	$40
R&D ($M)				$10	$10
ROI				-60%	-60%
G-1					
Market Share	30%	20%	20%	20%	25%
Revenue ($M)	$240	$100	$60	$20	$420
R&D ($M)	$10	$1	$1	$1	$13
ROI	140%	900%	500%	100%	223%

American market, both the national competitor (A-1) and the global competitor (G-1), which is also an American company, each have 30 percent.

Assume that the total market for the new product is $1.7 billion in the four markets over its entire life-cycle. Also assume that the $10 million development costs are the same for each competitor. The global competitor (G-1) incurs an additional $1 million for customizing and qualifying the product in each additional market. In order to isolate the effect of global R&D leverage, it is assumed that each company makes 10 percent profit on sales. In reality, manufacturing and distribution economies of scale would favor the large competition even more.

Figure 8–1 shows the differences in the competitive economics. The American competitor (A-1) and the Japanese competitor (J-1) achieve a good return (simple ROI with no consideration of the cost of capital) on their investment in developing this product, 140 percent and 100 percent respectively. The competitor from the United Kingdom (U-1) receives some investment return (20 percent) but not significant enough to justify the risk. The Italian competitor (I-1) loses money. The global competitor (G-1), on the other hand, does extremely well, achieving a 223 percent return on investment, and capturing 25 percent of the global market.

This analysis leads to some interesting conclusions relative to a global product strategy:

- Global competitors have a significant economic advantage.
- Competitors that focus exclusively on smaller national markets cannot afford to develop many high-technology products because the return on investment is insufficient.
- Global competitors need to have a significant share of major markets, particularly their own. This is an advantage for competitors from large markets.

These conclusions led to the formation of the European Economic Community (EEC). Indigenous competitors in individual European countries could not compete against larger global competitors, and they could not themselves become global competitors without having a larger "domestic" market.

A telephone switching system, for example, costs approximately $1 billion to develop. In Europe, five different companies previously developed switches for the unique standards in their own countries. Each investment was spread over a much smaller base than the equivalent investment in a telephone switch for the American or Japanese market. Even in a large market, R&D costs are a high percentage of the cost of a telephone switch. AT&T, for example, estimates that R&D can run 8 to 15 percent of the price of a switch.[2]

The same is true for a new pharmaceutical drug. With development costs estimated at $200 million to $300 million for a new drug, it is likely that global competitors will be the only ones that can afford the R&D investment.

Competitive advantages can be gained by developing a product to be successful in most major worldwide markets. However, the problem is that product requirements do differ internationally.

International Differences in High-Technology Products

There are many varied reasons for international differences in products. Some of these are unavoidable, yet others may be managed in the right circumstances.

Certification requirements.   Government agencies require numerous certifications of high-technology products. For example, telecommunication products in Europe must be approved by the various national telephone systems (PTTs). The process of adapting and certifying foreign designs to meet these telecommunication standards, called homologation, can be quite extensive and varies among countries. Medical, pharmaceutical, and biotechnology products require approval from regulatory agencies in individual national governments. Some of these requirements are being standardized in Europe with EEC unification practices. Different approval requirements affect the design of these products. They need to be incorporated into the initial design or modified later to meet each country's requirements. Extensive approval processes can also delay the release of new products in some countries. For example, the United States has one of the longer new drug approval cycles, and new drugs are frequently introduced first in other countries before becoming available in the United States.

Standards.   Differing standards are a major problem in high-technology markets. Standards vary by country or groups of countries, and products that work in one country may not work at all in another. Televisions and VCRs made for the United States will not work in Europe. Three standards were originally developed for color television broadcasting: NTSC (National Television Standards Committee) in the United States and Japan based on the original RCA technology with 525 scanning lines per screen, SECAM (segmented color memory) with 825 lines per screen in France, and PAL (phased alternate line) with 635 lines per screen in Germany. The three standards continue to be used throughout the world but remain incompatible.

Cellular telephone provides a current example. In 1988 there were 18 cellular networks in Europe, which served over one million subscribers with six different and incompatible standards. NMT (Nordic Mobile Telephone) was developed by the Scandinavian PTTs in the late 1970s. Variations of this (NMT-450 and NMT-900) were implemented differently in several countries. TACS (Total Access Communications Systems) was a refinement of the American 800 MHz AMPS system. It was used in the United Kingdom and Ireland. Radiocom 2000 was developed by Matra and used in France. C-450 was developed by Siemens in 1985 and used in Germany. RTMS was the Italian standard, and COMVIK was a unique network used in Sweden.[3]

Variations in standards such as these in the European cellular industry in 1988 make it very difficult for a company to design and market a global product. The products are technically very different. This is intentional. Each country wants its "national champion" (the company based in its country) to be the company that dominates its national market, not foreign competitors.

However, the EEC recognized that this practice also handicapped national companies from developing the economic leverage to become global competitors. As a result, it formed the GSM (Groupe Special Mobile) to develop standards and specifications for a Pan-European digital cellular system. This was feasible since new standards were needed for the next cellular platform that would be based on digital rather than analog technology. The systems and equipment for this were developed by joint ventures of European suppliers. This would enable a common standard throughout Europe, but it would still be different from the digital cellular standards in other countries.

Many standards will come together over time, particularly as changes in technology require new ones. Some standards that are deeply entrenched, such as electric power specifications and left- versus right-drive cars, may never change.

Language differences.   Languages differ among countries, and products sold to customers in multiple countries need to accommodate a variety of languages. In high-technology products, language differences are important in user instructions, training materials, control panels, and user-interfaces in computer systems.

English can be used as a universal language in some products, particularly those that are more technical. Complex technical support manuals used by a limited number of customers are an example. However, in most products the benefit of translating user instructions and manuals into the most common foreign languages is worth the added cost. Apple Computer, for example, translates most of its user manuals into 10–15 foreign languages.

Computer software products have more difficulty with foreign languages than other high-technology products. The user interface that appears on the computer screen is language specific, and it is difficult to translate all words and messages.

Differences in use.   Products are varied to accommodate the different ways that people throughout the world prefer to do things. For example, in some countries, supermarket check-out clerks stand as they work, while clerks in other countries sit. The configuration of automatic supermarket scanners needs to be varied accordingly.

Differences in use can also come from a difference in infrastructure. For example, newer technology can have very different applicability in less developed countries. In some cases, new technology may even have a broader market where it overcomes the lack of existing infrastructure, as evidenced by the explosion of cellular phones in Latin America and China where the existing phone systems are primitive. In other cases, new technology may not be successful, as is seen in low sales of disposable syringes in less developed countries because they are more expensive than reusable syringes.

Eventually, many of the ways people throughout the world do things may be standardized by technology. To some extent, cultural difference is an excuse used by country managers within multinational companies to get specific product models designed for each country. Whirlpool challenged these differences with good results. Cultural preferences indicated that people in every European country wanted a different type of washing machine. The French preferred top-loading machines, for example, while the Germans preferred front-loaders. However, Whirlpool found that customers would trade these cultural preferences for machines that had superior performance, were easier to use, and were more economical. By devising a uniform product line, Whirlpool eliminated half of its European warehouses, simplified distribution, and increased profits by 27 percent.[4]

Demographics. Demographics such as population distribution, income levels, and income distribution differ by country. For example, 1993 income per capita was $23,000 in the United States, but only $3,000 in Latin America. The richest 10 percent of the population in Brazil had more than 50 percent of the national income, while the same proportion had only 25 percent of the U.S. income.

Differences in demographics can create dissimilar market segmentation from one country to another. In the pharmaceutical industry, for example, the market is affected by the size and composition of the population, as well as the standard of living. Age distribution changes the market size for particular products. For example, an older population shifts the emphasis to geriatric-related drugs.

The size of the pharmaceutical market in a country is directly related its standard of living. As a result, the U.S. market is many times larger than the Chinese market. In fact, most of the worldwide pharmaceutical market is centered in the United States, Japan, and Western Europe, particularly France, Germany, and the United Kingdom.

There are also differences in business market segmentation among countries. The differences in computer-buying patterns in Europe provides an example. Italy, with numerous midsize companies, has a larger midsize computer segment. Computers such as IBM's AS/400 are very popular. The United Kingdom progressed faster than other European countries in the application of desktop computers. Some European countries, particularly Germany, continued to maintain the old centralized approach to management, and because of this they continued to prefer large, centralized mainframe computers.

National preferences/protectionism. Customers in most countries prefer to buy products that were made in that country. They see the local company as being more committed to their country by providing jobs. This preference will become even more important as global unemployment increases.

National preference is particularly important when the customer is a national government or government-owned company, which is the case with many high-technology products. Besides the obvious defense products, most telecommunications products are purchased by government agencies. In many countries, the government is the primary customer for medical and pharmaceutical products since it provides health care.

National governments also influence buying practices to entice foreign companies to locate facilities (jobs) in their country. Several major computer companies, for example, have received computer purchase inducements to locate facilities in a particular country. After building a new plant, they received large orders from government agencies and educational institutions.

Trade barriers such as tariffs and quotas are used by countries to protect their local industries. The motivation behind these barriers is simple: preserve jobs. All countries want to support companies that provide jobs to their citizens.

Subtle protectionism is often behind other stated reasons why a product cannot be sold in a foreign country. For example, one telecommunications company was the leader in its own country but could not get the approval authority in a foreign country to approve its communications switch. Finally, it met with the minister of trade in that country to resolve the issue. The company was told that the real reason was that it did not invest enough in the country. So it acquired a local company that was going bankrupt, preserved 1,500 jobs, and its communications switch was approved.

Sometimes, protectionism is not so subtle. In the early days of the computer industry, Japan placed a high tariff on imported computers and refused to let IBM build a manufacturing facility in Japan until it agreed to Japanese restrictions. Likewise, Texas Instruments was prohibited from producing semiconductors in Japan until it licensed its technology to Japanese companies and agreed to limit its penetration of the Japanese market.[5]

FIGURE 8–2

Elements of Global Strategy. Each element is closely coupled with the others.

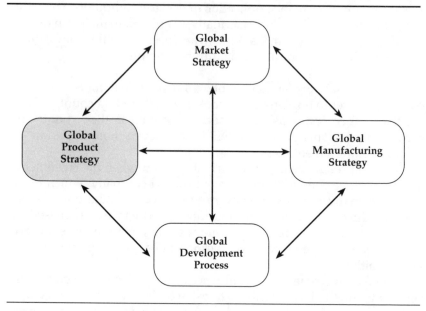

Elements of Global Strategy

Global product strategy is so closely coupled with other global strategies that it is difficult to succeed at one without integrating the others. This close coupling has led to confusion and frustration by some companies trying to make progress on improving one element of global strategy without addressing the others. Decomposing the different elements of global strategy helps to clarify the role of each. Figure 8–2 illustrates these elements.

Global market strategy defines the national and regional markets in which a company will compete. Global manufacturing strategy determines where a company locates manufacturing facilities and how its global supply chain functions. The global product developmentprocess provides the framework for how products are developed for worldwide markets with worldwide resources. Global product strategy defines which products are developed and how the characteristics of these products address global requirements. That is the focus here, but before getting into more detail, the other strategies need to be explained.

Global market strategy. Global market strategy determines where a company will sell its products. It is primarily a sales strategy, although it affects product strategy because of its implications concerning product variability and product priorities.

While there are numerous country-markets throughout the world, high-technology products are marketable primarily to developed countries, considerably limiting the number of country-markets. In addition, the developed country-markets vary by size, and the smaller markets may not be economically attractive. The advantages of selling products into multiple markets is offset by the costs of entering each market.

Most high-technology companies concentrate on the triad of regions: North America, Western Europe, and Japan, which constitute the dominant portion of the global market for most high-technology products. Usually a company is based in one of these regions and then expands into the others. Expansion into Europe, which was previously done country by country, has become Pan-European in the 1990s.

Some companies go beyond the triad of major markets into smaller developed and larger undeveloped country-markets. Companies relentlessly pursuing this expansion strategy enter one or more new country-markets each year. There are advantages to this strategy. Smaller markets tend to be less competitive, and in some there is no competition at all. Moreover, once a company dominates a small market, it discourages competitors from entering. Eventually, a sufficient number of smaller markets can increase the overall global volume needed to achieve economic advantage.

Emerging country-markets have long-term potential; some of them can eventually grow to be larger than the triadic markets. For example, the pharmaceutical market in China is very small today (estimated at only a few billion dollars); however, it could be a $20 billion market by 2000 and possibly the largest pharmaceutical market in the world by 2050.

From a product strategy viewpoint, the sequence of expansion should be based on the size of the country-market, the strength of competitors, and the suitability of current and planned products. From a sales strategy viewpoint, it is typically based on the feasibility or ease of expansion into targeted country-markets.

Global manufacturing strategy.   A global product strategy is tightly linked to global manufacturing strategy in two ways. First, a company needs to have an international manufacturing capability as it adopts a more global product strategy. International manufacturing is helpful in implementing a customized global or universal global product strategy, although a universal global strategy does not require international manufacturing unless there are significant trade barriers. The second link comes from the leverage provided by manufacturing

FIGURE 8–3

Relationship of International Manufacturing to Foreign Sales. Companies increase manufacturing in foreign regions to increase foreign sales.

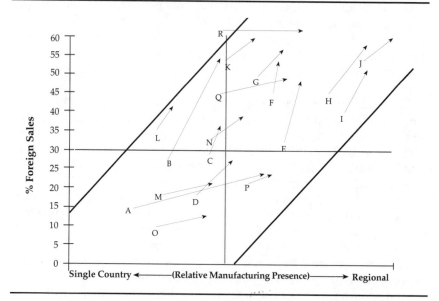

products in foreign markets. Companies with foreign manufacturing are much more successful in achieving foreign sales than those that do not manufacture in their target markets.

A study of international manufacturing strategy by Pittiglio Rabin Todd & McGrath (PRTM) illustrates this relationship. Figure 8–3 analyzes the relationship of foreign manufacturing to foreign sales for 18 electronics companies. The horizontal axis shows the relative presence of manufacturing in foreign countries, while the vertical axis shows the percentage of foreign sales.

The position of each company (A through R) on the chart clearly shows the relationship between these two factors in 1986. The arrows show the movement of each company from 1986 to 1990. To be successful internationally, a company needs to operate manufacturing facilities in the major foreign countries where it does business. PRTM's study looked at the relationship between manufacturing locations and sales leverage by individual region and country, applied statistical correlations, and reviewed specific case studies. The conclusion is that foreign manufacturing clearly leverages foreign sales.

There are several reasons for this leverage. In many countries, customers prefer a product manufactured locally over an imported product. In some countries, protectionism in the form of tariffs or informal barriers provides advantages to locally manufactured products. Local manufacturing facilitates the understanding of local requirements and enables a faster response to changes in customer preferences. Finally, local manufacturing provides a focal point for customer visits, allowing a company to demonstrate the care and quality that goes into producing products.

Global product development process. Developing products globally requires a product development process that leverages resources scattered throughout the world. Many companies find this difficult to accomplish, as is illustrated in the following scene, one that is typical in many high-technology companies.

The project team in an American high-technology company was proposing a new product, primarily for the American market. While the company was international and had a stated goal of becoming more global, the product requirements and sales forecasts for the product were based solely on the American market.

"Will this product be successful in Europe?" the CEO asked.

The team leader responded, "We believe it will be, but we don't have much information on the European market."

"What does the European marketing manager think about the product?" the CEO asked the team leader.

"He said he had other priorities and that he would look at it when it was close to completion."

"I think we need to understand the worldwide requirements for this product," the VP of Engineering said. "We don't have the resources to re-engineer this for the European market."

"What about the requirements for the product in Japan and Brazil?" another executive asked.

"We don't know anything about those markets," the marketing member of the project team responded.

At this point, the VP of North American Sales jumped into the conversation, "We can't delay development to find out what other countries want." "We need this product yesterday. If they can't define what they need, that's their problem. The cost benefit is sufficient, and I think we should just go ahead and develop it. Then we can modify it to fit their needs later."

After more discussion, the CEO said, "We keep saying we are trying to become more global. Eventually, we need to begin making decisions on a global, not a national, basis. I think we need to start now."

The other executives agreed, and they declined to approve the project until it integrated worldwide requirements. The CEO said that he would contact the marketing organizations in the other countries and get their participation.

To be successful, a global product development process must, at a minimum, accomplish the following:

- Priorities for assigning resources to new product opportunities must be determined at a global level. This is a subtle, but difficult, change for most companies that are used to decentralized decision making. They need to place product approval authority at a worldwide executive level.

- Product marketing tasks such as product specification, competitive positioning, and sales forecasting need to be done through global collaboration. This requires coordination among multiple marketing and sales managers throughout the world, which is not an easy task for most companies.

- Worldwide sales organizations need to make commitments to support the product launch, sell the product, and achieve sales forecasts. This requires early involvement and coordination of all sales organizations throughout the world.

In addition, a company may perform development globally with design, engineering, testing, and so on being done in multiple countries. This enables balancing resources throughout the world and leveraging critical skills without restriction to where they are located. However, this is not required to develop a global product.

GLOBAL PRODUCT STRATEGIES

In general, a company should try to leverage as much of its product development effort as is possible by selling products throughout the world. However, at the same time, it must sell competitive products in each foreign country. This leverage ranges from selling the exact same product in all countries to simply coordinating some research activities. In between, a company could leverage product platforms, modules, or technology. This leads to a range of four alternative strategies for globalizing products.

Generic Global Product Strategies

- Develop a regional product.
- Leverage a regional product into new regions.
- Develop a customized global product.
- Develop a universal global product.

Global product strategies are applied on an individual product-platform basis, and a company with multiple platforms can follow multiple global product strategies simultaneously. Competitive advantage can be achieved by applying a better global strategy than competitors; the catch is the degree of variation that restricts these strategies. Where there is a low level of R&D investment required, a global product strategy has less impact, and any global strategy can be equally as effective.

The characteristics of products can change over time as they progress through their life-cycle, and these changes can shift the competitive advantages of one strategy over another. For example, in the early days of the personal computer industry, R&D costs were relatively high. Over time, however, these costs declined as companies moved to standard components and volumes increased. This change reduced the advantages of a more global strategy.

Strategy: Develop a regional product.

Products designed for customers in a single country or a few directly related countries follow a regional product strategy. This is sometimes referred to as a local or domestic strategy when the product is developed for only a single country. Most high-technology products, however, are at least regionally focused, developed for the North American or European markets, for example.

An international variation of this strategy is used when a company develops multiple products, each designed separately for an individual region, usually by a company's business units in these regions. This is referred to as a multiregional product strategy. Since there is little difference between a local, regional, or multiregional strategy from a product strategy perspective, they are collectively referred to as a regional strategy.

With the regional strategy, product development priorities are established to achieve regional objectives. Product requirements and specifications are based on what is necessary to be successful in the targeted region. There is little or no sharing of product requirements from one region to another and no reason to consolidate requirements. Each product is essentially developed in a vacuum, although there may be some sharing of common experience.

This is an appropriate strategy for some products. Take power transformers as an example. ABB (Asea Brown Boveri), with $1 billion in revenue, is the leader in designing these products used in the transmission of electricity over long distances. ABB does not see this as a global business, but as a collection of local businesses with intense global coordination. ABB transformer factories concentrate on maximizing design and production flexibility and focus tightly on the needs of domestic customers.[6] Product strategy is regionally focused, but there can be indirect leverage from global coordination in other activities. Global coordination includes consolidation of material requirements to gain advantages from suppliers and shared learning on common processes and problems. ABB has become excellent at attaining this leverage.

Developing multiple regional products can be an inefficient strategy since it does not leverage development resources. This was the mistake made by a company that designed and manufactured computer-based industrial control systems. The company was the leader in the United States, and it acquired the leading company in the United Kingdom. It wanted to implement a customized global product strategy but was unable to because each country had what appeared to be different requirements. American customers preferred a computer terminal interface with keyboard entry and output displayed on the computer screen. The British preferred system controls with individual knobs, buttons, and switches.

Because of these perceived differences, the company used a multi-regional product strategy. In the end, this cost the company over $20 million and prevented it from gaining an economic advantage over local competitors. Ironically, the difference turned out to be a design trade-off, not a significant cultural difference. A local competitor in the United Kingdom was successful with a computer terminal interface.

Strategy: Leverage a regional product into new regions.

This is a subsequent strategy to the previous one. After a company develops a product for a specific region (typically domestic), it then decides to sell it to another region (typically foreign). To do this it needs to re-engineer the product. This is also the traditional export strategy. Companies develop a product for their home market and simply export it to foreign markets. Sales agents in those foreign countries make the changes necessary and then resell the product.

Generally, this is not a good strategy since the re-engineered product is usually not as successful and is always more expensive. Unfortunately, this is one of the more popular strategies because of the organizational structure and product development process limitations of most companies. Product development decisions are frequently made on a regional basis, and marketing involvement is restricted to regional responsibility.

A medical diagnostic equipment company illustrates the inefficiency of this strategy. The company had facilities in multiple countries, each developing products for regional markets. When it began selling an American-designed product in Europe it needed to re-engineer the product design and remanufacture each product sold to fit local needs. Completely tested diagnostic equipment was shipped by the factory in the United States to the factory in England. When received there, it was torn apart and rebuilt to meet British and European requirements. The necessary changes included additional shielding, the substitution of approved materials to meet local government standards, and replacing the power supply and related components. The equipment was then retested and put into inventory. Because this was a medical product, testing was a significant cost.

When shipped to a particular European country, the equipment was again modified for local needs and then retested. This process of remanufacturing and retesting more than doubled the cost of the equipment. Eventually, the company found that it was able to design and test one product for global requirements. Some of the additional requirements were easier to put into all products instead of remanufacturing them.

This strategy may be appropriate when there is a significant difference in the maturity or critical characteristics of regional markets. In this case, the timing of market entry may be so different that common requirements cannot be considered without causing a costly delay in entering the primary market. The Japanese PC market provides an interesting example.

The Japanese PC was significantly different from others up until the middle of 1993. PCs could not handle *kanji*, the Japanese character set, so Japanese computer manufacturers "Japanized" standard PC hardware and operating systems. Since they had their own variations, the result was incompatibility among computers and software. Using a keyboard was also unusual in Japan since *kanji* required thousands of pictograms instead of phonetic characters. Handwriting was used instead of typing. Computers made typing possible, but the market evolved as stand-alone word processors (*wahpuro*) instead of multipurpose computers. PCs were used in Japan much less often than in the United States—only 9.9 per 100 Japanese workers compared to 41.7 per 100 American workers.[7]

In 1993, Microsoft introduced a new Japanese-language version of Windows, Windows 3.1J. This version was fully bilingual and could run on almost any manufacturers' hardware. It also provided the easy-to-use capabilities that made Windows so successful throughout the rest of the world. Japanese companies could no longer compete using locally developed operating systems. Microsoft's economic advantages were just too significant. Microsoft implemented this strategy by changing the Japanese market to some degree. Alternatively, it could have followed a multiregional product strategy and designed a unique product for the Japanese market.

In this case, there were also strategic implications for computer hardware and software companies. Windows 3.1J made a customized global product strategy possible for them because the Japanese market became similar enough to the American and European markets. They could sell their existing products after modifying them for language differences. The ability to use a customized global strategy provides significant advantages to global competitors such as IBM, Dell, and Compaq, which had only 15 percent of the $6 billion Japanese market.[8] Local competitors like NEC, Fujitsu, and Toshiba were put on the defensive by the feasibility of a customized global product strategy instead of a regional strategy.

Strategy: Develop a customized global product.

The customized global product strategy is perhaps the most successful. It involves designing a base product that is then customized for local requirements with the minimum amount of effort. The cost advantages and R&D leverage can be significant. The key to this strategy is balancing changes to fit local market requirements and changes to the local market to fit global product requirements.

The customized global product strategy begins with a design that considers the requirements of all relevant national markets. Common requirements are designed into the base product, and variations are added as part of the final configuration.

A manufacturer of cable TV set-top boxes executed this strategy brilliantly. It designed a common product platform for worldwide requirements. This enabled high-volume, low-cost production of the electronics and set-top box. Variations for different markets (the United States, Mexico, Brazil, Hong Kong, and Europe) were implemented prior to shipment by inserting the appropriate software code, enabling the common electronics to interface with the different protocols and transmission formats.

Xerox implemented a customized global strategy when it developed the Xerox 5100 copier in 1990. The design incorporated the requirements for U.S., European, and Japanese markets with input solicited from customers in each of these markets. In the past, Xerox had developed unique products for each market because the requirements for a successful product differ in each region, particularly in Japan. Copiers in Japan need to accommodate a lighter weight paper, Kanji characters are much more difficult to copy, and the use of blue lead pencil is common. The Xerox 5100 copier was introduced in Japan in November 1990 and in the United States in February 1991. It was the fastest global roll-out for any new product at Xerox, and it saved Xerox $10 million in development costs.[9]

Key to the design of a customized global product is maintaining commonalty for as long as possible. Country-specific variations are then added at the latest possible stage in the manufacturing process, preferably after the product had been tested. Some companies use "country kits" for software, accessories, plugs, and so on, to accommodate the unique country-specific differences.

One computer printer manufacturer had a creative approach. The only remaining differences in its product were the power converter and electrical plugs used in different countries. It left a small hole in the shipping box after the product was manufactured and put in the appropriate converter plug as the product was shipped to the customer.[10]

Biotechnology and pharmaceutical companies generally follow a customized global strategy. The basic drug is the same, but the dosage format and packaging may be different for each country. The approval process is also unique, so the product needs to be approved individually in each country. Because of this, a key aspect of a customized global strategy is the up-front planning of coordinated approval in multiple countries.

Strategy: Develop a universal global product.

Developing a common product for all worldwide markets provides the highest leverage, both in development and in manufacturing. It enables a company to design a product once, eliminating costly, after-the-fact redesigns each time a company enters a new market. Unfortunately, developing a universal global product is not always possible.

Raw material and component products can use this strategy. Many electronic components, such as semiconductors and disk drives, do not change based on the requirements of national markets. Advanced materials and specialty chemicals products are generally global.

Some products require relatively small modifications so they can be developed as universal global products. Mainframes and supercomputers, for example, require minor modifications for power and environmental factors in each country, but this is so insignificant when compared to their cost that they are virtually global products.

Still another class of product must have interoperability on a global basis. Data communication hubs and routers need to accommodate most international communication standards, so they are universal global products by requirement.

RISKS OF GLOBAL PRODUCT STRATEGIES

The primary risk of product strategies that are less global, such as regional or leveraged regional strategies, is that competitors will gain an economic advantage with a more global strategy, such as customized global or universal global. However, there are also risks involved in strategies that are more global.

Failure to Execute

It is very difficult to execute global product strategy. Many companies forget this and formulate their global product strategy independent of their overall global capabilities. Then they fail to execute because they lack the necessary capability.

As was previously discussed, global product strategy is closely coupled with other global strategies. If a company does not have the right global manufacturing or supply-chain capability, it cannot efficiently build or deliver a global product. If it does not have a global product development process, it cannot develop a product that would be successful in multiple country-markets. And if it does not have a global distribution capability, it cannot sell the product in country-markets even if it was designed as a global product.

Execution of a global product strategy is not easy, even for the best companies. Microsoft's attempt to penetrate the Chinese software market provides an interesting example. It introduced a Chinese version of its Windows software, called P-Win. But by early 1994, it faced many obstacles. The powerful Ministry of Electronics Industry (MEI) promoted another operating system called Chinese Star, developed by SunTendy, a Chinese company. (Interestingly, Chinese Star required both Microsoft DOS and Windows.) The MEI wanted Microsoft to drop P-Win and endorse Chinese Star so that Microsoft could not dominate the Chinese Software market. It was reluctant to give licenses allowing software companies to write software for P-Win.

Microsoft had other problems with P-Win as well. Instead of developing P-Win in China, Microsoft decided to develop it in Taiwan, which is viewed as a renegade province by the Chinese. The Taiwanese also used a different set of Chinese characters and a different way of typing them into a computer. P-Win lacked the most popular Chinese-input methods and did not support many application software products. On top of all this, software piracy was a major problem in China. Shenzhen University was involved in making unauthorized copies of Microsoft products. Microsoft estimated that 650,000 copies were made, costing it $30 million. The university was fined $260.[11]

Insufficient Proximity to National Requirements

Not all high-technology products can be successful as universal global products. Choosing this strategy and designing a product for all worldwide markets can backfire. For example, customers in major global markets may not be willing to trade advantages in price or capabilities for less customization to their individual needs. Or a product developed to meet the requirements of so many country-markets becomes overly complex compared to products developed for one country-market. An applications software company fell into this trap when it developed one accounting software product to meet the needs of more than a dozen national markets.

For high-technology products, the magnitude of investment in product development is an indicator of the likelihood that a product will be successful as a universal global product. This correlation is an extension of the economic advantages discussed earlier. Supercomputers, for example, are successful universal global products because of their high level of R&D investment per unit. However, this is not always the case. An example is Japanese consumer electronic companies that developed analog-based, high-definition television expecting their investment to give them a competitive advantage in the American and European markets. These markets decided to use a digital-based standard, and the Japanese products would not work.

The universal global product needs to maintain sufficient proximity to national products. The advantages of lower price or better capabilities need to offset the advantages of a product designed to specific national requirements.

SUMMARY

Differing requirements for high-technology products across international markets are beginning to converge. As they do, the convergence provides an opportunity for global product strategies where a product is developed for worldwide markets. The economic benefit of product globalization is so significant that global competitors may eventually dominate regional competitors. Global product strategy is interdependent with the other elements of global strategy. It needs to be managed in conjunction with global market strategy, global product development, and global manufacturing. It also needs to consider international differences.

There is a range of four different global product strategies: regional products, regional products modified for another region, customized global products, and universal global products. Each progressively leverages the investment in product development. A strategy that is more global is preferable to one that is less global—as long as the strategy is feasible. There are risks to selecting a strategy that ignores real national requirements or cannot be successfully executed.

NOTES

1. Theodore Levitt, *The Marketing Imagination* (New York: The Free Press, 1986), p. 28.

2. John J. Keller, "AT&T's Network Equipment Unit Is Bouncing Back," *The Wall Street Journal*, December 2, 1993.

3. John A. Quelch, Robert D. Buzzell, and Eric R. Salama, *The Marketing Challenge of 1992* (Reading, MA: Addison-Wesley, 1992).

4. William Echikson, "Inventing Eurocleaning," *Fortune*, Autumn/Winter 1993.

5. Clyde V. Prestowitz, Jr., *Trading Places* (New York: Basic Books, 1988), pp. 34–35.

6. William Taylor, "The Logic of Global Business: An Interview with ABB's Percy Barnevik," *Harvard Business Review*, March–April 1991.

7. Andrew Pollack, "Now It's Japan's Turn to Play Catch-Up," *The New York Times*, November 21, 1993.

8. Brenton R. Schlender, "U.S. PCs Invade Japan," *Fortune*, July 12, 1993.

9. For more information, see Michael E. McGrath and Richard W. Hoole, "Manufacturing's New Economies of Scale," *Harvard Business Review*, May–June 1992.

10. European consumers are used to assembling the plugs on appliances.

11. Jeffrey Parker, "Can Microsoft Bust China's Protectionist Strategy?" *Reuters World Report*, March 17, 1994.

Chapter Nine

Cannibalization Strategy

C annibalization[1] is a recurring strategic issue for high-technology companies, caused by emerging technology that drives them to continuously upgrade and replace existing products. Cannibalization occurs when a new product replaces an existing product. This is normal with high-technology products, but cannibalization becomes a particularly difficult strategic issue when the new product is economically unfavorable compared to the existing product. This was the case in the following company.

The project team was proud of what they had accomplished; after all, they had been working on the new product for almost 18 months. They expected that it would be completed and ready for release in another 6 months. When released, it would be a very competitive product, with 80 percent of the capabilities of the company's existing product at less than 50 percent of the price, and these were the capabilities that were most important to customers.

Their afternoon status presentation to the executive committee went very well. The Engineering VP was pleased with some of the innovative design features, and the Sales VP thought that the product would sell well. Only the Chief Financial Officer (CFO) seemed to be concerned. He kept asking questions about the impact on the company's existing product. It was like he was in another meeting, they thought. The existing product was not their responsibility.

They were obviously shocked, to say the least, when they were told two days later that the project had been canceled. The prevailing opinion seemed to be that senior management was either crazy or incompetent. The reason for cancellation, they were told, was to avoid cannibalization of the existing product.

"This is stupid," they responded. "Our new product is a much better value for the customer. If we don't keep up with what the customer wants, the competition will."

They knew that the CFO was behind all this and asked for a meeting with him to try to change the decision. He started by explaining his analysis to the team. He took their forecast that 5,000 units would be sold over the next three years, and then explained that 80 percent of these sales would come at the expense of the existing product.

"No kidding," the lead design engineer thought sarcastically, *"we have al-most 70 percent of the market; where else is it going to come from?"*

"As you know," the CFO went on, *"the profit on the new product is a lot less than that of the existing product." "When you compare the results of launching this new product to keeping the existing one, we would lose almost $50 million in profit. If you include the cost of excess and obsolete inventory on the existing product and incremental manufacturing overhead, this loss could go up to $65 million."*

"What about expanding the market with the lower price?" someone asked. *"No, the market for our products is pretty well fixed in size,"* the marketing team member responded. *"There is little or no price elasticity."*

"What about the threat of competition?" another engineer asked.

"This is unlikely for the time being," the marketing team member re-sponded. *"Our existing product is only 18 months old, and the competition isn't expected to have a product in this range for at least two years."*

"All of this work was wasted then," one of them said in frustration.

"We were asked to see what elements of the design could be used to cost-reduce the existing product," the team leader said. *"Maybe some of it can be used there."*

As they got up dejectedly and began to walk out of the room, one of the en-gineers asked the CFO, *"Couldn't this analysis have been done sooner?"*

"Yes," he responded. *"It could have been done at the very beginning, but it wasn't. Everyone was too excited about getting started and didn't think through the impact of cannibalization."*

BASIC CONCEPTS OF CANNIBALIZATION

Cannibalization is perhaps the most misunderstood or most over-looked product strategy in high-technology companies. Very few com-panies appear to understand the basic concepts of cannibalization.

- Cannibalization can be either a normal aspect of product strategy or a major strategic dilemma.
- Cannibalization problems can have several causes.

Cannibalization: Normal or Dilemma?

Cannibalization can be a normal aspect of product strategy: An im-proved product replaces an existing one. It can also create a dilemma: The new product will be less profitable than the product it replaces.

In the normal case of cannibalization, an improved version of a product or a new product platform replaces one currently being sold. As is illustrated in Figure 9–1, the original product approaches the end

FIGURE 9–1
Normal Product Replacement Cycle. Illustrates a typical replacement cycle.

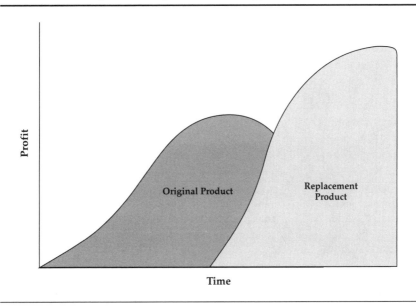

of its life-cycle, sustaining sales by reduced price over the last couple of years. The new replacement product is introduced, typically at a higher price, and the company implements an orderly transition, using the price difference between the old and the new products to manage the sales mix between them. This enables manufacturing to phase out production and reduce inventory of the older product while ramping up production of the new product.

The issue of cannibalization occurs when there is not an orderly or profitable transition. The replacement product kills the original product before its time. However, cannibalization can also be good. New products within a product line generally cannibalize other existing products within the same product line. Companies make their strategic mistakes in not understanding when cannibalization should be avoided and when it is appropriate.

Figure 9–2 illustrates how cannibalization can reduce profits. The original product is still successful when the replacement product is released, but sales and profits begin to decline as sales are transferred to the replacement product. However, the replacement product profit in this example is lower than what the company would have made by continuing to sell the original product. This difference can be caused by lower prices or higher costs of the replacement product. The darkly shaded section represents lost profit.

FIGURE 9–2

The Cost of Cannibalization. Illustrates the profit lost through cannibalization.

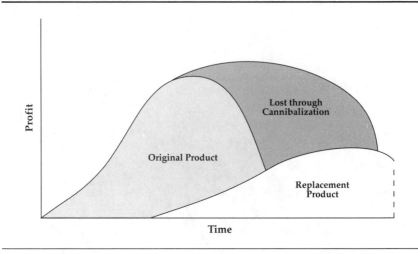

Cannibalization is particularly important for the market leader. Introduction of a new product at the expense of the most successful product in the market usually has little upside potential. Yet, failure to introduce a new product or technology can provide an opportunity for a competitor to attack the market.

Causes of Cannibalization

Cannibalization should be avoided, or at least approached cautiously, when it has an unfavorable economic impact. Lower profit contribution, unfavorable economics, significant retooling, or higher technical risk are typical cannibalization problems.

Lower profit contribution.   A new product can generate a lower profit contribution than the product it cannibalizes when the new product is sold at a lower price with a resulting lower profit per unit, *and* the lower price does not sufficiently increase market share or market size. The new, lower-priced product must create sufficient incremental unit sales to offset the lower profit per unit. Incremental unit sales above those of the existing product can be achieved through a higher market share and/or by increasing the size of the market.

Unfavorable economics.   Technology changes can sometimes cause cannibalization by a completely different type of product. The following is a case in point. Business forms is a $6 billion market that is likely to be cannibalized by personal computers. Using personal computers, information can be entered directly, and the completed form can be printed all much more easily than typing on a form. The information can be edited, entered automatically, and integrated into other computer systems without retyping. Many forms, particularly multipart forms, are thrown away without being used. Computer-generated forms can eliminate this waste.

One company that was a leader in multipart forms for financial services faced this issue of cannibalization. A team of computer-savvy forms designers proposed a new software product that would automate one of the company's most popular forms, permitting the company to expand into application software. Discussions with customers showed a high interest in the software product.

The product was completed and released to the market 18 months later and proved to be a success. In the first two years, $15 million of product was sold, returning ten times the development costs. Unfortunately, the company's sale of the form that it cannibalized were reduced by $30 million in the second year. When the company examined the economics of this cannibalization, they saw something similar to the following ($ million):

Year	Software Revenue	Software Profit	Lost Forms Revenue	Lost Forms Profit	Change in Profit
1	$6.0	$3.0	$5.0	$1.5	$1.5
2	$9.0	$4.5	$30.0	$9.0	($4.5)
3	$10.0	$5.0	$50.0	$15.0	($10.0)
4	$6.0	$3.0	$60.0	$18.0	($15.0)
5	$5.0	$2.5	$80.0	$24.0	($21.5)

The analysis showed that the new software product was a one-time sale, but it was cannibalizing an ongoing revenue stream. By the time the company realized the economic impact, it was too late. The cost was almost $20 million per year. Although this cannibalization may eventually be necessary, dilemmas such as this are what make cannibalization such an important strategic issue.

Significant retooling. When the new product requires a different manufacturing process, incremental profit is lower because of the investment in that process and because of the write-offs associated with closing current manufacturing plants. One company facing such a problem was the market leader with a medical device that had 85 percent market share. The company manufactured the product in high volume at three plants. Researchers saw the opportunity to redesign the device using a new material that would provide additional safety advantages to its customers.

While devices made from this new material were better, customers were not willing to pay very much more for them. Medical reimbursement schemes prevented customers from passing along higher prices. So the company had an opportunity for improving its product, but could not increase prices. Also, it had invested more than $50 million over the last ten years to automate its manufacturing to reduce its product costs as much as possible. The new material used in the proposed device would make these manufacturing facilities obsolete, and the company would probably need to close these facilities completely and relocate production. The new product would require an investment in new manufacturing plants of more than $40 million over the next three years.

After developers produced a prototype of the new device, the company delayed its decision to complete development because of cannibalization. Management of the company was split on this issue. Some believed the company had to introduce the new product regardless of the financial consequences. If it did not, a competitor would, and the company would lose its position in the market. Others believed that cannibalization would only cause disruption and a significant reduction of profit for the next three years. To them, it was pure stupidity.

After many months of discussion, the company finally decided on a compromise strategy. It completed development using the new material but only in a limited format—one aimed at a very small market segment where the company did not have significant penetration. That way, it could test the customer reception to the device with the new material and develop production using incremental capacity.

Higher technical risks.   The new product may provide a favorable economic impact, but it may introduce much higher risk. In this case, a company can cannibalize its position in the market with a failed product. Again, the market leader has the most to lose.

A manufacturer of test equipment suffered this problem. It developed a new fully automated test system that would handle 50 tests simultaneously, compared to the one-test-at-a-time capacity of its semi-automated test equipment. It would be first to market with a fully automated system and would increase profits even though it would cannibalize its semi-automated equipment. The advanced technology and high performance would enable the company to charge a premium and reap higher margins.

This advanced technology had higher risks, which the company failed to recognize. After it successfully introduced the new system and had more than 100 customers, it discovered a fatal software problem. When a power interruption occurred, the new automated system got confused and mixed up the reported results. One test sample would get the reported results of another. Customers stopped buying the new automated system as well as the previous semi-automated instrument. Instead, they purchased a new highly reliable semi-automated instrument from a Japanese competitor. A year after introducing the new automated system, the company had gone from a 75 percent market share to less than 30 percent.

CANNIBALIZATION STRATEGIES

Cannibalization is not always bad. Deliberate cannibalization can be a key element of product strategy. For the attacker, the fear of cannibalization may be the defender's Achilles' heal. For the defender, controlled cannibalization may be a reluctant, but necessary, strategy to repel competitors.

Cannibalization Attack Strategies

Since cannibalization hurts the market leader, it can provide attackers with an advantage. The attacker, either a new market entrant or a competitor with a much smaller market share, has less to lose than the market leader.

Generic Cannibalization Strategies

Cannibalization Attack Strategies
- Cannibalize the market to attack the market leader.
- Introduce new technology first.

Defensive Cannibalization Strategies
- Cannibalize yourself before competitors do it.
- Introduce cannibalization to continue as the technology leader.
- Manage the rate of cannibalization through pricing.
- Minimize cannibalization by restricting introduction to specific market segments.

Strategy: Cannibalize the market to attack the market leader.

Cannibalizing an existing market is a successful strategy for attacking an entrenched market leader. By upsetting the market, the attacker erodes the position of the dominant company, although the attacker cannibalizes its own products in the process. The attacker hopes to compensate for its cannibalization loss with increased market share in the redefined market.

Sega Enterprises' attack on Nintendo's dominance of the $3.5 billion American video game market included a strategy to cannibalize its own video game software with a new form of software distribution. Sega formed a joint venture with Time Warner Entertainment and Telecommunications Inc. in 1993 to offer Sega's video games through cable television networks. The joint venture's Sega Channel provided Sega's 100 or more video games for a monthly fee of $20.[2]

This strategy could have significantly cannibalized Sega's own game software revenue, since it would receive a much lower license fee for software distributed this way. However, as the market attacker instead of the leader, Sega's strategy was to increase its overall market share in both game players and software by redefining the market. To be successful, the higher volume needed to offset a lower profit per unit. This strategy also positioned Sega for future technology improvements when interactive cable will enable video games to be played together by groups of cable subscribers.

In this product strategy, the attacker is willing to make the sacrifice of cannibalization since it has less to lose and more to gain. Cannibalization favors the attacker rather than the market defender. High-technology companies that have a small market share, but desire to increase it, should consider alternative cannibalization strategies rather than simply trying to compete directly with the market leader.

High-technology markets are unique in this regard. Constantly changing technology offers the opportunity to redefine products in a way that cannibalizes the market and delivers a competitive blow to the market leader that is forced to sacrifice more.

Strategy: Introduce new technology first.

The market leader has a vested interest in maintaining the current technology as long as possible. After all, this is usually the most stable and profitable time in the product platform life-cycle. When the market leader considers introducing replacement technology, cannibalization usually makes the financial return and risk unattractive. So the leader waits.

This delay provides an opportunity for an attacker to move first in introducing the new technology. The attacker can use this strategy, which is a variation of the first-to-market strategy, to leapfrog the market leader. Sega used this strategy when it introduced its 16-bit Genesis video game player ahead of Nintendo, which was content to continue with its 8-bit player as long as possible. Nintendo's share of the U.S. market dropped from 90 percent to 50 percent, while Sega's increased from 7 percent to almost 50 percent. Ironically, because Sega was successful, it has more to lose in the implementation of the previous cannibalization strategy.

This strategy of attacking a market leader with new technology while the leader is trying to hold on to the old technology is common in high-technology industries. The minicomputer companies used it against mainframe computer companies. PC companies used it against the minicomputer companies.

Defensive Cannibalization Strategies

Cannibalization can also be a defensive strategy for the market leader. In these strategies, the market leader uses cannibalization as a defense similar to burning sections of a forest to create fire breaks to stop a forest fire.

Strategy: Cannibalize yourself before competitors do it.

Cannibalization of a company's own products may be necessary as a defensive strategy to keep an attacking competitor from being successful. Under this strategy, a company chooses to cannibalize itself rather than let a competitor do it.

The drug industry provides an example of cannibalization as defensive strategy. Drug companies maintain high prices on patented drugs to generate the income necessary to cover research costs. They could reduce the price, but would subsequently starve their research and development efforts. However, once a drug comes off patent, ferocious price competition starts. At this time the drug company usually phases out of the market for the drug and supports its business through other patented drugs.

However, Merck began to implement a strategy of intentional cannibalization of some of its products as they came off patent. In a joint venture with Johnson & Johnson, it introduced an over-the-counter version of its popular ulcer drug, Pepcid. Merck also entered the generic drug market with diflunisal, made from the same compound as its branded arthritis drug, Dolobid. Both of these products were made in the same plant in West Point, Pennsylvania.[3] Rhone-Poulenc Rorer, Marion Merrell Dow, Glaxo, and Warner-Lambert initiated similar strategies to selectively cannibalize their off-patent prescription drugs.

Timing is the key to successfully implementing cannibalization as a defensive strategy. If it is implemented too soon, cannibalization will cause unnecessary lost profits. If it is implemented too late, attackers will seize the market.

Sometimes a company can create a strategy to fend off competition without significantly cannibalizing itself. Eastman Kodak's creative defense of its film and film processing market provides an example. Under the threat of digital photography and camcorders, Kodak developed the photo CD. Many companies in Kodak's position would have reacted by introducing a digital camera and cannibalizing their film and film development businesses. But Kodak found a way to integrate this business into its solution. It designed the photo CD player to use CDs prepared by the Kodak photofinisher from normal 35mm film. A photographer takes pictures with existing camera equipment and film and then requests a copy on CD, at an extra charge. The CD can be viewed on normal television, using the photo CD player.

Strategy: Introduce cannibalization to continue as the technology leader.

The technology leader in a market regularly cannibalizes its existing successful products just as its competitors begin to catch up. Intel, for example, cannibalized its two-and-a-half-year-old 8088 microprocessor with its 80286 processor in February of 1982. It replaced the 80286 with the 386 in October 1985 and replaced the 386 with the 486 in April 1989. Finally, it replaced the 486 with the Pentium in May 1993.

Regular cannibalization by the technology leader is successful when the underlying technology continuously advances. When it does, the technology leader can pace the market by establishing regular product life-cycles. In the Intel example, it was able to establish the following half-life[4] life-cycles:

- 8088 2 years 8 months
- 80286 3 years 8 months
- 386 3 years 6 months
- 486 4 years 1 month

Intel also lengthened the life-cycle of the 486 by several months when it delayed the introduction of the Pentium because competition had not yet caught up. With this delay, Intel reduced cannibalization of the 486 and increased profits. One analyst estimated that for every new Pentium chip, Intel could churn out up to a dozen more 486 microprocessors, and the delay increased profits by more than $112 million in 1993.[5]

Strategy: Manage the rate of cannibalization through pricing.

Pricing is used most often as the mechanism to control the rate of cannibalization. In cases where cannibalization is an issue, the price for the new product is set at a level that encourages a particular sales mix of the existing and new products. If the price of the new product is relatively higher, the rate of cannibalization will be lower. Reducing the price of the new product will usually increase the rate of cannibalization.

Strategy: Minimize cannibalization by restricting introduction to specific market segments.

The medical device company discussed previously applied this strategy to minimize cannibalization by restricting introduction of its new product to specific market segments.

Some market segments are less vulnerable to cannibalization because the company either has more to gain or less to lose in this segment. By tailoring the new product to this segment, a company gets the benefits without the loss. It also has the opportunity to get experience with the new product.

Sometimes, however, a product drifts into another segment. The aircraft industry provides a good example. In 1990, Boeing was uncomfortably aware of the threat that the Airbus A340 long haul aircraft posed to its product line and began development of the Boeing 777. Early sales for the 777 were encouraging, showing comparable performance against the Airbus product. However, orders for the larger 747 "jumbo" plummeted, resulting in an order intake of just two in 1993. There were many factors involved, such as deregulation of the airline industry, which resulted in many more direct city-to-city flights with lower-capacity requirements (so-called "long, thin routes"). The high-capacity jumbos were in more demand when regulation permitted only the hub-spoke arrangement, where all passengers flew into one international airport and took connecting flights to their destinations. However, upgrade plans for the 777 indicated a passenger capacity of 550 against a 747 "jumbo" limit of 566, and the 777 started to become more of a competitor than a complement.[6]

RISKS OF CANNIBALIZATION STRATEGIES

The risks of cannibalization strategy are quite clear: cannibalizing when it is not necessary and not cannibalizing when it is necessary. The strategic challenge of cannibalization strategy is knowing when to do it and when to defer it.

Premature Cannibalization

Premature cannibalization is the primary cannibalization risk. In some cases, the costs incurred by cannibalization are more significant than the costs to develop the new product.

Why do companies do this to themselves? Usually, it is not because they thought about it but made the wrong choice. Surprisingly, it is because they did not think about it before doing it.

Avoiding Necessary Cannibalization

Some companies—particularly those that are conservative market leaders—err in the other direction. They avoid cannibalization too long and let competitors get an advantage. Instead of introducing new technology first, they let competitors bring it to market.

IBM made some severe mistakes by avoiding cannibalization because it was the market leader, letting competitors succeed where it had developed new technology. It developed RISC technology but delayed introduction, in part because it would cannibalize current products. It also intentionally restricted the capabilities of the PCjr so that the product would not take sales away from the PC. These restricted capabilities contributed to the failure of the PCjr. Lou Gerstner, the new CEO of IBM, recognized the problems created by IBM's avoidance of cannibalization, "We've got to eradicate out of anybody's mentality in IBM that we don't cannibalize our product."[7]

ANALYTICAL FRAMEWORK

Companies frequently stumble in trying to evaluate the impact of cannibalization, and in doing so they end up making the wrong strategic decision. They may think they have a great opportunity when it is not so great because of the impact of cannibalization. They may decide against introducing a new product because of cannibalization and then lose market share that was not factored into their analysis.

Figure 9–3 provides an illustration of the alternative ways used to analyze the impact of cannibalization. Many companies use one of the first two alternatives (usually they progress from the first to the second), but the third is the correct alternative way to analyze cannibalization. The financial analysis is somewhat simplified to illustrate the main point.

The first alternative is a straightforward financial analysis of the new product opportunity. Fifty thousand units will be sold in 1996, 400,000 the next year, and so on. Assuming a net income of 15 percent (to simplify the analysis), the new product will make a profit of $375,000 in 1996, increasing to $12 million in 1999 and 2000. Assuming an initial investment of $10 million to develop the product, it will fully recover the money in 1997 and make a net profit of more than $24 million. It appears to be a great opportunity!

However, the second analytical approach (Alternative 2) considers the impact of cannibalization. In 1997, 300,000 of the 400,000 units sold are expected to come from sales of the company's existing product. This is inevitable since the company is the leader in the market. In the analysis, net income from the previous analysis ($375, $2,700, etc.) is the starting point, and the effect of cannibalization is an adjustment. The selling price ($40) for the current product is multiplied by the estimate of unit cannibalization to compute the revenue loss from cannibalization. This revenue loss is then used to estimate the net income cannibalized and the estimated income net of cannibalization.

Cannibalization reduces estimated net income in 1997 from $2.7 million to $900,000, and it continues every year. For simplicity sake, this assumes the same profit margin, even though this is not usually the case. Considering cannibalization, the investment of $10 million is never fully recovered, leaving a loss of more than $1 million at the end of the year 2000.

What about the sales that would be lost if the company does nothing? Considering this is necessary, and it is in alternative 3. This alternative includes an estimate of lost sales for the existing product. These are sales that would be lost to competition if the company did nothing. Sales would begin to erode in 1998 with an estimated 500,000 units expected to be lost. This will increase to 1 million in 1999.

This analysis begins with the income net of cannibalization from Alternative 2 and makes the adjustments necessary to consider the impact of sales that would be lost by doing nothing. The estimated units of lost sales are multiplied by the selling price and percentage of net income to compute the expected lost income. Netting the sales that are expected to be lost against cannibalization yields a net income of

FIGURE 9–3

Alternative Analytical Approaches. Illustrates three alternative methods to analyze cannibalization. Alternative 3 is the correct one.

Alternative One	1996	1997	1998	1999	2000
Revenue:					
Units (000)	50	400	1,200	2,000	2,000
Selling Price	$50	$45	$42	$40	$40
Total Revenue ($000)	$2,500	$18,000	$50,400	$80,000	$80,000
Net Income %	15%	15%	15%	15%	15%
Net Income ($000)	$375	$2,700	$7,560	$12,000	$12,000
Net Investment ($000)	($9,625)	($6,925)	$635	$12,635	$24,635

Alternative Two	1996	1997	1998	1999	2000
New Product Inc. ($000)	$375	$2,700	$7,560	$12,000	$12,000
Cannibalization:					
Units (000)	0	(300)	(1,000)	(1,500)	(1,500)
Selling Price	$40	$40	$40	$40	$40
Rev. Cannibalized ($000)	$0	($12,000)	($40,000)	($60,000)	($60,000)
Net Income %	15%	15%	15%	15%	15%
Inc. Cannibalized ($000)	$0	($1,800)	($6,000)	($9,000)	($9,000)
Inc. Net of Cannibalization	$375	$900	$1,560	$3,000	$3,000
Net Investment ($000)	($9,625)	($8,725)	($7,165)	($4,165)	($1,165)

Alternative Three	1996	1997	1998	1999	2000
Inc. Net of Cannibalization	$375	$900	$1,560	$3,000	$3,000
Expected Lost Sales:					
Units (000)	0	0	500	1,000	1,000
Selling Price	$40	$40	$40	$40	$40
Lost Revenue Expected ($000)	$0	$0	$20,000	$40,000	$40,000
Net Income %	15%	15%	15%	15%	15%
Lost Income Expected ($000)	$0	$0	$3,000	$6,000	$6,000
Inc. Net of Cannibalization	$375	$900	$4,560	$9,000	$9,000
with adj. for lost sales					
Net Investment ($000)	($9,625)	($8,725)	($4,165)	$4,835	$13,835

$9 million in 1999. Overall, the new product may again be attractive, returning the $10 million investment by 1999 and generating a positive net investment of more than $13 million by 2000. However, this return must be considered against other potential investments. It would also be a much more attractive investment if it was delayed two years to extend the life-cycle of the current product.

By using this analytical framework, a company can do a sensitivity analysis to determine critical break-even points, such as the level of cannibalization where a new product becomes uneconomical or the level of erosion where cannibalization makes sense.

SUMMARY

Cannibalization is a particularly important strategic issue for high-technology companies. It occurs when a company introduces a new product that kills its own successful product. Cannibalization creates some unique problems. Sometimes it is a strategic necessity; sometimes it should be avoided.

This dilemma leads to interesting product strategies, both attack strategies and defensive strategies. Companies frequently stumble in evaluating the impact of cannibalization. They cannibalize prematurely or avoid necessary cannibalization because they do not do the proper analysis.

NOTES

1. The term *cannibalization* is used in product strategy in a similar sense to the typical definition of "eating one's own."

2. *Nikkei Weekly*, April 19, 1993, p. 8.

3. Shawn Tully, *Fortune*, May 3, 1993, p. 66.

4. Half-life is used here as the time period from when the product is originally introduced to when cannibalization starts. That is when the life-cycle decline begins.

5. Richard Brandt, *Business Week*, February 22, 1993, p. 40.

6. *London Sunday Times*, January 9, 1994.

7. Judith H. Dubrzynski, "An Exclusive Account of Lou Gerstner's First Six Months," *Business Week*, October 4, 1993.

Chapter Ten
Expansion Strategy

C reate and launch a continuing series of products that open new markets and fuel rapid growth. This is the dream of most high-technology companies. Expansion into new markets was behind the growth of success stories such as Motorola, 3M, IBM, Hewlett-Packard, and Microsoft. While some companies were more like "one-shot wonders," relying on a single successful product line, these companies were able to continually expand in multiple directions.

For example, Motorola expanded its original AM (amplitude modulation) car radio business into FM (frequency modulation) radios in 1940. FM technology led Motorola from car radios and into two-way-radio businesses such as Handie-Talky radios for the army during World War II and police radios. The skills and experience developed from these products eventually led to cellular phones and pagers. Motorola's cellular business was estimated at $6 billion in 1993.

By consistently building upon its core competencies over several decades, 3M became a very large, extremely diversified company. By 1992, it had more than 50,000 products and $13 billion in revenue. It expanded from adhesive products into products as diverse as magnetic tape, medical supplies, medical devices, and medical instruments. Its adhesive skills also led to the famous Post-It note business, as well as materials for safety products such as traffic signs and license plates.

Lotus Development Corporation and Microsoft followed very different growth strategies in the late 1980s. This comparison illustrates the difference between a strategy for expanding into related markets and one that primarily focuses on a single product platform. Lotus rode the success of its 1-2-3 spreadsheet application software product to significant growth. From a $157 million company in 1984, it grew at a 25 percent annually compounded rate to $900 million by 1992. Most of this growth came from variations of its one successful product. Expansion into new markets was limited, and where it tried to expand into unrelated fields such as stock market data transmitted over radio waves, it was not successful. While very successful with its primary product, Lotus did not follow a product strategy of growth through expansion.

FIGURE 10–1

Comparative Growth of Lotus and Microsoft. Microsoft grew much faster because
of its expansion strategy.

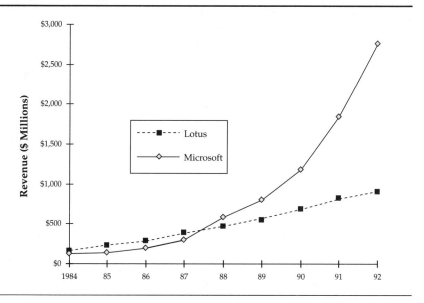

Microsoft's strategy contrasted with that of Lotus. In 1984, Microsoft, with $125 million in revenue, was a little smaller than Lotus. How-
ever, Microsoft pursued a strategy of growth by expansion into related
markets. The result was a compound annual growth rate of 45 percent
and revenue of $3.7 billion for the year ended June 30, 1993. Microsoft
grew to become more than three times as big as Lotus. This difference
is illustrated in Figure 10–1.

In addition to being much larger than Lotus, Microsoft's pretax
income was $1.4 billion compared to $120 million at Lotus. Its market value was $23 billion compared to approximately $2 billion.
Microsoft was more diversified, developed more core competencies, and created more potential expansion paths that it could follow
in the future.

This is not to take anything away from Lotus. It is a very successful
company. The comparison simply illustrates the benefit of a growth
strategy by expansion into new markets. This difference was not lost
on Lotus. It began to follow an expansion strategy of its own in the
early 1990s with Lotus Notes. This very exciting expansion path fueled
most of its growth in 1993 and accounted for an estimated 15–20 percent of its revenue.

Why is an expansion strategy so attractive? Some companies have been successful with a single product platform but want to continue growing and need to expand into new markets to fuel this growth. Polaroid faced this dilemma when the instant photography market began to run out of steam. The company tried to expand into several new markets, but its efforts were unsuccessful. In 1982, Polaroid tried to expand by acquisition and development into unrelated areas such as fiber optics, ink-jet printers, and medical diagnostics. All of these expansion efforts failed, some after significant investment.

In 1993, Polaroid continued its expansion into new markets, trying to build a $2 billion electronics business by the year 2000. Its CEO, I. MacAllister Booth, believed that, "There are many more opportunities in the business world than just selling cameras and films."[1] However, the initial results of its lead product for this expansion, the Helios Laser Imaging System, were disappointing. Introduced in 1990, it was not readily accepted by hospitals or medical equipment manufacturers. The primary problem was that it made an 8-by-10 print instead of the 14-by-17 print preferred by doctors who read X-rays and CAT scans.[2]

Expansion into new markets is sometimes necessary for survival. High-technology markets have a unique characteristic: They appear and disappear relatively quickly. When a market begins to disappear, companies relying on it need to expand into a new one or face extinction themselves. For example, Wang replaced its calculators with word-processing systems and then expanded into minicomputers. However, the next time it was not as successful. Wang was not able to expand into another market in time to replace its disappearing word-processing and minicomputer businesses.

The rapid decline of present markets makes expansion into new markets very important to high-technology companies. Without expansion, a company could end up following the hundreds of other high-technology companies that went out of business when their primary market disappeared.

Sometimes, companies fueled by their success in one market confidently expand into new ones, only to fail. All too frequently, this failure also drags down their existing products by diverting limited resources. Take WordStar, for example. Its pioneering word-processing program made it one of the early software success stories with revenue of $67 million in 1984, which was significant for a software company at that time. Then it tried to expand into new markets such as database and spreadsheet products. While diverting resources to its expansion efforts, WordStar let its word-processing products become less competitive. By 1993, it was roughly half the size it had been ten years earlier, losing nearly $20 million in nine months.[3]

Why are some companies successful at expanding into new markets while others fail? Experience, case examples, and research studies show that the answer is leverage. Companies following expansion strategies that leverage their market knowledge and product technology have been much more successful than those following strategies with little leverage. In what was perhaps the best study on the success and failure of new high-technology products, M. A. Maidique and B. J. Zirga determined that leveraging a company's technical and marketing experience was one of the key determinants of new product success. This study, which was part of an innovation project at Stanford University, looked at 158 products—half successes and half failures.[4]

To successfully expand into new markets, a company needs to leverage its strengths, particularly its core competencies. Leverage provides the basis for a framework to plan and evaluate expansion strategies.

LEVERAGED EXPANSION

Leveraged expansion builds upon what a company already does well. For example, a company may have underlying core technology or unique expertise in selling products into a particular distribution channel. By leveraging these capabilities, generally referred to as core competencies, a company has some advantages to build upon in its expansion.

On the other hand, when a company expands without any leverage at all, it is only providing capital and has no more of an advantage than any other investor. In most cases, it may not be as good at being an investor as others, such as venture capitalists. What makes expansion into an unknown market so deceptively alluring is that a company really does not know what it is getting itself into.

Core competency leverage can be viewed as two basic directions: a product/technology direction and a market/channel direction.[5] Figure 10–2 illustrates these two directions, expanding to the right and up from the starting point of existing products.

Leveraging Product and Technology Competencies

The horizontal direction in Figure 10–2 involves leveraging product and technical competencies; the further along this direction, the lower the leverage.

Product platform.   The strongest, easiest, and fastest form of leverage is using an existing product platform to enter new markets.

FIGURE 10–2

*Leveraging Core Competencies. Illustrates the degree of leverage along both
dimensions.*

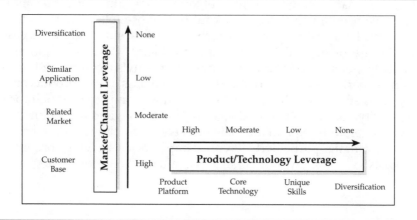

There are several ways of doing this. It can be done by creating a derivative platform, such as a portable computer platform from a desktop computer platform. The product platform can be modified for unique foreign market requirements. In some cases, an existing platform, such as an innovative materials-based platform, can be used for additional applications.

Using an existing product platform as the starting point, a company can usually create a new product quickly, enabling earlier expansion into the new market. Existing product platforms have other advantages. They are proven in both manufacturing and customer use, reducing many new product risks.

Core technology.   When a product platform cannot be applied to a new market, the underlying technology can sometimes create a new product platform. In this case, leverage comes from core technology.

The form of core technology varies by product. It could be critical subassemblies in an electronic systems product. It could be software modules in an application software product. It could be the type of composite material in a materials-based product. For example, fiber-based core technology used to reinforce aircraft bodies could also create golf clubs and bicycle wheels. The degree of leverage depends on the importance of the existing technology to the new product platform. Defining technology provides the most leverage. Leveraging only ancillary or supporting technology provides little advantage.

Unique skills.   Unique skills form the third layer of technical leverage. Generally, these are the same skills used to create the core technology in previous product platforms. Examples of unique skills are Microsoft's skills in writing software, and cable TV equipment company General Instrument's skill in analog design.

To be of significant value, the skills need to be reasonably distinguished. Existing or potential competitors should not have the same, or possibly better, skills. Here again, skills related to the defining technology are most successful. Finally, the skills should already exist, as opposed to a latent capability that can be acquired through new experience.

Leveraging unique skills differs from leveraging core technology. In skills leverage, there is little or no use of existing modules or proprietary technology, only the skills used to create previous technology.

Leveraging Marketing and Distribution Competencies

The vertical direction illustrated in Figure 10–2 provides the leverage that comes with market knowledge and distribution experience. A company uses its understanding of customers and markets to design a new product that leverages this understanding. It uses its presence in the channel of distribution to bring a product to the customer the same way it has with other products.

Customer base.   Selling a new product to the existing customer base provides an opportunity to leverage both the market knowledge and the channel of distribution. The combined experience of knowing what these customers want and knowing how to sell it to them can provide powerful leverage in expansion.

The same customers may purchase other products through the same channel. For example, customers who purchase personal computers also purchase the application software for those computers. The degree of customer-base leverage depends on the breadth of the products purchased by that customer base. Some customers purchase a range of products, while the purchases of others are more limited.

There are some subtle, but critical, differences in access to customers that affect the strength of the customer base as an asset. For example, companies that manufacture and sell to resellers are not close enough to the final customer to have significant leverage.

Some companies are in the envious position of having strong relationships with a large, fertile customer base. H&R Block is a case in point. Through its 9,500 tax offices, it prepares tax returns for 18 million people. Through its CompuServe on-line computer service, it has a 1.5 million household subscriber base. Combined, these two channels give Block access to both low-end and high-end consumers through which it can leverage expansion into new markets.[6]

Related market. Related markets are those adjacent to the current market. Notebook computers and laser printers, for example, are related markets to the desktop computer market. Expansion into a related market is easier than expansion into one that is unrelated because a company has some understanding of the related market. It has some experience with related customer needs and desires through the products it already sells. It may be able to leverage its reputation. It may also be able to use its same distribution channel.

The significance of leverage to related markets varies along a spectrum, depending on how closely they are related. Some are directly related, whereas others are only partially or indirectly related.

Similar application. When a new market is not related, the only remaining source of leverage comes from having a similar application for the product. Leverage comes from understanding how to meet the needs of a different customer with a similar application. For example, electronic scanners for package tracing is an application similar to retail scanners, which were originally developed for supermarkets.

The distinction between a directly related market and one with a similar application is critical. The directly related market offers significant leverage in either the direct knowledge of the market or the distribution channel, sometimes both. In a market with a similar application, leverage is much lower, and risk is higher. Some experience may apply, but then again it may not. Only the eventual success will determine if it does.

EXPANSION STRATEGIES

The concept of leverage provides the basis for constructing a framework to analyze and, more importantly, plan strategies for expansion into new markets. Figure 10–3 illustrates this framework. Existing products are positioned in the lower left-hand corner of the framework, at the intersection of the customer base and product platform. The framework defines expansion strategies by their emphasis in each of the two directions: product/technology leverage and market/channel leverage.

Strategies along the horizontal direction emphasize changes from current platforms. The greater the distance along that direction, the greater the change from the current platform and technology. Eventually there is no leverage at all from existing product platforms, core technology, or unique skills. Product diversification occurs at this point.

Generic Expansion Strategies

- Use core technology to develop a new product for the same customer base.

- Use unique skills to develop a new product for the same customer base.

- Use the existing product platform to expand into a related market.

- Use the existing product platform to expand into a new market with a similar application.

- Leverage core technology into a related market.

- Leverage core technology into a new market with a similar application.

- Use unique skills to expand into a directly related market.

- Use unique skills to expand into a new market with a similar application.

- Diversify into a completely new market.

- Diversify into a completely new business venture.

- Diversify into completely different products.

Strategies along the vertical axis represent changes from the current market and channel of distribution. The greater the distance along this direction, the greater the change from current markets and channels of distribution. Eventually there is little or no leverage from experience and reputation in either the market or channel of distribution. Market diversification occurs at this point.

Diagonal strategies represent changes in both dimensions simultaneously. Expansion a short distance in this direction enables a company to leverage both technology and marketing. Eventually, expansion along this path loses all leverage, becoming what is essentially a completely new business venture.

While leverage diminishes along a path, opportunity may increase. Going further along an expansion path provides more opportunities since the scope of opportunities becomes broader. This implies that intermediate paths—those just far enough away to be interesting, but not too far to be dangerous—are frequently the best opportunities.

FIGURE 10–3

Framework for Expanding into New Markets. Illustrates expansion paths based on the type and degree of leverage.

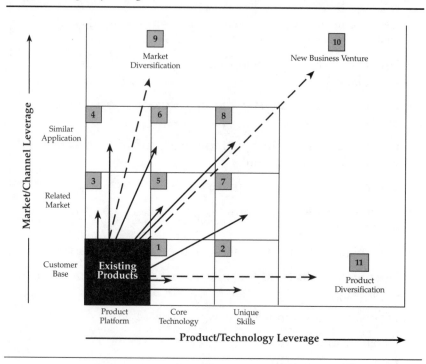

Using this framework, expansion strategies can be viewed as a series of alternative paths, each offering a different type of opportunity. By defining these alternative strategic paths, a company can evaluate the opportunities and challenges associated with each. Along each strategic path, a company knows what it can leverage and what it needs to learn. The expansion framework defines 11 different strategic paths, grouped into four categories.

Customer-Base Paths

The first two strategies lead to expansion by introducing new products into the present customer base. The paths differ to the extent of product/technology leverage. The core technology path provides a higher degree of leverage, but good opportunities along this path are usually more difficult to find. By leveraging unique skills, the number of potential opportunities is greater, but the degree of leverage is smaller.

Market risk is usually low with these two expansion paths, and the challenge, therefore, is to develop a product that is competitive. A strong reputation with the customer base can sometimes offset some advantages of competitive products already in the market.

Strategy: (1) Use core technology to develop a new product for the same customer base.

By following this strategy, a company leverages its understanding of both the market and how to sell the product since it is already selling to the same customer base. When combined with leverage derived from using proven core technology, the result is likely to be a successful product—if the opportunity is large enough. The problem with this path is not the risk involved in expansion, but the lack of opportunities at the end of it. Core technology applied to the same customer base tends to resemble the same product.

In some cases, expansion along this strategic path can be combined with expansion into a related market. Such was the case when Apple introduced its PowerBook notebook computer. The PowerBook used the operating system and microprocessor core technology of the Macintosh to develop a derivative platform. Part of the customer base was the same (those who wanted a PowerBook as an additional computer), but part was different (those whose priority was a notebook computer, not the Macintosh platform).

With the PowerBook, Apple was able to expand along two paths: core technology into the existing customer base and into a related market. Either of these would have been a successful path for Apple, but together they were very successful, providing it with $1 billion in additional sales in the first year.

Strategy: (2) Use unique skills to develop a new product for the same customer base.

Similar to the previous strategy, this path leverages presence in a market to define new products for existing customers. These new products use some of the same unique skill competencies but do not rely on an existing core technology.

Compaq Computer's 1992 expansion into laser printers provides a good example of this strategy. By using its unique skills in designing and manufacturing high-quality low-cost electronic systems, Compaq developed a line of printers that appealed to its customer base. It leveraged sales by selling these printers to its same customers where it had already developed a reputation. "We wanted to have a Compaq printer for anybody who wanted to have a Compaq PC," claimed David Black, general manager of Compaq's peripheral division. However, even leveraging an existing customer base does not ensure success. After a fast start, capturing 10–15 percent of this market segment, Compaq's sales stalled.[7]

It was a distant second to Hewlett-Packard, which already had an established reputation, and Compaq was forced to reconsider its printer business. David Black was replaced, and a number of new printer projects were canceled in order to reduce losses. By December 1993, Compaq abandoned the laser-printer business even though it sold $120 million in 1993 and had 15 percent market share. It realized that it needed to invest much more to be successful outside of its current customer base and concluded that the continuing investment required to support this additional core technology could be better used in the company's personal computer business.

Eastman Kodak used its skills in digital graphics to partially change a mature market where it had a strong customer base: 35mm photography. In 1992, it introduced the photo CD player, which stored 100 photos on a CD prepared by local photo finishers. In addition to the consumer market, the photo CD could be a tool for businesses such as real estate firms and retailers, creating the opportunity for Kodak to expand into a directly related market at the same time.

Similarly, IBM, Digital Equipment, and Hewlett-Packard expanded into the market for RAID (redundant arrays of inexpensive disks) disk drives. These drives use multiple lower-capacity disks to perform the data storage function of a high-capacity drive. They sold these primarily to their own customer base, optimizing the drives to work with their own computer systems.

Product-Platform Paths

The next two expansion strategies build upon existing product platforms, leveraging them into new markets. Product platform expansion can usually be initiated rapidly and requires less investment since this is the highest form of product/technology leverage. Expansion along these two paths is usually managed as part of a product-line strategy since the same product platform is used.

Strategy: (3) Use the existing product platform to expand into a related market.

Directly related markets can sometimes offer opportunities for expansion by simply applying an existing product platform and varying it for unique needs. Foreign variations of products are typical of this type of expansion. The platform generally remains unchanged, with only minor variations. Application software products, for example, are modified for foreign markets by translating the documentation and user interface.

AutoDesk scaled down its very successful AutoCAD computer-aided design software to run on personal computers at a lower price. It aimed AutoCAD LT at a related market: architects, designers, and engineers who needed a design tool that did not require more advanced features or development tools. The goal of AutoCAD LT was to increase revenue by expansion into a related market.

Next Computer and Sun Microsystems used this expansion strategy when they unbundled their operating systems and modified them for a different, but related, market: the IBM PC compatible computer market. For these two companies, this expansion strategy started when they realized that their core technology was really software, not hardware. Next discovered this the hard way through the failure of its computer hardware business. Nonetheless, Steve Jobs launched this expansion with the same vigor he launched the Macintosh computer with. In 1994, Apple Computer announced its intention to follow a similar strategy with its Macintosh operating system.

Strategy: (4) Use the existing product platform to expand into a new market with a similar application.

The opportunities along this path can be limited since most product platforms are not versatile enough to provide new product opportunities in a similar application but unrelated market.

Component and material suppliers tend to have more opportunities in this category than companies building final products. Flat-panel displays are an example. Originally developed for portable computers, the flat-panel product platform has been successfully expanded into other unrelated markets that have a similar application, such as video cameras and automobile navigation systems.

Advanced composite materials created new product platforms that found initial product applications in the space program (for the Space Shuttle and satellites). These materials offered greater stiffness at a lower weight than aluminum or steel. Later, these advanced composite materials platforms were applied to the related aircraft market. But, they are also being increasingly applied in similar applications in unrelated markets, such as automobiles. The opportunity for growth by expanding the application of advanced composite materials into new markets is limited only by creativity.

Combined Leverage Paths

The next four expansion strategies combine leverage in both directions. These strategies are usually the most exciting because the range of opportunities is broad, while the combined leverage is significant enough to enable success. Continually following these strategies has the added advantage of developing new core competencies while managing risk to reasonable levels.

Strategy: (5) Leverage core technology into a related market.

With this expansion strategy, core technology, not the existing platform, leverages expansion into a related market. Historically, this has been a prolific expansion path with many opportunities at the end of it. Motorola, IBM, Hewlett-Packard, and 3M consistently used this strategy in their expansion.

Adobe followed this strategy when it leveraged its core technology in printing to expand into a related market with its Acrobat product. Acrobat is software for information distribution that eliminates the need for printing. It enables information prepared by almost any application to be displayed on a computer without the original application software. For example, using Acrobat, a newsletter can be produced by page-layout software, distributed throughout a network, and viewed just as it would have been printed.

Adobe built Acrobat on its Postscript core technology by creating data files in a portable document (PDF) format. In doing this, Adobe essentially used its technology to do "pseudo printing." It sold Acrobat to a directly related, but different, market. Although the customers of Acrobat ran it on their PC just as other Adobe products, it had an entirely different use. Adobe's previous channel of distribution was OEMs (who built Postscript into their products) and resellers such as dealers. Acrobat was sold to dealers and system integrators who used it to provide large, integrated systems.

Going back to the RAID disk-drive example shows another application of this strategy. Data General used a different expansion strategy from that used by IBM, Digital Equipment, and Hewlett-Packard. Its CLARiiON product line was not targeted only at its own customer base, but for use with other UNIX systems. This gave Data General a much broader market opportunity, although it had less leverage. It took advantage of the opportunity and achieved considerable success with this strategy.

Related markets enable leveraging of experience, but even this can be misapplied. IBM found this out when it expanded into the home personal computer market with the IBM PCjr. The PCjr's awkward keyboard, lack of appropriate software, slow processing speed, and high price caused one of the highest profile failures in IBM's history.

Strategy: (6) Leverage core technology into a new market with a similar application.

This strategy provides many opportunities for expansion, as a company leverages its core technology into new opportunities. It can be particularly successful for companies that have robust core technology.

For example, AT&T applied the same core technology used in its network systems switching business to expand into ATM (asynchronous transfer mode) switches. ATM switches provide high-speed links for interactive networks that simultaneously carry voice, data, and video. AT&T combined existing core technology in switching, while developing new ATM technology. The application is similar—switching—but the market is different from central-office telephone switches. AT&T expected its ATM business expansion to grow to $150 million in 1994.[8]

This is the primary strategy followed by defense contractors looking for ways to expand into commercial markets. Take microwave technology as an example. The U.S. Department of Defense funded the development of gallium-arsenide-based core technology for monolithic microwave integrated circuits through development funding and purchases of devices for communications and smart bombs. With the market for these devices greatly curtailed, manufacturers are trying to expand into new markets for products that can use this core technology for wireless communications.[9]

Raytheon used its microwave circuit core technology to develop devices for satellite television broadcast receivers and microwave systems for satellite-based communication networks. M/A-Comm expanded into components for wireless phones and collision-avoidance systems. Alpha Industries expanded into components for wireless phones and automotive systems.

Following this strategy for expansion into new markets with similar applications presents the risk of misunderstanding what the market wants, particularly trying to "force" core technology on the new market. Most companies are biased toward their own core technology. For example, Polaroid assumed that its wet chemistry core technology was just what the market for instant movies wanted. It developed Polavision at a significant investment, only to discover that the market preferred videotape technology.

Strategy: (7) Use unique skills to expand into a directly related market.

Expansion opportunities in directly related markets are sometimes found by combining existing skills while developing some new ones. This strategy builds on knowledge of related markets more than technology, although skills for developing the key technology are necessary.

For example, when AT&T expanded[10] into the video telephone market with its VideoPhone 2500, it combined existing design skills with new skills it had developed for video communications. The Video-Phone 2500 was further leveraged by selling it into a directly related market: telephone customers who wanted to see each other during conversations.

EMC Corporation was moderately successful building add-on memory boards for large computers. In 1988, it decided to build upon its unique skills to expand into data storage systems. This was a directly related market that required a totally new platform. EMC's storage system platform was designed using many small disk drives strung together to create a large, efficient data storage capacity. This new platform was tremendously successful, and EMC expanded to become one of the fastest growing companies in the U.S., achieving $780 million in revenue in 1993.

This strategy is also useful for defense contractors trying to expand out of the military market. Canada's CAE Inc., a manufacturer of flight simulation equipment, used its unique skills in designing simulation systems to expand into commercial markets. It saw an opportunity to apply its unique skills to develop simulators to train medical practitioners in emergency procedures. Its first product was a simulated anesthesiology mannequin that simulates abnormal reactions to drugs administered by an anesthetist. The mannequin's pupils dilate, its thumbs twitch, its lips turn blue, and it vomits.[11]

Strategy: (8) Use unique skills to expand into a new market with a similar application.

This expansion strategy combines a little leverage in each direction. It is clearly the weakest of the leveraged expansion strategies since it does not leverage very much. However, it can be successful in certain cases and is less risky than diversification.

Cirrus Logic Inc. provides an excellent example of how this type of expansion strategy works. The company's CEO, Mike Hackworth, has positioned the company to grow by developing a wide range of semiconductors for controlling peripheral functions. The expansion strategy is based on leveraging unique skills: the company's Storage/ Logic Array (S/LA) VLSI design software. Cirrus Logic's initial products were disk-drive controller chips for disk-drive manufacturers such as Seagate and Conner. Next, it expanded into Video Graphics Array (VGA), controllers for PC manufacturers. Continued expansion followed with controllers for flat-panel LCDs (liquid-crystal displays), data-fax modems, and graphical user-interface (GUI) accelerators.[12]

Similarly, Texas Instruments (TI) used its component technology skills to expand into radio-wave based anti-theft devices for automobiles. These devices are built into the car key and send a radio signal to a receiver in the steering column. The car's ignition system will work only if the correct signal is sent. Ford Europe was TI's first customer for this product.[13]

The same risk of misunderstanding the preferences of a new market with a similar application occurs along this expansion path. DuPont discovered this with Corfam, a synthetic leather that it hoped would be as successful for shoes as nylon was for stockings. That it was not was the lesson it learned at a cost of more than $80 million. Similarly RCA's Videodisc failed because it could not record television programs.[14]

Unleveraged Paths

There are three other expansion strategies, but these offer little or no leverage. Consequently, the success rate of these expansion paths is much lower. Of the few successes in unleveraged paths, the most common method is through acquisition, alliances, or licensing in order to gain access to technology or channels of distribution.

Strategy: (9) Diversify into a completely new market.

This expansion strategy brings a company into completely uncharted territory. It knows little or nothing about the market. Unfortunately, just like amateur explorers who do not know where they are going or what terrain lies ahead, it may underestimate what it needs to be successful in this new market.

For example, Texas Instruments (TI) tried to expand into new markets in the 1970s to leverage its calculator technology and get away from the increasing price competition for basic calculators. Leveraging its calculator platform, TI sold a math instructional package with calculators to school systems. This was a terrible failure; TI found out that it did not know how to sell to school systems.

Following this experience, Texas Instruments decided to follow a more leveraged expansion strategy and developed the Little Professor.

The Little Professor was a calculator in reverse. It presented the math problem, and the child entered the answer. TI introduced the Little Professor in 1976, and it could not make enough of them for the Christmas season. It then leveraged this into new expansion with additional products like the Speak and Spell that helped children learn how to spell.

Strategy: (10) Diversify into a completely new business venture.

The upper right-hand corner of the framework in Figure 10–3 shows an expansion strategy with no leverage at all. This is a diversification strategy so different that a company has nothing unique to bring along on the journey. Being more successful than others requires luck rather than skill.

An automotive electronics company decided that it would expand by diversifying into marine electronics. This was an entirely different market with no commonalty in channels of distribution. The company had experience in designing consumer electronics, but little of its technology or unique skills applied to marine electronics. It lacked any experience in required technologies such as designing waterproof systems. The expansion effort was a failure that cost the company millions. Later, the company attributed its failure to the lack of leverage in its expansion efforts.

Strategy: (11) Diversify into completely different products.

This final expansion strategy leverages the market knowledge, channel of distribution, and possibly even the customer base. However, there is no product or technology leverage. Expansion is with a totally unrelated product.

Adding accessories or supporting products to provide a complete product line is typical of this expansion strategy. In this simplest case, a company resells a product that is developed and manufactured by someone else. It takes advantage of the leverage in its distribution channel and overcomes weaknesses in product/technology by purchasing it from someone else.

CASE STUDY IN GROWTH BY EXPANSION: MICROSOFT

Microsoft Corporation provides an exciting example of applying expansion strategy to grow into new markets. Over a 15-year period, expansion strategy has been the driving force behind Microsoft's

FIGURE 10–4

Microsoft's Expansion Paths. *Illustrates how Microsoft expanded from 1979 to 1992. The dollar figures represent approximate revenue by category in 1992. (Sources: Microsoft, The Making of Microsoft, and Gates. See footnote 15.)*

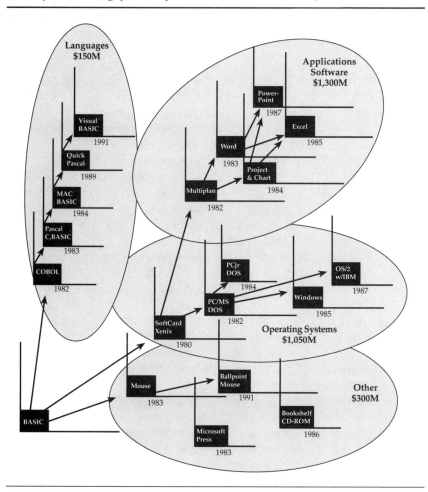

rapid growth. Starting from its early skills, Microsoft expanded from $2.5 million in 1979 to $2.7 billion in 1992. Figure 10–4[15] illustrates the expansion paths that led into four directions: languages, applications software, operating systems, and other. Using the framework introduced earlier, the figure shows expansion in the approximate direction that leverages market or technology. Each expansion path establishes a new position for future expansion.

In 1979, Microsoft began its growth from a small ($2.5 million) base by building on its core technologies in microcomputer languages and knowledge of microprocessors. This included the early experience of founders Bill Gates and Paul Allen in trying to build a traffic-counting computer in their Traf-O-Data venture. Microsoft developed a Convergent Technologies version of its existing BASIC compiler platform and a new assembler language using its skills in developing language software. Both of these expansion paths were closely related to its existing business.

In 1980, Microsoft expanded into a similar, but not directly related market with Softcard, a hardware emulation board enabling an Apple II to run the CP/M operating system. It sold more than 100,000 Softcards. More importantly, while this expansion strategy utilized some of its unique skills, it also required Microsoft's programmers to learn more about operating systems. With these new skills, it launched development of XENIX, a version of UNIX for microcomputers.

This new core competency in operating systems led to the most significant expansion path in Microsoft's history, perhaps one of the most significant expansion moves in business history. In 1981, Microsoft developed its first major operating system, PC-DOS (MS-DOS for the Microsoft version) for IBM.

Microsoft actually did not have the experience or time to develop this product on its own. So it licensed 86-DOS from Seattle Computer to form the core for PC-DOS. IBM originally approached Microsoft only to develop languages such as BASIC, FORTRAN, and COBOL for the new IBM computer. However, Bill Gates saw a big opportunity for expansion when he realized that IBM did not have the operating system it needed. Microsoft made a deal with IBM to develop four languages and PC-DOS, retaining the right to resell DOS to other companies as MS-DOS.

The following year, Microsoft completed development of COBOL and FORTRAN for DOS. It also followed a new expansion path in operating systems by licensing MS-DOS to fifty other computer manufacturers. And, somehow, Bill Gates and Microsoft found the time to embark on a totally new expansion strategy, applications software. It developed its first application product, Multiplan.

Expansion along these diverse paths shows that massive resources are not always necessary for expansion. Microsoft was a small company with limited resources, but it intuitively had a clear strategic direction.

Microsoft's strategy of growth by expansion into new markets accelerated in 1983 as it pursued expansion paths in many varied and exciting directions. It developed the mouse for personal computers, reflecting its skills in operating system interfaces and its knowledge of user needs. This also required new skills in hardware development. It launched Microsoft Word, one of its most successful application software products. The remaining languages—Pascal, C, and BASIC— were completed for MS-DOS during 1983, and it completed XENIX 3.0. Finally, Microsoft followed an unleveraged expansion strategy, Microsoft Press, to publish guidebooks for personal computer users. It was generally an unprofitable venture for Microsoft, showing again that unleveraged expansion has more risks than benefits.

Microsoft's expansion was not any slower in 1984, as it turned its attention to the new Macintosh computer. Multiplan and Word were converted to the Macintosh platform, as was the BASIC language. Microsoft continued its expansion into new applications with Microsoft Project, Microsoft Chart, and Microsoft File. It also pursued the path of a derivative platform with DOS for the IBM PCjr. Even Microsoft does not always pick successful paths.

Microsoft began to pursue fewer expansion paths in 1985. However, the two that it pursued were major successes. In September of 1985, it released Excel for the Macintosh, eventually beating out Lotus Jazz as the most successful spreadsheet application on the Macintosh. It sold Excel into an existing customer base (Macintosh spreadsheet users who were already being sold Multiplan). Excel was a completely different platform from Multiplan, but used Microsoft's unique skills.

Windows was a completely new user interface for the DOS operating system. Windows development began in 1981 as the Interface Manager project, and it was first announced by Microsoft in 1983. After many delays, Microsoft finally released it in November 1985. Windows was a highly leveraged expansion strategy. Microsoft sold it to a directly related market—DOS users—and it leveraged Microsoft's unique skills in both operating systems and applications software development.

1986 was a relatively slow year for Microsoft's expansion, as it tried to digest some of its major expansion strategies of the previous two years. However, it did launch its first expansion into multimedia with establishment of a CD-ROM division and the development of Bookshelf, a CD-ROM product.

In 1987, Microsoft returned to exploring new strategies for expansion. It acquired Forethought's PowerPoint presentation software. It released the IBM PC Windows version of Excel, leveraging Excel's core technology into a directly related market. Microsoft Works for the Macintosh, an integrated application aimed at beginning users, was released in September 1987. This leveraged several existing platforms into a directly related market. Finally, in 1987 Microsoft released the OS/2 operating system developed jointly with IBM.

Its pursuit of expansion strategies began to slow in 1988. Building on the success of Works, Microsoft released the PC version. It also released two OS/2 related products: LAN Manager with 3Com and

Presentation Manager. In 1989 Microsoft pursued relatively minor expansion paths with Quick Pascal, SQL Server, Excel for Presentation Manager, and the acquisition of printer driver software. In 1990, the company also launched some relatively unleveraged expansion by forming a consulting division.

Microsoft returned to expansion using some of its traditional technology in 1991. It developed a new mouse, the Ballpoint mouse for laptop computers, and it developed Visual BASIC.

MANAGING CORE COMPETENCIES

The expansion framework provides a way for a company to manage its expansion into new markets. Each strategy identifies opportunities for expanding into new markets using core competencies. Understanding this framework for expansion leads to an important conclusion: Companies with more and better core competencies have a greater capacity to expand. Therefore, a business strategy for expansion into new markets requires effective management of core competencies.

Companies that manage their core competencies can leverage expansion into new markets. NEC, for example, grew from less than $4 billion in 1980 to more than $21 billion in 1988 by managing its core technologies. NEC actually viewed itself in terms of core technologies, developing technologies in semiconductors, communications, and computing.[16]

Managing core competencies requires a long-term, sustained, strategic commitment to their development. This can be viewed as a three-part process.

1. *Understand core competencies.* This understanding begins by developing an inventory of current core competencies. A company needs to ask itself, "what really are our core competencies?" Current core competencies include both product/technology and market/distribution experience and skills.

When inventorying core competencies, some companies are deluded by wishful thinking. They perceive some of their capabilities as core competencies, when most are no more than basic capabilities. To be considered a core competency, a characteristic must be competitively strong, relatively unique, and strategically important.

Product/technology core competencies should involve the defining technology, not just supporting or ancillary technology. Defining technology, as discussed earlier, is the underlying technology of a product platform. Market/distribution core competencies come from understanding specific market trends and controlling or influencing channels of distribution.

2. *Nurture core competencies*. A company that wants to grow by expanding into new markets must nurture its core competencies as part of its expansion. It needs to keep them progressing to stay ahead of competition. Stale competencies are not core competencies.

Nurturing core competencies requires investing in them. Typically, a company directs a portion of its R&D budget to developing core technology as a strategic building block. Frequently, this also requires setting priorities for which core competencies are most important since resources for developing them are limited. Most companies can only afford to develop or nurture a handful of technical core competencies.

Expansion into new markets can also expand core competencies since a company may develop new competencies as part of its expansion. Then, after it develops these new competencies, it can use them to expand again along new expansion paths. This was what Microsoft did. Each time it expanded it developed a new core competency, which it then leveraged into more expansion: Languages into applications, applications into different applications, languages into operating systems, operating systems and applications into user interface software.

3. *Explicitly plan to leverage core competencies*. Managing core competencies also means using them. Unused core competencies are wasted. Why would a company waste its core competencies? The incidence of wasted core competencies is high, and the reason behind this is that companies simply do not consciously plan to use them.

Each core competency should be explicitly managed. Where will it be used? How will it be used? What is the payback on maintaining or improving this core competency? The answers to these questions need not be extensive, but somebody in the company should think about them.

JOINT VENTURE EXPANSION STRATEGIES

Joint ventures of various forms, including alliances, distribution agreements, technology licensing, and acquisitions may be necessary to attain the appropriate leverage to pursue expansion opportunities. Through joint venturing, a company can acquire the leverage it lacks so it can successfully expand along a desired path.

The framework introduced in Figure 10–3 can be used to plan and evaluate expansion into new markets using joint ventures. It can be used to position what each party in the joint venture provides and to show how the combined skills change an unleveraged expansion path into one that is leveraged. This combination (illustrated in Figure 10–5) is what was traditionally referred to as synergy.

FIGURE 10-5

Synergy from Joint Ventures. Through a joint venture, the combined expansion leverage is increased for Companies A and B.

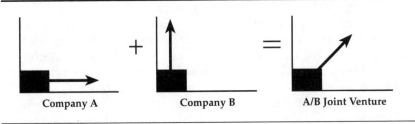

An example of this combined leverage is the HP95LX Jaguar palm-top computer with 1-2-3 that was developed jointly by Hewlett-Packard (HP) and Lotus. Lotus used the core technology of its 1-2-3 software, incorporating this into a calculator-like computer. The existing base of 1-2-3 customers was a primary market. On its own, however, Lotus lacked the skills necessary for developing an electronic product and could not distribute the product through its distribution channels. HP provided the leverage from its unique skills in designing, building, and selling calculators. It designed the hardware portion of the product. It also sold the HP95LX through its distribution channels.

The result of this joint venture was successful expansion for each company in a direction that they could not have pursued individually. This strategy changed what would have been a highly risky and insufficiently leveraged expansion path for each company into a highly leveraged one.

A company with core technology can grow into a new but unfamiliar market by incorporating its technology into another company's product. An example of this expansion path was seen when Bose Corporation expanded into the audio side of video conferencing with its Acoustimass speaker systems. Bose is known internationally for high quality audio products for the home and car markets. It had previously expanded successfully into car stereos by designing and selling them directly to auto manufacturers.

Bose expanded into video conferencing in conjunction with PictureTel Corporation, a leader in this technology. Entering the market in this way was the only approach for Bose since it had no distribution capability in video conferencing, either for initial sales or as add-on equipment. The Acoustimass speaker was originally provided as an option for the PictureTel System 4000 E-Series video-conferencing products. The speaker incorporated some of Bose's underlying core technology, such as its bass module, which eliminates sound distortion in larger rooms.

SUMMARY

Expansion into new markets is one of the most exciting strategies for high-technology companies. However, it is not always successful. Leverage is the key to expansion strategies for growing into new markets. It comes from two directions: product/technology and market/channel of distribution. These directions can be combined to create a framework that defines alternative strategies for expansion. These strategies can be viewed as different paths, and new market opportunities lie at the end of each path. The journey down each path is unique in its risk and its use of leverage.

A company can use this framework to map out its alternative paths to new market opportunities. It can systematically select expansion strategies that are most attractive, understand the capabilities it is building on, and pursue the path with confidence that it knows where it is going.

Expansion into new markets is behind some very successful companies. The Microsoft case study is a good example of growth through expansion strategy. The expansion framework illustrates how Microsoft grew from $2.5 million in 1979 to $2.7 billion in 1992.

The degree of expansion leverage depends on a company's core competencies, since core competencies determine a company's capacity to expand. Increasing the capacity to expand comes from a long-term sustained commitment to managing core competencies. Finally, the expansion framework is not limited to individual companies. It is also a useful framework for evaluating the synergy of joint ventures.

NOTES

1. Gary McWilliams, "A Radical Shift in Focus for Polaroid," *Business Week,* July 26, 1993, p. 66.
2. Gary McWilliams, "A Radical Shift in Focus for Polaroid," *Business Week,* July 26, 1993, p. 67.
3. *Boston Globe,* August 18, 1993.
4. Robert A. Burgleman and Modesta A. Maidique, *Strategic Management of Technology and Innovation* (Homewood, IL: Richard D. Irwin, Inc., 1988), p. 321.
5. H. Igor Ansoff also utilized a similar matrix with the added dimension of geography to describe strategic portfolio strategy and mission. See H. Igor Ansoff, *Corporate Strategy* (New York: McGraw-Hill Inc., 1965, revised 1987).
6. Matthew Schifrin, "H&R Block's Crown Jewel," *Forbes,* December 6, 1993.

7. Kyle Pope, "Compaq Is Revamping Its Printer Line," *The Wall Street Journal*, August 13, 1993.

8. John J. Keller, "AT&T's Network Equipment Unit Is Bouncing Back," *The Wall Street Journal*, December 2, 1993.

9. Aaron Zitner, "Cutting the Cords," *Boston Globe*, August 24, 1993.

10. Actually this was not a new expansion. AT&T first demonstrated a prototype of the video telephone 28 years earlier at the New York World's Fair.

11. Larry M. Greenberg, "Shrinking Aircraft Market Forces CAE to Branch Out," *The Wall Street Journal*, August 24, 1993.

12. Bill Arnold, "Cirrus Takes PC Market by Storm," *Upside*, August 1993.

13. Kyle Pope, "Ford Taps Texas Instruments to Supply Security Device for Cars Sold in Europe," *The Wall Street Journal*, August 25, 1993.

14. "Flops," *Business Week*, August 16, 1993.

15. Sources: Microsoft company literature; Daniel Ichbiah, *The Making of Microsoft* (Rocklin, CA: Prima Publishing, 1993); Stephen Manes and Paul Andrews, *Gates* (New York: Doubleday, 1993).

16. C. K. Prahalad and Gary Hamel, "The Core Competence of the Corporation," *Harvard Business Review*, May-June 1990. This is a good reference on core competencies.

Chapter Eleven

Innovation Strategy

I nnovation is more prevalent in the high-technology industry than in any other, and innovation strategy is a more important element of product strategy for high-technology companies. Emerging technology creates opportunities for new types of products that establish entirely new markets. Companies that are both creative in seeing new possibilities and persistent in pursuing them can be rewarded by taking advantage of these opportunities. This is the intent of innovation strategy.

The meaning of innovation and its application to product strategy is sometimes confusing. Here it has a specific meaning. Innovation is the act of creating something really new. An improved or more competitive product may be new for a company, but it is not really new in the sense that there was nothing like it before. Innovation is used here in the context of product strategy to mean developing a new type of product that creates an entirely new market.

Innovation should not be confused with invention. Invention is the discovery of a new device, method, or process based on study and experimentation. Inventions can lead to innovations, but all innovations are not based on immediately preceding inventions.

Why are some companies innovative when others are not? While there are many reasons, they primarily revolve around innovation strategy. More innovative companies do not just sit around and wait for innovation to happen; they cultivate it.

Conceptually, innovation can be described as a combination of inspiration and evolving technology. Both ingredients are necessary. New technology without an idea of how to apply it will not lead to innovation. Much has been invested by governments, universities, and businesses to develop new technology that has no practical application. Likewise, an inspiration for a new product that is not technically feasible is simply a folly. Figure 11–1 illustrates this combination of technology evolution and inspiration.

This combination has another characteristic. Innovation using newer technology does not require as much creative inspiration, while innovation using mature technology requires more. For example,

FIGURE 11–1

Ingredients of Innovation. Innovation stems from the combination of inspiration and the evolution of a new technology. Innovation is more dependent on inspiration as the technology matures.

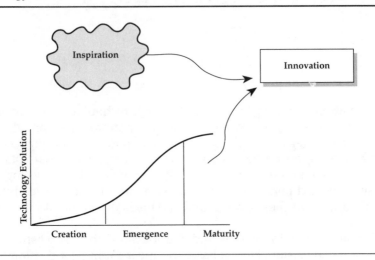

when polypropylene was first introduced, companies instantly found numerous applications for it because it was more flexible and easier to use than previous forms of plastic. They used it in building materials for roofing, pipes, and upholstery; appliance components for dish-washers, clothes washers, and refrigerators; automotive parts; cloth-ing; and consumer products such as videocassettes.

Technology in its rapidly emerging stage provides a fertile source that inspires new applications. The increasing power and declining costs of microprocessors provided the inspiration for numerous innovations in products that previously did not use any electronics. By the time a tech-nology matures, most of its more obvious applications have been intro-duced. The burden of innovation using mature technology shifts to crea-tive inspiration. New ways of solving customer problems or generaliz-ing from the solution to specific problems becomes the driving force.

This conceptual framework, though somewhat simplified, provides the basis for understanding specific strategies for innovation. Innova-tion strategy is unlike other strategies in that it is not initiated to directly achieve an anticipated result. Innovation cannot be scheduled. The goal of innovation strategy is to increase the likelihood of innova-tion. Innovation is more than simply stumbling across a good idea. Yet, it can be achieved without investing extraordinary amounts into sci-entific discovery. Innovation is a set of strategies.

INNOVATION STRATEGIES

All high-technology companies would like to be innovative. The issue is how to do it. Innovation strategies are based on the source of the innovation. They define where companies should look for innovation opportunities. Innovation strategies are classified into three groups; opportunity-driven, prediction-driven, or technology-driven. Each classification comes from a primary approach to innovation.

Opportunity-Driven

These two innovation strategies take the solution to a specific problem and generalize it to provide a solution for other related problems. In this way, the solution becomes a product rather than a customer-specific solution or a limited fix to a specific problem. The two strategies differ by their source. Customers are the source for the first strategy, while any problem is the source for the second.

Strategy: Identify general opportunities by listening to specific customer needs.

Customers are an obvious source of innovation opportunities. They are the ones living with the problems that innovation can solve, and they

---

Generic Innovation Strategies

Opportunity-Driven

- Identify general opportunities by listening to specific customer needs.

- Identify opportunity by generalizing a solution to a specific problem.

Prediction-Driven

- Identify opportunities based on the declining cost of technology.

- Identify new applications for emerging technology.

- Look for opportunities at the intersection of multiple emerging technologies.

Technology-Driven

- Efficiently search for solutions to perceived problems/opportunities.

- Stumble over a technology breakthrough and apply it.

are the eventual market for the innovation. In some cases, a customer may challenge a company to solve a particular problem, and, in doing so, the company is forced to an innovative solution. There may be opportunities to then generalize this solution to create an innovative product. Such was the case with one of the major innovations of the 20th century: the microprocessor.

The birth of the microprocessor began in 1969 when now defunct Japanese calculator manufacturer Busicom asked Intel to design a set of chips for a family of programmable calculators. The original design called for at least 12 custom chips, but Ted Hoff, the Intel engineer assigned to the project, thought the configuration was unduly complex. His solution was to develop a single-chip, general-purpose logic device that would retrieve its application instructions from semiconductor memory.

Hoff and Bob Noyce, who was a co-founder of Intel, realized that with the trend toward custom-designed logic chips, the number of chips would eventually exceed the number of circuit designers. Hoff's vision was transformed into silicon nine months later. The 4004 microprocessor consisted of 2300 transistors and was 1/8-inch wide by 1/6-inch long. It had the processing power equivalent to the first electronic computer, the ENIAC, which filled 3,000 cubic feet with 18,000 vacuum tubes when it was built in 1946. The 4004 could execute 60,000 operations in one second, primitive by later standards, but a major innovation at the time.

However, Intel had a problem with this innovation. Busicom owned the rights to it, having paid Intel $60,000 to design the chip set. Knowing that Busicom was in financial trouble, and sensing the opportunity for the microprocessor as a generalized product, Intel offered Busicom the $60,000 back in return for exclusive rights to the product. Busicom accepted, and the rest is history.[1]

In many cases, customers may even specify exactly what they need to solve a specific problem. When development is completed, the customer may have no interest in generalizing the solution for others.

This was the case in the late 1950s when IBM designed and built the first component insertion machine for printed circuit boards. After building and testing the design in-house, IBM contracted with a local machine builder for eight machines according to its specifications. Perceiving that this was an innovation, the machine builder received permission from IBM in 1962 to market the X-Y table component insertion machine to others. This innovation was successful for the company, which became a leader in the market.[2]

Identifying innovation opportunities from listening to customers does not mean taking a poll or doing customer surveys. Rarely, does the average customer provide such insights. Instead it is the customer in the forefront solving emerging problems, who identifies these opportunities. The key is to identify these customers and invest time in listening to them.

Strategy: Identify opportunity by generalizing a solution to a specific problem.

The world is full of problems—big and small—and sometimes the solution to an individual problem can be generalized to solve other similar problems. This generalization can lead to the innovation of exciting, new products.

One of the most publicized cases of innovation came about by generalizing specific solutions when Art Fry of 3M became frustrated with trying to mark his place in his hymnal while he was singing in the church choir. He used little scraps of paper to mark the pages for upcoming songs, but they usually fell out. In frustration with his problem, he thought back to a discussion he had earlier with Dr. Spencer Silver, a 3M chemist who had mistakenly created a low-tack adhesive while trying to develop a super-strong one. "What I need," Fry thought to himself, "is a bookmark with Spence's adhesive along one edge. It would stay in place when I needed it to, but it wouldn't be so sticky as to damage the pages when I removed it."[3]

The solving of this individual problem eventually led to one of 3M's most famous products, Post-It Note Pads, which has generated hundreds of millions of dollars in revenue for the company. The key to this innovation was the transition from an individual solution to a generalized solution.

The transition from specific to general is not usually easy, and it was not in the Post-It Note example. Not everyone saw the opportunities for using Post-It Notes. It took an all-out sampling campaign with some 3M offices and the town of Boise, Idaho, to show that there were many similar applications for this potential product.

Prediction-Driven

Three additional innovation strategies stem from projecting trends into the future. By looking far enough ahead, it is possible to see a potential innovation before someone else does. The underlying assumption behind these prediction-driven strategies is that the trends can be projected into the future. These innovation strategies take advantage of the predictability of emerging technology. Scientific breakthroughs are not predictable, but the continued advance of emerging technology can be.

For example, Gordon Moore of Intel projected the rate of improvement in computer memory chips in the early 1970s by looking at the historical rate of improvement. He forecasted that capacity would double every two years. This showed a progression from 1K bit chips in 1971 to 1 MB chips in 1991. Moore's forecast was, and continues to be, accurate. Many companies failed to apply this forecast and missed the opportunity to innovate new products. Others, such as Microsoft, internalized these trends and innovated new products based upon the forecasted change in technology.

Cost trends are the focus of the first strategy in this group. The next two strategies project the potential application of emerging technology.

Strategy: Identify opportunities based on the declining cost of technology.

The declining cost of an emerging technology creates opportunities as new applications become possible where the technology was not previously cost-effective. This is illustrated in Figure 11–2. The initial market for a new technology is typically small, focusing on select applications where the benefit is so high that cost does not matter. When the cost declines, a secondary market provides a larger opportunity. Subsequent opportunities may occur in a third major market and potentially additional ones. Each subsequent market is progressively larger than the preceding one.

Global-positioning technology provides a good example of progressive opportunities created by declining costs. This technology was originally developed by the American Defense Department for military applications such as determining the location of a ship, airplane, or smart bomb. Using 24 satellites, global positioning can identify the exact location of a receiver with accuracy of a few feet. Each satellite constantly transmits its position and time of transmission. By taking the readings from the four closest satellites, the receiver plots its longitude, latitude, and altitude.

Early global-positioning receivers were very expensive, and the initial market, military applications, was small. As costs declined, secondary markets became feasible with the application of global positioning as a navigational aid for commercial airlines, private airplanes, and recreational boating.

Major market opportunities are expected in the future. In 1993, receiver prices were as low as $700 to $1,700, opening up opportunities for recreational uses such as hiking and cross-country skiing as well as use in automobiles. Avis Rent-a-Car, for example, began testing the possibility of using global positioning in its fleet. Eventually, global positioning systems could be as widespread as car phones. By the end of the 1990s, the major market (consumer products) is expected to exceed $3 billion.[4]

FIGURE 11-2

Expanding Opportunity as Cost of Technology Declines. The declining cost of an emerging technology creates progressively larger opportunities.

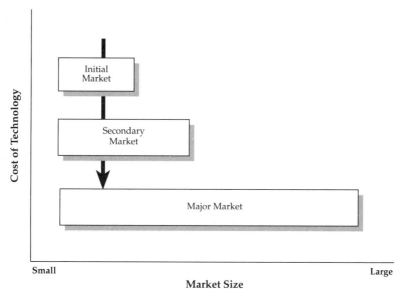

Predictability is the key to this innovation strategy. The rate and extent of cost declines can be forecasted by understanding the under-lying technology. Opportunities for innovation can be identified at each lower cost level. At $200, will every car have a global positioning system?

Strategy: Identify new applications for emerging technology.

New markets can be created by incorporating new technology into an innovative product. In some cases, the technology may be so innova-tive that no one is actually sure how it will be applied. The strategy here is to identify these opportunities and introduce an innovative product before anyone else.

This was the case with Apple Computer when it launched its Newton personal digital assistant (PDA) technology in the Newton MessagePad. The goal of this product was to create an entirely new market—the pocket-computer market—that was expected to be the next leap in personal computer technology.

Apple created Newton by predicting the applicability of handwriting-recognition technology in new products. It evaluated several product opportunities using this technology, and Newton was the result.

Another example comes from identifying new opportunities for emerging genetic engineering technology. The market for fresh tomatoes exceeds $3 billion, and it has not changed much since the creation of tomatoes. Biotechnology changed it, establishing a new market in the process—genetically engineered tomatoes. These new tomatoes—such as DNA Plant Technology's VineSweet tomato and Calgene's Flavr Savr tomato—have an improved taste and texture, a longer shelf life, and can be grown year round.

Natural tomatoes have a built-in enzyme that accelerates rotting, and because of this, tomatoes are picked green and ripen during transport to the grocery shelves. Since a tomato is juicier when it is allowed to vine-ripen, this early picking results in lower quality store-bought tomatoes. Calgene's Flavr Savr tomato resists rotting because it reverses the DNA sequence used to manufacture the rotting enzyme, giving it a longer shelf life and improved taste and texture.

New technology can also create the opportunity for new services. Shopping by cable TV was created by Home Shopping Network in the late 1970s along with QVC in 1986. By 1993, the shopping-by-cable-TV market had expanded to more than $2 billion. Cable TV technology of the 1980s enabled this market, and new technology will accelerate the opportunity even further. Cable television systems will significantly increase their capacity to 500 or more channels in the future, making a variety of shopping channels possible. Digital technology will also create interactive cable, enabling viewers to request information and place orders by television.

Shopping by cable TV has taken only 1–2 percent of the retail market by 1993. However, as technology advances, more of the retail market will shift to cable shopping. This is a classic case of creating new markets by riding the technology wave.

Strategy: Look for opportunities at the intersection of multiple emerging technologies.

The combination of two or more emerging technologies can also create exciting innovation opportunities. Each emerging technology can perform more advanced functions; together they can do things that nobody ever thought of before. This innovation strategy, more than others, requires creativity to be successful. Innovation comes from challenging, "How can something be done better by combining new technologies to do it a different way?"

The Wright Brothers applied two emerging technologies when they innovated the airplane. The first was the gasoline engine designed in the mid-1880s to power early automobiles. The second was advancements in aerodynamics that were developed through experiments with gliders. Each of these emerging technologies was developed independently, but the Wright Brothers combined them into a new innovation.

Innovation can create totally new ways of doing something. The manufacture and distribution of compact disks (CDs), for example, seemed like an established process, but IBM and Blockbuster Entertainment saw the opportunity to improve it through innovation. They formed a joint venture in 1993 to manufacture and market automated retail systems to make and dispense audio CDs on demand at retail stores. Retail stores would not need to carry a large investment of CDs in inventory; instead, they would reproduce them directly for customers from a large computer database of titles. The record companies would not need to produce and distribute vast quantities of CDs; instead they would simply receive a royalty for every title reproduced.

This innovation combined several emerging technologies including computer processing, large-scale data storage, and compact-disk recording. These technologies had advanced to the point where it was possible to create such a system. For IBM, creating this new market presented the opportunity to sell application-specific computers to thousands of retail stores. For Blockbuster, this strategy could dislocate already well-established retail CD store competition operating on the "old" practice of inventorying CDs. This technology could also be the basis for expansion in the future into sales of computer games, computer software, and other products as well.

In another example, the modern PBX (private branch exchange) or switchboard was created from the convergence of two technologies: telecommunications and computing. By combining these two technologies, it was possible to automate and simplify the task of answering and switching telephone calls. Later, these technologies were combined with the emerging technology to digitize voice to create voice-mail systems.

The strategy of innovation by combining multiple technologies is based on understanding and applying the right combination of technologies to the right alternative opportunity. It requires a rich understanding of emerging technologies and their trends. With this understanding, a company can continuously examine numerous opportunities for doing things differently. It can challenge existing products and processes, seeking a more innovative solution.

Technology-Driven

Technology-driven strategies are typically associated with invention or discovery. These strategies lead a company to find or discover a new technology and use it to innovate new products. To some extent, this is also the traditional innovation approach of a new technology solution in search of a problem.

Strategy: Efficiently search for solutions to perceived problems/opportunities.

Innovation can result from a deliberate search for a solution to a perceived opportunity or problem. This is the scientific approach to innovation.

DuPont followed this approach to innovation when it developed nylon. Under Wallace Hume Carothers, DuPont investigated opportunities for making synthetic fibers through polymerization—building larger molecules out of smaller ones. Scientists had made new fibers, such as rayon, from cellulose but had never synthesized them from simple chemicals.[5] After methodically trying different chemicals, DuPont eventually settled on amides—the same chemical that forms the protein in wool, silk, and other animal fibers. By carefully controlling the reaction, its scientists built up polyamides into strong, flexible fibers. This innovation led to nylon stockings, clothing, tires, parachutes, and many other products.

Edison also used this strategy in innovating the artificial lighting system using incandescent lamp bulbs. The problem was that no one had been able to make a strong, effective, high-resistancy lighting element. After methodically trying numerous types of materials, Edison and his staff were able to find material that worked. In addition, Edison had to build electric generators, inexpensive transmission lines, methods for connecting the bulbs, and methods for installing wires into a house. This innovation by Edison was not a blinding flash; it was a lot of work.

Strategy: Stumble over a technology breakthrough and apply it.

Historically, many technical discoveries are found by someone "stumbling over" them. While this analogy is descriptive of the process, it is not really a process based upon luck. People can only do this if they are going somewhere and there is something to stumble over. What this means is that they are involved in research of some type, and they recognize the importance of what they run into.

For example, Alexander Graham Bell stumbled over the break-through necessary for the telephone. On June 2, 1875, Bell was working on research involving telegraph signals, using magnetized steel reeds to transmit a fixed frequency signal. Watson, his assistant, accidentally made the reed vibrate, causing the reed at Bell's end to also vibrate and emit a noise. The original vibration caused an electromagnetic current to be transmitted through the wire, resulting in a vibration at the other end. The vibration reproduced the sound along the wire. However, Bell recognized the importance of what he "stumbled over," because of a theory that he had developed a year earlier. He had developed a theory for electrically reproducing speech, but he could not figure out how to make an electric current change in proportion to the sound of the voice. This lucky accident solved his problem.

A similar process of stumbling over a discovery was involved when Kary Mullis discovered the process for Polymerase Chain Reaction (PCR) one Friday night in 1983 as he was driving in Northern California. PCR is a biological process for amplifying a particular molecule of DNA from a few to millions. Without amplification, it is not possible to detect the presence of molecules in low concentration. However, when amplified a million times, diagnostic instruments can detect the presence of any targeted molecule. PCR, and similar technologies such as Strand Displacement Amplification, enable major new innovations in diagnostic instruments. DNA identification can diagnose diseases such as tuberculosis in three hours instead of the up to six weeks needed for traditional bacterial culturing methods.

Kary Mullis' discovery came while he was working on research to determine the identity of a nucleotide at a given position in a DNA molecule. He was thinking about his experiment while driving to Mendocino county late one night, when he realized a problem with the experiment. The experiment would cause the number of DNA molecules to double. While this was a problem with the intended experiment, Mullis saw the possibility of progressive doubling to amplify the molecule to large numbers.[6]

Sony also innovated its famous Walkman through this process. In 1978, engineers at Sony's tape recorder division were trying to develop a small, portable tape recorder for journalists, called "Pressman." Unfortunately, they were unable to fit the recording mechanism into the required unit size, so they used it to listen to cassettes as they worked. Masaru Ibuka, Sony's honorary chairman, saw this incomplete tape recorder and admired the quality of its stereo sound. Remembering and unrelated project where Sony engineers were working to develop lightweight portable headphones, he wondered about combining them. The combination, he realized, would dramatically increase sound quality. Maybe it could be a successful product without a recording capability. In 1979, the Walkman was introduced and went on to become one of the most successful consumer products of the 1980s.[7]

People such as Bell and Mullis and companies such as Sony who innovate through discovery have a common trait: They are continually pondering possibilities limited by current technology. When they see a solution to remove the limitation, they recognize it. Once more they are in environments where they may "stumble over" it. This innovation strategy is dependent on having these types of people in a company. It is then necessary to provide a creative enough environment for them to be working on related research with time to follow up on hunches or possibilities.

INNOVATION IN ACTION:
THE APPLE NEWTON CASE STUDY

In August 1993, Apple Computer introduced the Newton MessagePad, its first all-new computer in nearly ten years. The Newton makes a good case study in innovation because it (along with a few similar products) created a new market and because it is more like regular innovation than the rare breakthrough innovation. The Newton is classified as a personal digital assistant (PDA), which is a product somewhere between a calculator and a notebook computer. There were many parallels between the Apple Newton and the Apple Macintosh (along with the Lisa, which preceded the Macintosh). Both were innovative products targeted at new markets. Both introduced new technology that changed the traditional way of working with computers. The Lisa and the Macintosh were perceived to have limitations, and so did the Newton.

The Newton also introduced some innovative technology. Handwriting recognition was the most notable innovation. Newton captured and interpreted handwriting and sketches. It also introduced a seamless object-oriented approach to its operating system, which made transparent the traditional computer concept of running programs. Through its operating system, Newton introduced an intelligence capability that anticipates what the user intended.

Apple initiated development of the Newton in 1987 when Steve Sakomen led a small group to rethink the future of computing. The project began losing momentum at the beginning of 1990 until April when Steven Capps, the project leader at the time, prepared a model for Apple CEO John Sculley. Apple at that time was desperate for a new product platform. The Macintosh was aging and becoming less differentiated from other computers. Sculley approved the Newton project, but gave the team only two years to develop it. The deadline (which was not based on a development plan) was April 2, 1992. At that time, Apple had not yet defined the specific concept for what was to become Newton. There were many alternatives from wall-sized to pocket computers. Eventually, in February 1991, the current Newton product concept was defined by Sculley and a marketing manager. The new concept excluded some of the planned features but was feasible to develop.

Apple needed to convince the outside world, particularly the stock market, that it had upcoming innovations, particularly in light of its heavy investment in R&D. It described the Newton in January 1992 and demonstrated a prototype in May 1992. However, Newton development proved to be more difficult than planned. The original deadline could not be achieved. The development, particularly the software, took much longer. The Newton team worked long days, nonstop and under tremendous pressure. Many gave up and left Apple for a more sane position elsewhere. One committed suicide. Another had a breakdown. Eventually the project got the necessary leadership to complete the work, and the Newton was introduced in August 1993.[8]

Newton initially received mixed reviews. It was innovative and its capabilities were unique. Yet it lacked sufficient applications to justify its $700 price. Its handwriting recognition was unique, but unreliable. A popular comic strip even made fun of it. To some extent, Newton disappointed critics because it lacked some of the capabilities such as wireless communication that were anticipated from its earlier promises. Apple sold 50,000 Newtons in its first four months, but sales appeared to taper off as criticism mounted. By early 1994, estimated sales were fewer than 10,000 per month.

The Apple Newton development reflected many characteristics of other innovations. When development began, the market and product concept were not very clear, the product was designed around unproven emerging technology, and its development took a great deal of hard work and sacrifice.

Apple followed a prediction-based innovation strategy in developing the Newton. It combined the opportunities of declining technology costs (the microelectronics), emerging technology (handwriting recognition, object-oriented software, and pen-based computing), and the intersection of multiple technologies (microprocessor and eventually wireless communication).

By early 1994, Newton was far from being a successful innovation, but many innovations take time to be successful. Apple's president, Michael Spindler, compared it to the early days of television when the technology was awkward and incomplete and gave no hint of the immense societal changes to come.[9]

BARRIERS TO INNOVATION

Successful innovation is very difficult because there are many barriers in the way.

Failure to Have a Strategy for Innovation

The most fundamental barrier is the lack of any strategy for innovation. Without a strategy, a company should not be surprised if it does little innovation.

A company may have no innovation strategy because it never thought about having one. Perhaps it never expects to innovate. Sometimes companies do not have any innovation strategy because they do not understand innovation. They just expect it to happen. In many cases, a company invests in innovation by allocating funds to research, but it does not have a systematic strategy for innovating. It may be learning about and refining technologies without applying them.

While a company may have some strategy for innovation, it may be pursuing the wrong strategy. The innovation strategy needs to be appropriate for its market, core competencies, and vision. One company, for example, pursued a technology-based innovation strategy, investing heavily in finding new technical solutions for perceived opportunities. However, its competitor pursued a more successful opportunity-based innovation strategy. The customer base was rich with ideas for innovative products. The company did not find these in the lab, but its competitor found them in the marketplace.

Failure to Implement

Innovation is work. While all product strategies require a lot of work to implement, innovation strategies suffer most from the misconception that "It will come to you." A study of innovation clearly shows that it does not happen that way, so once a strategy is chosen it needs to be implemented. Work needs to be done.

Implementation begins by assigning responsibility. An individual or team needs to have the responsibility and resources to implement the innovation strategy. One company following a strategy of generalizing from customer needs, for example, assigns someone to continuously visit customers to solicit new ideas. This is a one-year rotating assignment, which provides a fresh look at opportunities each year. The opportunities are reviewed by a cross-functional team that helps to refine and prioritize them, and the most promising opportunities are introduced into the company's phase review process for approval.

Innovation is not just work; it is hard work. Too many companies that launch an innovation strategy start developing the first opportunity they come across. Why would they expect that the first opportunity is the best? They must all just be lucky. The truth is that they just stop when they find one. Some people shop for a gift that way. They walk into a store and buy the first thing that seems appropriate. Others comb the aisles and go to many stores to find the right gift. Finding the right innovation to invest in is like finding the right gift. Many opportunities should be identified and reviewed. Only the very best should be funded.

Lack of Vision

Strategic vision is necessary to guide any innovation strategy. It indicates which opportunities fit the company's strategic direction and which do not. Without a vision to guide innovation strategy, the results could be totally inappropriate.

An earlier example discussed a consumer electronics company that launched an innovation strategy for expansion. Because it did not have a strategic vision, it pursued opportunities that were far afield. It went into markets and technologies where it had no experience and failed. At the same time, it overlooked some excellent opportunities that were within its own domain.

An outdated vision can also hinder innovation. One company making mainframe computer peripheral equipment had the opportunity and technical talent to develop local area networking systems for workstations and personal computers. Even though management saw the decline in mainframe sales, it could not bring itself to work on something that was not part of its strategic vision. As a result, by early 1994 the company was downsizing to 30 percent of its former size and still trying to eke out a profit following the decline of the mainframe market.

Inadequate Core Competencies

As was explained in the previous chapter, expansion into new markets requires a strong base of core competencies to provide sufficient leverage. This is also true of expansion through innovation strategies. Without sufficient core competencies, it is difficult for a company to identify innovations that it can successfully pursue. If a company has limited core competencies, it needs to restrict its innovation strategy. In the extreme case, a company may need to strengthen its core competencies before it initiates any innovation or expansion strategy.

Market Resistance to Change

The biggest barrier to innovation is resistance to change. People do not change readily, and customers are people—either directly or indirectly.

One interesting historical example of resistance to change involves an improvement to the typewriter or computer keyboard. The current "QWERTY" keyboard used in typewriters and personal computers was invented by Christopher Latham Sholes in 1873 to slow typists, thereby reducing the chance of jamming by having two typewriter keys rapidly struck in succession. By laying out the letters this way, it was more difficult to type, and jamming was reduced. This design was so successful that it was used in all typewriters.

By 1932, typewriters were more mechanically efficient and jamming was not a significant problem. Professor August Dvorak designed a more efficient keyboard, arranging the keys differently. The most frequently used keys were located in the most convenient places, and the load was distributed to the generally stronger right hand instead of the left hand. Dvorak's innovation, the Dvorak Simplified Keyboard (DSK), dramatically increased productivity. However, this innovation was never adopted by typewriter manufacturers. Nobody wanted to upset the way things were being done and be incompatible with training or experience.[10]

SUMMARY

Innovation comes from the combination of inspiration and evolving technology. Innovation strategy is a form of expansion strategy that creates totally new products and markets. By understanding the sources of innovation, companies can create specific strategies.

Opportunity-based innovation strategies generalize solutions to specific problems. Prediction-based innovation strategies stem from the predictability of emerging technology. Technology-based innovation strategies apply technology to perceived problems.

Innovation is not easy. There are many barriers, such as no innovation strategy, failure to implement, lack of vision, inadequate core competencies, and resistance to change. Innovation is illustrated in a case study on the Apple Newton.

NOTES

1. Provided by Intel.
2. Eric A von Hippel, "Has a Customer Already Developed Your Next Product?" *Sloan Management Review,* Winter 1977.

3. William E. DeGenaro, Director of Innovation Resources at 3M, "Encouraging Innovation," *Prism* (Arthur D. Little, Summer 1989).

4. Roy Furchgott, "Wondering Where You Are? Try Asking the Satellites," *New York Times*, December 5, 1993.

5. *Inventors And Discoveries*, (Washington, D.C.: *National Geographic Society*, 1988.

6. Kary B. Mullis, "The Unusual Origin of the Polymerase Chain Reaction," *Scientific American*, April 1990.

7. P. Ranganath and John M. Ketteringham, *Breakthroughs* (San Diego: Pfeiffer & Company, 1994), pp. 115–136.

8. John Markoff, "Marketer's Dream, Engineering Nightmare," *New York Times*, December 12, 1993.

9. James Daly, "Apple Tries to Fire up Newton Developers," *Computerworld*, December 13, 1993.

10. Stephen Jay Gould, "The Panda's Thinking of Technology," *Readings in the Management of Innovation*, ed. Michael L. Tishman and William L. Moore (Ballinger, 1988).

Chapter Twelve

Strategic Balance

M ost high-technology companies have unlimited product opportunities. They can expand existing product lines, develop new
product platforms, and create new vectors of differentiation. They can
explore paths for expansion into new markets or even innovate entirely
new markets.

The problem, of course, is that a company cannot do everything it
would like to do. It must choose. It must set priorities and allocate
scarce resources. It must achieve a strategic balance among numerous
opportunities for new products.

This requires making trade-offs between short-term and long-term
opportunities, between current platforms and new platforms, between
diversification and focus, between expansion into new markets and
increased competitiveness in current markets, and between research
and development.

Portfolio management techniques that analyze characteristics such
as project type, product category, and risk help to profile and understand the mix of current development projects. However, where most
companies fail is setting priorities at the strategic level: defining the
mix of development that strategically makes the most sense. They typically spend most of their time profiling their current portfolio mix and
very little time deciding what the mix should be. They need to do both,
and when they do, they can make adjustments to bring the mix into
strategic balance.[1]

Strategic balance is an important concept in product strategy. If a
company's product strategy is balanced, it is pursuing the proper mix
of opportunities. If its product strategy gets out of balance, it may not
achieve its overall vision, even if the individual strategies are appropriate. For example, it could become preoccupied with short-term
opportunities while unknowingly sacrificing its future, or it could take
on more high-risk projects than it realizes, coming up empty handed
on new products while revenue declines.

Strategic vision defines the goal and provides a framework for
achieving it. This vision has to be reconciled to reality; specifically, it
needs to fit to the resources available. Strategic balance reconciles a

company's unlimited product opportunities to its limited resources. This is done at a strategic level, above the level of individual products and prior to portfolio management.

STRATEGIC BALANCE

To achieve strategic balance, individual product strategies must be implemented in the right proportion. This requires making trade-off decisions among various strategic considerations. Some of these are interdependent; a decision on one trade-off affects another.

Companies can classify new product projects in different ways. For example, Wheelwright and Clark introduced four primary classifications that differ by the degree of change: enhancements, next generation platforms, radical breakthroughs, and advanced development. This structure helps to clarify strategic thinking.[2]

Figure 12–1 illustrates the concept of strategic balance, using the metaphor of an electronic scale. Periodically, a company needs to check the mix of its product development portfolio according to the criteria it thinks are important. This example illustrates seven. According to the readings on the dials, two are in the acceptable range, four are outside the acceptable range, and the financial return is measuring 20 percent.

For purposes of achieving strategic balance, the following seven trade-offs are typical of what a company needs to consider:

Focus versus Diversification

Focus involves concentrating resources on a specific product platform or set of products. By focusing, a company is less likely to dilute its resources on other, less important efforts, thereby increasing its chance of competitive success in its primary focus. Focus can be especially critical in rapidly emerging markets, as the following example shows.

Steve Hui founded Everex Systems in 1983, building the IBM PC clone-maker to more than $425 million in revenue by 1991. But while its competitor, Dell, was focusing solely on the PC-compatible business, Everex lost its strategic focus. The company launched developmental efforts for a new microprocessor, computerized drafting tables, a modified version of UNIX, a Macintosh clone, and a Sun Microsystems' clone.[3]

In 1989, both Dell and Everex were approximately the same size. Both sold PC clones through telephone sales. At the end of 1992, Dell was four times larger, and Everex filed for Chapter 11 bankruptcy.

Diversification, on the other hand, involves having a range of product development initiatives, each with independent risk and success

FIGURE 12–1

Strategic Balance Scale. Illustrates the trade-offs that a company needs to achieve strategic balance. For example, short term/long term is in balance, but focus/diversification is not.

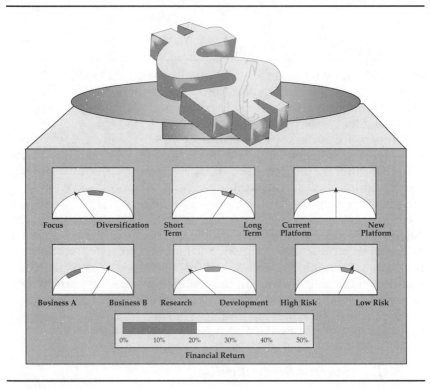

factors. Failure in one is, at least statistically, likely to be offset by success in another. A good example of the extremes in focus versus diversification can be seen in comparing Centocor Corp. and Genzyme Corp. Centocor followed a strategy of focusing on one or two big products that would turn it instantly into a major company. Genzyme, on the other hand, established a product strategy of pursuing smaller niche markets using a variety of technologies with good odds for commercialization.

The high expectations for Centocor's first big product. Centoxin, drove the market value of the company's stock to $2.2 billion, even though revenue was less than $100 million. When the FDA rejected the drug, the company's market value dropped by 85 percent. Then on January 18, 1993, Centocor suspended Phase III trials for Centoxin and ceased foreign sales of the product because of an excess mortality rate on patients treated with the drug. Centocor had gambled by putting most of its eggs into one basket and lost. Genzyme continued steady growth with a diversified product portfolio.

Short Term versus Long Term

The definition of short versus long term is relative to a company's perspective. Short-term product opportunities are generally aimed at achieving results within the upcoming two or possibly three years. These opportunities are typically product-line extensions or product enhancements.

Current competitive pressures drive companies to emphasize short-term projects to achieve immediate gains. A new feature or performance improvement will quickly make a product more competitive and boost sales. However, with a short-term focus, a company sacrifices longer-term opportunities, often without considering the consequences. The result can be a vicious cycle: The immediate crisis is followed by another because the company failed to invest sufficiently in longer-term opportunities.

For example, one company making communications software products focused most of its development on small projects, tying up the engineering resources. Major growth projects did not get any attention because marketing and sales, which were focused on quarterly quotas, constantly screamed at engineering to "be more responsive." The company's dilemma became critical when competitors introduced new generations of products. Marketing and sales then claimed that the company had inadequate technical capabilities.

A continuous short-term focus can be a sign of a troubled company. A company becomes reactive, rather than proactive, and if it does not break out of this vicious cycle, it will eventually succumb to competitors. With an extreme short-term focus, significant product development resources are allocated to customer support to fix customer problems. In a sense, this is a backward investment, investing in product that is already sold.

Long-term opportunities are out into a future time period, typically five to ten years. Capitalizing on these opportunities involves development of a new product platform or even innovating new technology. Companies that are competitively comfortable for the time being can put more focus on longer-term opportunities. They can invest in future product platforms, expand core competencies to prepare for future expansion, or explore new markets.

Sometimes the other extreme occurs, where everything becomes strategic and no projects are targeted for near-term return. This was the problem at a data communications company where a vice president observed during a phase review, "This is the fifth consecutive project where we are looking at a low return because it is strategic. What projects are going to make us any money?" Given that jarring observation, the senior management team realized that they needed to bring their short- and long-term perspectives into balance.

Too much investment in long-term opportunities can also cause competitive problems, particularly if the majority of these opportunities are also high risks. While a company is experimenting with long-range ideas and technologies that may not pay off, competitors can achieve significant immediate advantages and force a company to shift to a crisis mode. When this happens, the company never realizes the result of its longer-term investments.

Current Platforms versus New Platforms

As was discussed previously, all product platforms have a life-cycle, and at some point a company needs to shift its emphasis and resources away from building upon a current platform and into developing a new platform. The timing of this shift is an element of strategic balance.

If a company shifts too soon, it fails to get as much as it should from the current platform. Competitors continue to improve their products and introduce new variations while the company is distracted by developing its new platform. When introduced, the new platform may prematurely displace the previous one, reducing the return originally expected. Introducing a new platform too early may also frustrate customers who were just getting used to the previous one. In some cases, developing a new platform too early could diminish the difference between it and the previous platform. The defining technology may not have advanced sufficiently, and customers may not see the difference, enabling competitors to leapfrog into the next generation.

If a company waits too long before shifting its resources toward a new platform, it may not complete the platform in time to remain competitive. As was seen in an earlier example, Data General had this problem. By taking too long to shift from its proprietary Eclipse platform to a UNIX-based platform, it did not have sufficiently competitive products in time. Revenue declined, and profits disappeared.

What makes this shift difficult is the continued pull on resources to improve and expand products using the existing platform. It can be too late if a company waits until the expected investment returns diminish on these opportunities. Ironically, some of the best perceived investment returns are seen in the later stages of a platform's life-cycle. Depending on the platform life-cycle and the investment required, a company may need to increase its overall investment or divert resources from other areas to achieve the proper shift.

One Business Unit versus Another

Many companies allocate R&D resources across business units, such as divisions or product lines, without assigning priorities or distinguishing any differences in opportunity. They provide each with equal access to R&D resources or allow each to spend an equivalent amount of revenue on R&D, even if the opportunities vary. In doing so, the companies fail to achieve strategic balance across business units.

This practice takes away one of the advantages of a multidivisional business, which is to shift the allocation of resources to business units with better opportunities. Instead, it tends to subsidize lower-opportunity businesses by letting them invest as much as higher-opportunity businesses.

To achieve strategic balance, a multidivisional business needs to establish priorities for allocating R&D to each business. Theoretically, this makes sense, but in practice it is difficult. The R&D staff resides in individual divisions and is not readily redeployed. In addition, it is not easy to measure the differences in various opportunities across divisions. For these reasons, strategic balance across divisions is usually phased in over time. A company may also choose to maintain a portion of its development resource at a corporate level to fund selected expansion opportunities. These opportunities could span multiple divisions or occur in a division with high-growth opportunities.

Research versus Development

Investments in product development are very different than investments in research. The end result of a product development investment is a new product. The goal is clear, and the activities followed to get there are reasonably well-defined.

Investments in research, on the other hand, are aimed at creating, acquiring, or improving core competencies that will be used in future products. The result of research efforts could be a new material, new process, new base chemistry, or new electronic module, which is then applied to establish innovative product differences or a new product platform.

As part of achieving strategic balance, a company must decide how to allocate its resources between research and development. This split varies depending on a company's objectives. If it focuses entirely on development with no investment in research, its core competencies may atrophy. Large companies perform this allocation in part by establishing a corporate research center to focus on pure research activities. The Palo Alto Research Center of Xerox, Becton Dickinson's Research Center, and Bell Labs at AT&T are examples.

High Risk versus Low Risk

Risk is involved in all product development efforts, but the magnitude of risk varies from product to product. While some companies are comfortable at higher levels of risk, others may prefer a more moderate risk profile. Managing the risk profile is an important part of strategic balance.

There are different types of risks that prevent a company from turning what is perceived as a good opportunity into a successful product:

- *Market risk.* This includes those risks associated with bringing the wrong product to market. It may not be what the customers really want. It could be priced wrong or insufficiently differentiated. It could be inferior to other competitive products. In any case, the market was misjudged.

- *Technical risks.* Running into technical difficulties reduces the success of a product. It may not meet performance expectations. It may cost too much to do what was expected. In the extreme case, the product may not work at all.

- *Manufacturing risks.* Some risks involve not being able to manufacture the product properly. In most cases, higher than planned manufacturing costs are the risk. In other cases, the risk may involve problems in making the quantity required or delays in getting manufacturing started.

- *Market introduction risks.* Problems can occur with a complex or innovative product's launch into the marketplace, especially a worldwide launch. These include promotion to educate the customer on the product's benefits, training the sales force, preparing the indirect sales channels, supporting value-added resellers and setting up the service process. Shortcomings in these areas can doom an outstanding product to mediocre sales.

- *Managerial risks.* These are primarily failures in execution. The product is right, but the company just cannot complete the necessary development as planned. The failing could be in the quality of the product or in completion to schedule.

The combination of the different types of risks provides an aggregate level of risk that can then be classified into the appropriate risk category. Typically, a company uses some form of weighting scheme to compute this aggregate risk.

Financial Return

Most companies use a financial measure such as return on investment (ROI) to estimate if an opportunity will earn a favorable return for the investment required. Many companies set some level of hurdle rate that each opportunity needs to achieve before it is approved. This hurdle rate establishes criteria for allocating resources and achieving strategic balance.

However, a single rate for all opportunities ignores the importance of other criteria and turns product strategy into a capital budgeting exercise. "As long as the return on investment is higher than the cost of capital" has led some high-technology companies to decline. For a new product opportunity, ROI is an approximate estimate that combines numerous projections such as unit sales, pricing, costs, and so on.[4] Despite this, ROI is frequently used as the ultimate decision criteria, assigning it preciseness that was never intended.

One company, for example, used a 15 percent ROI hurdle rate for all new product projects. New product proposals consistently projected an ROI of 15–20 percent in order to surpass the hurdle rate and get funding. Some, of course, failed to achieve the projections. A portion never came to market. None were more successful than anticipated. Overall, the company did not get a very good return on its investment in R&D.

This poor return could have been mathematically determined in advance. The company set diminished expectations for product development investments by automatically approving everything that met an adequate financial return. Financial mediocrity was incorporated into its strategic balance.

Overall, the portfolio of new products developed must increase profit, and each opportunity, with a few possible exceptions, needs to contribute to that profit. Some need to contribute more than others. In fact, some opportunities, particularly those that are not being pursued for other reasons, should require a much higher return than others.

THE R&D EFFECTIVENESS INDEX

What is good strategic balance? A clear, preferably quantitative, objective becomes important at this point. Assuming that all high-technology companies want to achieve long-term growth, increasing profitability, and exceptional returns on their investment in product development, then the R&D Effectiveness Index provides a reasonable quantitative objective.

In R&D Effectiveness Index is an aggregate measure of the overall success of a company's product development efforts.[5] It fills the void for an overall metric at a level above individual products and development projects, and provides management with a tool to measure the long-term effectiveness of product strategy and product development.

The R&D Effectiveness Index (EI) compares the profit from new products to the investment in new product development, using the following formula (all % are a percentage of revenue):

$$EI = \frac{\% \text{ New Product Revenue} \times (\text{Net Profit }\% + \text{R\&D }\%)}{\text{R\&D}\%}$$

FIGURE 12–2

R&D Effectiveness Index Distribution from the Study. Only 21% had an index
above 1.25, and only 39% had an index above 1.0.

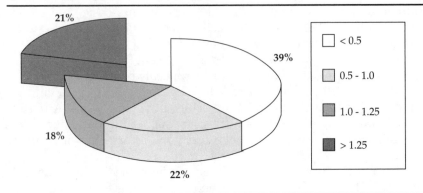

As a simple interpretation, the index computes the ratio of increased
profits from new products divided by the investment in product
development. When the index is above 1.0, the return from new products is running at a rate greater than the investment.

For example, assume that a company has a 9 percent net profit.
Also assume that it invests 6 percent of revenue in R&D and that
40 percent of its revenue is derived from new products. Its R&D Effectiveness Index would be 1.0 [computation: (40% × 15%/6%)]. On the
other hand, if this same company derived only 20 percent of its revenue from new products, it would have an index of 0.5 [computation:
(20% × 15%/6%)]. It would not be getting as much from its investment in R&D.

The definition of what is considered a new product varies from company to company, depending on product life-cycles. For computing the
R&D Effectiveness Index, a product is considered new if it is in the first
half of its life-cycle. For example, a product that typically has a four-
year life-cycle would be considered new for the first two years. Net
profit is the profit from new products, and the R&D percentage is as
reported on financial statements.

The R&D Effectiveness Index was computed for 45 electronic systems companies as part of a benchmarking study of product development.[6] The results were then analyzed and correlated to other
performance factors. Figure 12–2 shows the distribution of R&D Effectiveness Index values derived from the study.

Of the participants, 39 percent (21% + 18%) had an R&D Effectiveness Index greater than 1.0, indicating that new products were

generating more profit than the investment made in R&D. If any time value of money is considered, then only 21 percent (companies with an index greater than 1.25) generated a return on their investment in R&D.

Application of the Index

The R&D Effectiveness Index measures the productivity of a company's product development process and the success of its product strategy. The focus here is on using the index to measure the success of product strategy.

The R&D Effectiveness Index is best applied to measure relative performance, showing trends over time. A company or its board of directors can use the results to see if R&D is improving or declining. To a limited extent, the index can be used to measure ROI. An index value of less than 1.0 implies that a company may not be getting a sufficient return on its investment in R&D.

The R&D Effectiveness Index can also be used to measure performance across multiple divisions or business units. Differences in the index may indicate that some divisions have better opportunities than others. Some industries offer a much higher payback on R&D investments than others. In some cases, a low R&D Effectiveness Index may be more of an indication of an industry's potential than the performance of a particular company.

Characteristic of Companies with a High R&D Effectiveness Index

The benchmark study also provided an interesting analysis of the characteristics of companies with a high R&D Effectiveness Index. These characteristics help not only to understand the index, but also provide insights into what it takes to perform well.

Companies with a high R&D Effectiveness Index (> 1.25) outperformed the average of all companies in growth and profitability. While higher profitability is expected (since it is part of the computation), the magnitude of this difference is surprising. These companies were over ten times more profitable!

The difference in revenue growth also shows a strong relationship between growth and the R&D Effectiveness Index. Companies with a high index grew twice as fast as the average from 1988 to 1992. They also invested approximately a fifth less in R&D but had approximately a third more revenue from new products.

Companies with a high R&D Index balanced their opportunities differently. They invested proportionally more of their R&D budget on totally new product platforms—30 percent compared to less than 25 percent for the other companies.

The R&D Effectiveness Index provides a long-term aggregate measure of consistent success in product strategy. As an aggregate measure, it summarizes overall success, offsetting winning strategies with those that fail. Overall success requires more than just individual strategies; it requires the proper strategic balance.

SETTING PRIORITIES

Strategic balance is the result of the trade-offs. It is a strategic profile defining how a company chooses to balance its new product investments. Implementing this balance requires setting priorities.

Setting priorities for new product opportunities is a three-step process. The first step is strategic. It establishes the criteria for the preferred mix of opportunities that fits a company's strategy. This requires making the trade-offs discussed earlier, and specifying the desired balance: long term versus short term, high versus low risk, and so on. The result is usually summarized as a table.

The second step involves making a preliminary segmentation of development resources. This is not possible for all trade-off criteria, but can be done for some. For example, R&D spending can be allocated by business unit, and budgets for research can be defined separately from development.

The third step is the specific assignment of resources when new product opportunities are approved, typically using a phase review process. This is implemented by initiating and funding specific projects, typically at the phases of the phase review process. The summary of criteria for strategic balance, matched to the current portfolio of projects, is necessary input to those making phase review decisions.

CASE STUDY: ACHIEVING STRATEGIC BALANCE

The following provides an illustration of how a company can make adjustments to become more strategically balanced. It also shows how the R&D Effectiveness Index can be used to measure performance.

The company has six divisions, each developing related but different products. Its CEO was not satisfied with the results of its new product development efforts. He believed intuitively that the company was

TABLE 12–1

Division Performance. Shows the R&D Effectiveness Index and its elements for each division.

	New Product Revenue %	Profit % of New Products	Investment in R&D	Effectiveness Index
Division A	30%	25%	9%	1.13
Division B	15%	18%	7%	0.54
Division C	20%	10%	8%	0.45
Division D	30%	10%	9%	0.63
Division E	10%	10%	6%	0.27
Division F	5%	12%	7%	0.14

not getting enough in return for its research and development investments. "Our growth has been less than 10 percent per year," he said. "While the industry has been growing at 25 percent. Our profit margins are shrinking every year, and we don't seem to have as many new products as our competitors."

He did not know what to do. "The board of directors thinks I should cut R&D spending. They also believe that we shouldn't be investing the same relative percentage of R&D in each division, but they don't have any specific suggestions on how to shift it. Marketing and engineering, of course, say that we are not spending enough. Lately, I've begun to wonder if we have fundamental problems in our product strategy."

The CEO did not have a way to measure the performance of product development, and as a result he did not know how to fix it. The R&D Effectiveness Index provided him with the measure of performance that he needed. Overall, the company had an R&D Effectiveness Index of 0.5. Approximately 20% of its revenue came from new products, and the profit on these products was 12%. It invested 8% of revenue in R&D. The overall index was 0.5 (computation: (20% × [12% + 8%])/8%) but it varied widely by division, as can be seen in Table 12–1.

Even though it invested more in new product development, Division A had the highest index due to a higher percentage of new products and a higher rate of profitability. Divisions C and D also invested heavily in R&D, but their index was lower because profitability of their

new products was less. Division B, E, and F had a low percentage of
new products in their revenue and as a result had a low R&D Effectiveness Index.

No one, including the CEO, knew why each division invested what
they did in R&D. A budget of 6–9% seemed to be acceptable within the
company, and the R&D budget just continued from year to year,
increasing at about the same rate that the division grew.

The differences in the R&D Effectiveness Index across divisions was
not easily explained. Perhaps some had better markets than others.
Division A, for example, was in a "hot" market, while Division F was
in a mature market.

The CEO set an ambitious goal for improvement. Using the R&D
Effectiveness Index as the overall metric, he set a goal of improving
effectiveness from 0.5 to 1.4 over the next five years. Underlying goals
were to improve the new product content of revenue from 20 percent
to 40 percent, increase the profitability for new products from 12 percent to 15 percent, and reduce R&D investment from 8 percent to 6 percent. This would result in an index of 1.4 ($[40\% \times (15\% + 6\%)]/6\%$).
Each of these underlying goals, as well as the R&D Effectiveness Index,
were set by year. These were composite goals for the company as a
whole; each division had its own individual goals.

The company implemented a two-pronged program to increase its
Effectiveness Index. One focused on improving the product development process within each division. The second was aimed at changing
the company's strategic balance and deploying its R&D resource
differently.

Until now, the divisions had not set any criteria for deploying their
resources. They assigned resources on a project-by-project basis without reflecting on the overall mix. There was no strategic balance to their
product strategy; any balance or imbalance was the result of individual tactical decisions. The resulting profile of their current portfolio is
characterized in the Current Criteria column in Table 12–2.

The CEO set out to achieve a strategic balance. The short-term
emphasis of product development would be more evenly balanced
with long-term opportunities. Half of these long-term opportunities
would involve new product platforms to replace the current platforms.
More emphasis would be placed on diversification, particularly opportunities for growth by expanding into related markets.

The increased risk in this criteria was not a goal, rather it was a
recognition of the higher risk associated with the planned shift in other
characteristics. The criteria for financial return was segmented into
three levels. Most (60 percent) of the projects would require a ROI of 30
percent or greater. Some would be permitted an ROI of 20–30 percent,
but these opportunities would need to be prioritized using other criteria since only 30 percent of all projects would be funded at this level of
return. A limited number (10 percent) of projects would be considered

TABLE 12–2

Prioritization Criteria. *Illustrates differences between current and target criteria.*

	Current Criteria	Target Criteria
Short term vs. long term	Short term: 80% Long term: 20%	50%/50% split between short and long term
Current vs. new platforms	Current platforms: 95% New platforms: 5%	Invest at least 25% in new platforms
Focus vs. diversification	Focus: 99% Diversification: 1%	Selectively invest between 10% and 20% in diversification
Low vs. high risk	Low risk: 90% High risk: 10%	Allow high risk projects to be as much of 25% of total
Financial return	Hurdle rate of 15% ROI	60% of projects: 30%+ ROI 30% of projects: 15%-30% 10% strategic no ROI
Investment by division	6%-9% of revenue in each division	Reduce R&D in divisions E and F by half. Allocate 10% of R&D for company-wide opportunities.
Innovation vs. development	Innovation: 0% Development: 100%	Innovation: 10% Development: 90%

strategic, and no ROI would need to be estimated. Most of these were expected to be innovation or research projects.

The balance across divisions was also being changed, R&D in divisions E and F would be reduced by half. R&D investment in other divisions would be adjusted to fit their R&D Effectiveness Index targets. Finally, 10 percent of all R&D would be allocated companywide instead of by individual division. This would fund some of the diversification efforts. The CEO expected that it would take three years to achieve this targeted strategic balance.

While the work was just beginning, the CEO now felt like he was in control, having set a clear direction. "We certainly have our work cut out for us, but we know what we need to do and how we are going to get there. The R&D Effectiveness Index is our overall guide. There is no magic to the goal of 1.4. Perhaps we could do even better. However, I do know that an improvement of that magnitude is both achievable and badly needed."

SUMMARY

Strategic balance defines the characteristics and mix of new product opportunities which a company believes is appropriate. This balance requires making trade-offs such as focus versus differentiation, short term versus long term, current platforms versus new platforms, one business unit versus another, research versus development, high risk versus low risk, and the expected financial return.

Defining the appropriate balance requires setting an overall objective for the investment in new product development. The R&D Effectiveness Index provides a measurable objective. It is an aggregate measure of the overall success of a company's product development efforts.

Achieving strategic balance requires setting priorities to get to the desired balance. This is a three-step process: establishing the criteria, making a preliminary segmentation of resources, and assigning resources to specific projects. Achieving strategic balance and the R&D Effectiveness Index are illustrated in a case study that shows a company rebalancing its priorities.

NOTES

1. Strategic balance differs in emphasis from portfolio management. For a discussion of portfolio management, see Richard G. Hamermesh, *Making Strategy Work—How Senior Managers Produce Results* (New York: Wiley & Sons, 1986).

2. Steven C. Wheelwright and Kim B. Clark, *Revolutionizing Product Development* (New York: The Free Press, 1992).

3. Julie Pitta, *Business Week*, February 1, 1993, p. 75.

4. ROI is frequently calculated improperly, and the result is wrong. Despite this, it is still used to make decisions.

5. For a more detailed description of the R&D Effectiveness Index, see Michael E. McGrath and Michael N. Romeri, "The R&D Effectiveness Index—A Metric for Product Development Performance," *Journal of Product Innovation Management*, June 1994.

6. Pittiglio Rabin Todd & McGrath, *Benchmarking Study of Product Development Metrics* (Weston, MA: 1993).

Chapter Thirteen

The Process of
Product Strategy

How does a company actually do product strategy? Who does what? When do they do it? What skills do they need to do it well? How do the individual activities fit together? To answer these questions, product strategy needs to be defined as a management process.

It is a series of actions, activities, and decisions to bring about a result: a specific product strategy. Once defined as a process, a company can evaluate how it goes about doing product strategy and can make process improvements to create a better strategy. An effective product strategy process creates a better product strategy.

The process of product strategy is unique for every company since each has its own organization, different types of products, unique culture, and particular ways of operating. However, there are common aspects. This commonalty enables the product strategy process to be described generically, providing a framework to better understand it as a process. Besides defining the process of product strategy, it is necessary to understand the interaction of product strategy with other processes and to appreciate how product strategy depends on core competencies.

THE PRODUCT STRATEGY PROCESS

Figure 13–1 illustrates the process of product strategy. It shows how the strategies previously described (referred to here, in a process context, as *elements*) work together. The interrelationship of these elements is what makes this a management process instead of distinctly separate actions.

A description of any management process includes a definition of its structure, timing, and responsibilities. Structure defines what goes where. Timing delineates what elements precede others and how frequently each element of the process is executed. A management process also needs a clear definition of who is responsible for each

FIGURE 13–1

Overview of the Product Strategy Process. Illustrates the primary elements along with their interrelationships.

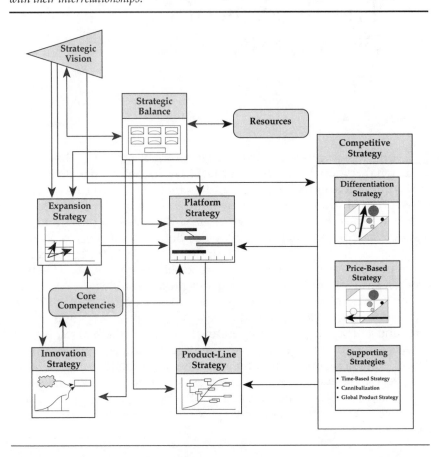

element of the process. Without a clear definition of responsibility, a process tends to flounder and lose momentum while waiting for somebody to do something. In addition, conflict can occur when different people end up doing the same task, or tasks "fall through the cracks" because everyone assumes someone else will take care of them. Finally, in product strategy, skill is a necessary ingredient that is more important here than other management processes.

Process Structure

There are six structural elements to the product strategy process. The first three—strategic vision, platform strategy, and product-line strategy—provide the basic structure. All product strategy flows either explicitly or implicitly through these three levels. Expansion strategy and innovation strategy are optional structural elements. A company only needs these if it wants to invest in expansion or growth. Strategic balance is the structural element that regulates the other elements to keep them within the desired mix objectives. Each of these elements was discussed in some detail; the focus here is how they work together as a process.

Strategic vision. Strategic vision provides a framework for product-platform strategy. The current platform strategy may not be adequate to achieve the strategic vision, and, if not, a new platform strategy is needed to achieve the vision. In some cases, a new platform strategy alone may not be sufficient, and expansion into new markets may be necessary. Strategic vision guides the extent and direction of this expansion.

Strategic vision also sets the tone for competitive strategy. It suggests the general direction for vectors of differentiation by indicating how products can be competitively successful. It implies the importance of price in product strategy and may indicate the need for supporting strategies. Strategic vision guides strategic balance. The mix objectives of strategic balance are an interpretation of the strategic vision. In some cases, there may also be some feedback to the strategic vision, particularly if the vision is not feasible because of resource limitations or other reasons.

The result of this initial structural element is a statement of strategic vision. While there is not a set format, a brief but clear statement of a few sentences is frequently effective.

Platform strategy. Platform Strategy is the element of the process that first articulates the strategic vision as a specific strategy. Failure to recognize this next step in the process inhibits implementation of the vision. It is this specific relationship that makes the strategic vision actionable. The software company CEO who out of frustration distributed a 53-page vision memo to all employees, did not understand how these process elements were linked. He did not have a process view of product strategy; he thought it just happened.

Since the result of expansion strategy is usually a new product platform, it can initiate platform strategy. Platform strategy is regulated by the strategic balance element. This keeps the portfolio of multiple platform developments in line with the overall balance objectives such as risk, long-term/short-term opportunities, and so on.

Competitive strategy is primarily implemented at the platform strategy level. This is where the vector of differentiation is created and the cost structure established. It is also where time-based strategy, global product strategy, and cannibalization are considered. The strengths of core competencies limit platform strategy.

The output of the product-platform element of the process is a product-platform plan for each platform. This is typically a summary of where the platform comes from and where it is going in the future.

Product-line strategy. Product-line strategy is a subset of product-platform strategy since the individual products within a product line generally stem from a common platform. Like platform strategy, product-line strategy is regulated by the strategic balance element to maintain the appropriate mix of investments. Product-line strategy is also driven by the elements of competitive strategy, but it is constrained by what was done at the platform level.

A product-line plan is the result of product-line strategy. This integrates with the product development process through the product-line development schedule.

Expansion strategy. Expansion strategy exists somewhat outside the basic structure. It is optional and not pursued by some companies. Since its focus is much broader than platform strategy, it is only loosely coupled to strategic vision and strategic balance, which guide its extent and direction. Expansion requires leveraging core competencies, some of which are available and others which need to be developed. Innovation is usually the route to improving or developing core competencies.

The result of expansion strategy is a prioritized list of potential new product platforms that will enable a company to expand. These are derived by evaluating the possible opportunities along various expansion paths.

Innovation strategy. Expansion opportunities and innovation are closely linked. Innovation efforts can be guided by the desired direction of expansion, and innovation may create the core competencies needed for expansion. Innovation is not driven by strategic balance, but it is limited by the funding allocated to the pursuit or nurturing of innovations.

The result of innovation strategy is less clear than the other structural elements. It is a set of changes to organizational practices and philosophies to stimulate innovation.

Strategic balance. The priorities established by the objectives of strategic balance serve to allocate resources and provide direction to platform strategy, expansion opportunities, product-line strategy, and innovation. This is generally a rough-cut allocation providing strategic guidance only. The specific assignment of resources to individual projects is done in product development through a phase review process.

Strategic balance performs the initial reconciliation between the strategic vision and the resources available. This may be an iterative process. Resources, particularly those related to product development investment, may need to be adjusted to achieve the strategic vision.

The output of strategic balance is typically expressed as a simple chart of the preferred mix or range of each category of new product investment. Typically, this is reconciled to the current product development portfolio to determine where it is out of balance.

Timing

The timing of the elements in a product strategy process is different from the timing of an annual planing cycle. That is one reason why annual planning, while necessary, is not sufficient for developing product strategy. The individual elements within the product strategy process have different cycles, but they need to be synchronized.

- *Strategic vision* tends to be relatively stable, changing only when a company needs to alter its direction. In high-technology companies, strategic vision changes more frequently than in other companies, but even here it typically changes only every five to ten years.

- *Strategic balance* should also be reviewed and updated annually, so it can be included in an annual planning cycle. A company should confirm its strategic balance at least once a year and periodically evaluate the strategic balance of its actual project portfolio to its preferred mix. Typically, this comparison is also referred to at most major product development phase reviews. The preferred mix of strategic balance is not changed very often, since it usually takes a while to make the shift. Most major changes in this balance occur when a company needs to make a strategic adjustment.

- *Product-platform strategy* is related to the life-cycle of the individual product platforms, so it does not change very often. However, when it is time to change, product-platform strategy needs significant attention.

- *Product-line strategy* is created when a new product line is launched from a new product platform. Subsequently, it can be reviewed and updated as part of an annual cycle.

- *Expansion strategy* is generally pursued based on resource availability, making allocation of sufficient resources through strategic balance very important. However, more aggressive companies will regularly launch intensive efforts to identify potential expansion paths as part of a more general growth strategy.

FIGURE 13–2

Product Strategy Process Cycle. Illustrates the different cycles of Strategic Vision (SV), Strategic Balance (SB), Platform Plans (A, B, C, X, Y), Expansion Plans (Exp-1, Exp-2), Product-Line Plans (A1, B1, B2, C1, X1, Y1), and Annual Plans (X).

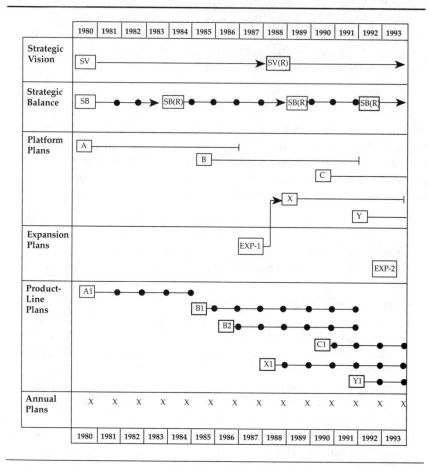

- *Innovation strategy* cannot be put on a set time schedule. It happens when the conditions are right and the opportunities arise. All a company can do is to create the best conditions that will cultivate innovation.

Figure 13–2 illustrates these cycle and timing differences over a 14-year period for a typical company. Its strategic vision (SV) was prepared in 1980 and not revised until 1988. It also determined its strategic balance (SB) in 1980 and then revised it three times over the following 13 years. It prepared a plan for platform A in 1980, and the platform lasted for six years, until 1986. It was eventually replaced by platform B, which was replaced by platform C.

The company also expanded into a new market with platform X, which was then replaced by platform Y. This opportunity was identified as a result of an expansion planning effort (Exp-1) during 1987 and 1988. The company initiated another effort (Exp-2) in 1993. Product-line plans (A1, B1, etc.) were initiated at the same time the related platform was completed. Platform B launched two product lines (B1 and B2). The company did annual planning at the end of each year (X), updating (-●-) product-line plans and comparing its product development portfolio to its strategic balance criteria as part of that process.

Product Strategy Responsibilities

In some companies, the responsibilities and authorities for product strategy are not clearly defined. These are not part of someone's job, or they may be done at the wrong level of authority and therefore not be effectively implemented. Lack of clear responsibility is one of the fundamental reasons for failures in product strategy.

The responsibility for product strategy varies even more than timing among companies. Besides organizational and product differences, there is a difference in ability. Some executives are good at product strategy, while others are not. Nonetheless, several guidelines can be suggested for assigning responsibility.

Strategic vision is usually the responsibility of CEOs, but they do not need to prepare a strategic vision by themselves nor do they need to do it in a vacuum. The views of others are important in forming a vision. Yet, developing a strategic vision should not be done by consensus, or a diluted or unnecessarily complex vision results. The CEO listens to others, evaluates alternative visions, crafts the final vision, and then preaches it to everyone.

Senior executives in a company are typically responsible for setting the strategic balance criteria, selecting the expansion paths to be evaluated, and approving platform strategy. Specifically, this is the responsibility of the senior executives who have the authority to set product strategy for the company.

The evaluation of specific expansion paths and the definition of potential innovation opportunities are typically done on an individual-project basis by small teams under the guidance of senior executives. Product-line strategy is usually the responsibility of product management for that product line, although frequent interaction with technical staff is usually expected.

Competitive strategies are defined as part of the product-platform strategy and the product-line strategy. These are guided by senior executives and reviewed by those with the authority for product strategy, such as a product approval committee, but marketing and technical views on alternative strategies are essential.

Skills

A company can have an adequate structure for product strategy in place, but without skillful execution it may not develop a successful strategy. Skillful execution begins with a conceptual understanding of product strategy. Without this understanding, those determining product strategy are more likely to make fundamental mistakes and errors in judgment. A mastery of the appropriate techniques and methodologies is necessary by those who prepare product strategy. These skills may not be needed by everyone involved, but those who are actively developing strategy should be competent in the relevant techniques.

Knowledge and appreciation of generic competitive strategies are also helpful. Generic strategies are derived from those used by other companies in the past. Understanding how these succeed and fail can prevent experiencing the same failure or overlooking an alternative strategy that could be successful. In the end, there is nothing like experience in applying product strategy. All companies should assess and improve their product strategy skills, just as they do skills in other areas.

A company also needs to achieve skill in the execution of the product strategy process itself. Everyone involved needs to talk a common language and understand their responsibilities in order to smooth the execution of the process. This requires that they all understand the company's structure of product strategy, its division of responsibilities and authorities, and the timing of each element.

INTEGRATION WITH OTHER PRODUCT DEVELOPMENT PROCESSES

The product strategy process does not exist in a vacuum. It is tightly integrated with other management processes, particularly product development and technology development. Its integration is depicted in Figure 13–3.

There are two principal ways that product strategy and product development are integrated. First, the product strategy process, through product-platform strategy, product-line strategy, and expan-

FIGURE 13–3

Integration of Product Strategy with Product Development and Technology Development.

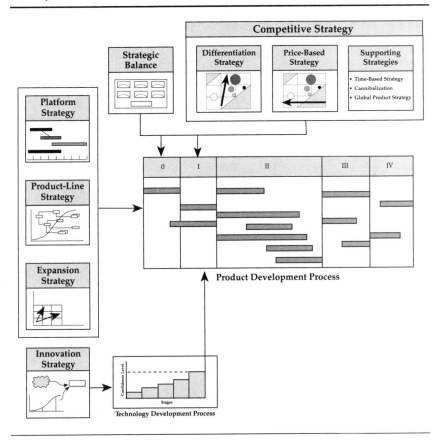

sion strategy creates the specific opportunities for new product development. These opportunities are clarified and reviewed as part of the concept evaluation phase (Phase 0) of product development. If they pass the review, opportunities become projects and proceed through development, usually through the framework of a phase review process.

In the two initial phases of the phase review process, a new product opportunity is evaluated for its strategic fit and its chance of competitive success. This is the second point of integration. Strategic balance and competitive strategy are considered before the opportunity progresses to later phases of development. They are used by the product approval committee in its decision process.

IMPACT OF CORE COMPETENCIES ON PRODUCT STRATEGY

As was previously discussed, core competencies can leverage or restrict product strategy. Core competencies in technology and marketing are directly applied to product platforms and individual products. However, there is also another type of core competency that is not directly applied to products; instead, it enables a particular product strategy. For example, a company with a core competency that enables it to develop products faster than competitors can implement time-based strategies that competitors cannot match because they do not have this competency.

Technical Core Competencies

Technical core competencies are used by companies to achieve sustainable vectors of differentiation. By developing, improving, or applying a technology better than competitors, a high-technology company can establish a vector for differentiating its product in a way that achieves competitive advantage. Without any particular technical core competency, a high-technology company is hard pressed to establish a vector of differentiation beyond a temporary feature or function that is easily copied.

Expansion strategies that employ product/technology leverage depend on technical core competencies. If a company has technical core competencies that are robust and rapidly improving, it should have many potential expansion paths. Microsoft was in this position and took advantage of its technical core competencies in its expansion strategies. If a company's technical core competencies have atrophied or become obsolete, it has very little leverage to expand in the product/technology direction.

Marketing Core Competencies

Marketing core competencies are usually related to unique advantages in the marketplace, particularly channels of distribution or close relationships with customers. A superior position in an important channel of distribution can provide a core competency that can exploit expansion paths in this direction.

A close relationship with customers may also provide a core competency for understanding the market, although this is more difficult to establish and sustain than other core competencies. A core competency in understanding the market can be used to identify a vector of differentiation not seen by competitors.

Management Core Competencies

Management core competencies are those in which a company is superior to its competitors at executing a particular process. For example, it can develop new products faster or manufacture products at a lower cost. Some product strategies are dependent on related management core competencies. Understanding the relationship between product strategies and management competencies is essential to implementing product strategy. The following are some of the more typical relationships.

Time-based strategy and product development competency. Chapter 7 explained why successful time-based strategy requires a core competency in product development. If a company has a better product development process than its competitors, it can pursue an exciting range of time-based strategies. It can be first to market, or it can be a fast follower. However, if it does not have a core competency in managing its product development process, its time-based strategy options are severely limited. It can only be first to market by starting way ahead of its competitors, and even then it needs to worry about eventually getting passed by faster competitors.

Price-based strategy and manufacturing supply-chain competencies. Manufacturing supply-chain competencies refer collectively to the integrated processes of order fulfillment through manufacturing to supplier management. Companies need to have a quick, low-cost supply chain to compete successfully using an offensive price-based strategy. Chapter 6 explained that a company needs to be the best at managing its product costs or it will simply lose money by competing this way. Managing product costs means managing the entire supply chain, not just one link, such as production costs.

Price-based strategy and product development competency. Price-based strategy may also require a management core competency in the product development process for a company to be a low-cost competitor. There are two reasons for this requirement. First, design for cost and the discipline to develop low-cost platforms need to be an integral part of the product development process. Second, in cases where development is a significant cost element, the product development process itself needs to be highly productive.

Global product strategy and global operations competencies. Chapter 8 showed how global product strategy is closely linked with a company's global operations capabilities, including its international manufacturing and its worldwide product development process. Without a core competency in these processes, execution of a global product strategy will be inefficient, although it may not be competitively threatening unless competitors can execute a global product strategy sufficiently better to achieve an economic advantage.

Differentiation strategy and product development competency. A differentiation strategy also may depend on a core competency in product development since clearly defining and implementing a vector of differentiation is not always easy. It frequently requires a disciplined and rigorous product development process that emphasizes differentiation throughout the phases of development.

SUMMARY

Product strategy is a management process, and as a process it can be continuously improved. The better a company's product strategy process, the more likely it will be to target the best opportunities and develop a successful competitive strategy.

Describing the process of product strategy involves defining the interrelationships among its structural elements, as well as its timing and assignment of responsibility. The process also requires skillful execution.

The product strategy process integrates with other processes, particularly product development and technology development. These points of integration enable seamless execution of product development. Product strategy is also leveraged or restricted by core competencies. These include technical core competencies, marketing core competencies, and management core competencies.

Defining product strategy as a process enables it to be implemented and improved. Product strategy no longer needs to be random or unpredictable. It can be managed!

Chapter Fourteen

Strategic Thinking

U nderstanding and applying the concepts and strategies described earlier may not alone be enough to create a truly successful product strategy. Truly successful product strategy requires strategic thinking. This type of thinking does not come easy to some. They seem stuck in a rut, unable to get beyond a "business as usual" procedural approach to product strategy.

This final chapter uses two approaches to stimulate strategic thinking. The first emphasizes what project strategy is not. The second looks to strategy in other areas as models for strategic thinking.

Real product strategy differs from other management activities that sometimes masquerade as product strategy. These activities have a useful purpose in the management of an enterprise but should not be confused with product strategy. One way of distinguishing between them and product strategy is to define what product strategy is not.

The formulation of strategy in other areas can provide useful models to stimulate strategic thinking in product strategy. Military strategy, game theory, sports strategy, and decision-making theory have been selected to illustrate some alternative models. This is not intended to be a complete application of strategic thinking in other areas to strategic thinking in product strategy—that would take a book of its own. Rather, it is intended to jump start strategic thinking.

ACTIVITIES THAT MASQUERADE AS PRODUCT STRATEGY

If asked about the product strategy, some companies respond by describing their annual planning process, pulling out a dusty binder, or showing a forecast of new product sales. Hopefully by now there should be little confusion that these are not product strategy, but for emphasis the following is a summary of what product strategy is not:

1. *Annual planning is not product strategy.* Product strategy is more than planning—in fact, it is entirely different than planning. In most companies, annual planning is a process for documenting expected

259

results, typically in a quantitative format. This usually includes projected revenue, expense, and profit, and it may be supplemented with a breakdown of revenue by product and a schedule of new product releases.

Product strategy, on the other hand, is primarily a structured thought process. Actually, it is both the thought process and the result of that thought process regarding how to achieve the strategic vision. It is a time-phased blueprint of anticipated actions, not results. Annual plans document the anticipated result of product strategy. However, the documentation process should not be confused with the thought process.

2. *Sales forecasting is not product strategy.* To some, product strategy is a revenue estimate for current and anticipated products. This is sales forecasting, not product strategy. Here again, companies confuse documentation of a result with the thought process to get to that result.

Sales forecasts are prepared from product-line plans, which, in turn, are the result of product-line strategy, product-platform strategy, and possibly expansion strategy. The way these products will succeed is shaped by competitive strategy. Sales forecasts lie at the end of a long and difficult strategic process. Some companies take a shortcut to get there. They skip the strategic thinking part and just go directly to the numbers. Their sales forecasts are put together in two or three days, with most of the time spent in calculating and formatting the numbers.

3. *Product requirement specifications are not product strategy.* Product requirement specifications are all too frequently used to develop product strategy. This is not product strategy; it is an element of the product design phase. However, if there is no product strategy process, product strategy decisions end up being made as product specifications are determined.

Here again, there is confusion between output and input. Product strategy is the input process. It defines which products should be developed and how they will be differentiated. Once a new product has a priority for development, a product requirement specification is prepared. Here again, skipping the strategy part and going directly to defining the details of the product is certainly easier. Product strategy can be very difficult. Rarely does this shortcut work, however. In most cases, companies end up developing the wrong product, or they develop a product that is not as successful as it could have been.

4. *Product strategy is not reactive.* Product strategy should be proactive. It should be aggressive, vigorous, and forceful. Companies that ignore product strategy always seem to be on the run, reacting to strategic moves by competitors and strategic shifts in the market. They are constantly in crisis mode.

Because they are continually trying to catch up, they have no time to do product strategy. It is a luxury they cannot afford. To them, product strategy becomes reacting to a new competitive product by discounting prices to retain sales. New product development is clear: Match the capabilities of competitive products in order to remain competitive.

5. *Product strategy is not tactical.* It is strategic. While these two terms—strategy and tactics—are closely related, they are virtual opposites. However, because of their close relationship, they are frequently confused. Strategy concerns the overall plan. It is long-term and general in nature. Tactics are the individual activities used to execute the strategy. They tend to be short-term, specific, and concrete.

Individual pricing decisions, for example, are tactics of an overall price-based strategy. However, in the absence of an overall price-based strategy, tactical pricing decisions are viewed as strategy. But they are not; they are still tactics, and there is no strategy.

6. *Product strategy is not the responsibility of strategic planners.* Product strategy is the responsibility of top management. Strategic planners can assist and facilitate the formulation of strategy, but, in the end, senior management must be responsible for evaluating the proper alternatives and making the strategic decisions.

Senior management leadership is particularly critical at strategic junctures where a company is being transformed in a new strategic direction. Andy Grove, CEO and founder of Intel, experienced this in 1985 when the company was making the transition to microprocessors from memory chips. "We had the very ridiculous system, common in America at the time, of delegating strategic planning to strategic planners." Until top management recognized the strategic shift and articulated it as a strategy, the best development people were still working on memory chips. Andy Grove refers to this as "strategic dissonance"—the strategic planners' plans, top management's vision and Intel's investments were not consistent.[1]

7. *Product strategy does not come from brilliant ideas by brilliant people.* Many believe that brilliant ideas for new products come from brilliant people, while dumb ideas come from dumb people. That is absolutely wrong. The difference between brilliant ideas and dumb ideas is how thoroughly they are thought through.

Successful products stem from ideas that are thoroughly thought through. The eventual product idea may be significantly revised from the original, or it may even be the culmination of a string of related ideas that were sequentially analyzed and discarded for a better one.

Products that fail are frequently born out of a lazy process where the original idea is implemented without sufficient thought or critique.

This explains the high leverage that experience provides in expanding into new markets. If a person does not know much about a new market, it is easier to assume that an idea for a new product in that market is brilliant.

MILITARY STRATEGY

Military strategy is most often looked to as a model of strategic thinking. After all, it has evolved over many centuries with a great deal of experimentation and reflections. Military strategy has also been applied in situations where the consequences were critical.

Military commanders and theorists throughout history have formulated what they considered to be the most important strategic and tactical principles of war. Napoleon I, for example, had 115 such principles. Some of the most commonly cited are the objective, the offensive, surprise, security, unity of command, economy of force, mass, and maneuver. Most are, like product strategy, interdependent. Military forces, whether large-scale or small-scale, must have a clear strategy that is followed despite possible distractions.[2]

Three famous writers on the strategy of war and conflict have been chosen to illustrate strategic thinking. The writings of Carl von Clausewitz in 1832 form the basis for much military strategy and have been applied to industrial strategy. Sun Tzu's *The Art of War*, written in China more than 2,000 years ago, was the first known attempt to formulate a rational or strategic basis for the conduct of military operations. *The Book of Five Rings* was written in 1643 by Miyamoto Musashi, undefeated dueler, master samurai, and teacher.

Carl von Clausewitz

The Prussian general Carl von Clausewitz (1780–1831) is one of the most recognized military strategists. His doctrines were originally published in *Vom Kreige (On War)* in 1832.[3] Clausewitz believed that strategy appoints the time, place, and force in a battle and that it does this in many ways, each of which influences the result. He emphasized the importance of the principles of mass, economy of force, and the destruction of enemy forces.

Superiority in numbers is the most general principle of victory. Clausewitz states that strategy fixes the point where, the time when, and the numerical force with which a battle is fought. History has shown that the competitor with a superior force has a decisive advantage. Therefore, the greatest possible number of troops should be brought into action at the decisive point.

The logic behind this is simple. For example, Army A has a force of 9,000 troops and Army B has 6,000. Assume that in combat each fires a round with an accuracy rate of one out of three. After the first round, Army A has been reduced to 7,000 and Army B has 3,000 remaining. By the end of the second round, Army A has 6,000 troops remaining, and Army B is almost wiped out, with only 667 surviving. Combat ends after the third round. Army B only has a chance if it has other advantages over Army A.

In product strategy, superiority in numbers relates to a company's presence in the market. This includes customer base, reputation, and distribution capability. Although this strategy of combat seems obvious, it is often overlooked by companies deciding product strategy without thinking strategically.

For example, one electronics company realized that a competitor had three times its presence in a market, but in spite of this it decided to introduce a new product that was comparable to that of its competitor. The company assumed that it would have a third of its competitor's market share, which would be acceptable. However, the company ended up with very little market share as its competitor defeated it soundly in the marketplace.

The principle of superiority is also behind the concept of market leverage in the strategy for expanding into a new market.

The best strategy is always to be very strong, first generally then at the decisive point. Clausewitz believed that there was no more imperative and no simpler law for strategy than to keep the forces concentrated. He thought that it was incredible, and yet it happened many times, that troops were divided and separated merely through "a mysterious feeling of conventional manner": By this he meant that it was just the way that things were done. This separation diluted superiority and reduced the chance of victory.

The mistake of dividing resources is also made frequently by companies in their product strategy. They fail to sufficiently focus their efforts, and they dilute their strength by trying to develop too many products at once. Interestingly, the description by Clausewitz that resources were divided by "a mysterious feeling of conventional manner" is very appropriate to what happens in many companies. They seem to try to do too many things out of a conventional manner without thinking about the strategic consequences.

When absolute superiority is not attainable, an army should try to produce relative superiority at the decisive point. When overall superiority is not possible, Clausewitz believed that relative strength at the decisive point was the next best strategy. He believed that skillful assemblage of superior forces at the decisive point had its foundations in the right appreciation of those points, in the judicious direction by which means have been given to the forces, and in the resolution required to sacrifice the unimportant to the advantage of the important.

In product strategy, as in military strategy, a company needs to identify the decisive point in both time and place in order to gain a relative advantage. This means identifying the market segment, product, and timing of introduction so as to have a relative advantage. It also means to identify the important from the unimportant and to be willing to sacrifice what is not important.

Surprise is one way to gain relative superiority since it catches a competitor unprepared. Clausewitz believed that secrecy and rapidity were the two primary factors in surprise. This applies in product strategy as well. The advantage of surprise is attained by the company that is first to market. Secrecy is also important to the element of surprise, yet many companies lose the strategic advantage of surprise by preannouncing new products well in advance of completion.

Sun Tzu

The essays in *The Art of War* by Sun Tzu form the earliest known treatise on military strategy. Sun Tzu's moderation contrasts with the emphasis on the absolute by Clausewitz. Two of Sun Tzu's strategies are discussed below.[4]

What is of supreme importance in war is to attack the enemy's strategy.   Sun Tzu believed that attacking the enemy's strategy was of higher importance than combat. By defeating the enemy's strategy, the army could be conquered before threats materialized. Sun Tzu also believed that determining the enemy's plans would indicate which strategy would be successful.

A competitor's product strategy can also be attacked before it is fully implemented or deployed. For example, a vector of differentiation can be neutralized by a similar, but incompatible, vector. An attempt to gain price leadership can be attacked by resegmenting the market. The key to this is understanding the competitor's strategy, something that very few companies appreciate.

The principles of product strategy can be used to analyze the strategy of competitors, thus pinpointing their weak points. If a competitor does not have a coherent product strategy, it can be exploited. At a minimum, individual elements of product strategy can be analyzed and the weaknesses individually exploited.

Generally, he who occupies the field of battle first and awaits his enemy is at ease; he who comes later to the scene and rushes into the fight is weary.   Sun Tzu believed that it is important to bring the enemy to the field of battle and not be brought there by him. This provides a competitive advantage.

This is also true in product strategy. One application is the first-to-market advantage. With this advantage, a company awaits the competition while occupying the field of battle. Another application of this theory is getting competitors to compete on a basis where a company has an advantage. For example, if a company that has a cost advantage can get others to compete on price, it gets them to compete on its "battleground."

Miyamoto Musashi

The Book of Five Rings by Miyamoto Musashi is considered one of the most important texts on conflict and strategy emerging from the Japanese warrior culture. Composed in 1643, it has become a well-known classic among business people, studied for its insights into the Japanese approach to business strategy. The two following selections provide an insight into Musashi's philosophy.[5]

Focus of the eyes in martial arts.   Musashi believed that the eyes need to be focused in such a way as to maximize the range and breadth of vision. Observation and perception are two separate things: The observing eye is stronger; the perceiving eye is weaker. A specialty of martial arts is to see that which is far away closely and to see that which is nearby from a distance.

Musashi's philosophy of the differences between observation and perception apply to product strategy. Some companies observe the details of important trends without perceiving them as trends. They see, but they do not comprehend, and therefore they do not act. To use a more modern expression, they cannot see the forest for the trees. Neither do they perceive what is nearby because they are too close to it. They may not comprehend an important action because the implications are too far away.

Knowing disintegration.   According to Musashi, disintegration is something that happens to everything that gets out of rhythm with the times. When a house crumbles, a person crumbles, or an adversary crumbles, they fall apart because they are out of rhythm. In large-scale military science, it is essential to find the rhythm of opponents as they come apart. At this point, they are most vulnerable.

Competitors are also most vulnerable to attack when they are out of rhythm with the market. Product strategy, particularly its timing, can be most effective when a competitor has this vulnerability. Markets also disintegrate. They get out of rhythm with the times and begin to crumble.

FIGURE 14–1
Prisoners' Dilemma. Shows that both A and B are better off by confessing.

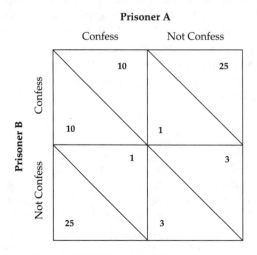

GAME THEORY

Game theory is a branch of mathematics and social sciences that focuses on decision making. It applies logic and reasoning in a structured way to understand how to out-think an adversary. Much of game theory can be applied to develop strategic thinking. Here are two examples.

Prisoners' Dilemma

Perhaps the best-known example of game theory, the prisoners' dilemma illustrates a game where there is the possibility of mutual advantage as well as conflict. The basic story behind the prisoners' dilemma is the arrest of two individuals who are charged with committing a crime together. They are separated and given the opportunity of confessing and implicating the other. If they do so, they would get a one-year sentence if the other does not confess or a ten-year sentence if the other does confess. By not confessing, they would receive a three-year sentence if the other does not confess, but a 25-year sentence if the other does confess. The alternatives are summarized in Figure 14–1.

Game theory holds that if they both are logical, they will each end up with a ten-year sentence. Prisoner A, for example, thinks through the alternatives and realizes that he is better off to confess whether prisoner B confesses or not. His sentence is less in either alternative (10 versus 25, or 1 versus 3). Prisoner B's logic is exactly the same. Thus they each serve a ten-year sentence instead of the three if they

FIGURE 14–2

Prisoners' Dilemma Applied to Pricing Decision. Shows that both A and B are better off reducing prices.

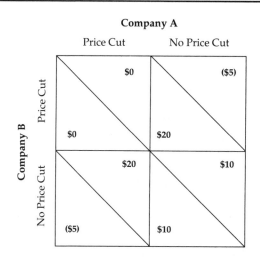

did not confess. To do this, however, they needed to communicate and agree to stand firm and not confess. Which, of course, is why they were separated.

The logic of the prisoners' dilemma is directly applicable to product strategy (Figure 14–2). Substitute competing companies for each prisoner, and look at the example of a possible price cut before a major trade show or contract bid. Neither knows if the competitor is planning to cut its prices, but by using the prisoners' dilemma logic, each knows that it is better off to cut prices in either case. If company A cuts its prices and Company B does not, then A achieves an advantage and higher profits ($20 million). If both cut prices, then A is better off cutting them also (even though neither would make a profit) since it would be better than a $5 million loss.

The best alternative would be for neither to cut prices. Both companies would be better off (each would make $10 million), but the logic behind the prisoners' dilemma indicates that they will both reduce prices and eliminate all profit from the market. This is the logic behind many price wars.

Creeping Incrementalism

Why do companies invest more in new products than they could possibly get back in profits? One reason is creeping incrementalism, as is illustrated in the game of bidding for a dollar.

The game goes like this. A group is invited to bid on a one dollar bill with the caveat that the second-highest bidder must pay his or her bid without winning the dollar. This simulates a sunk cost situation. By the time the bidding gets to approximately 95¢, everyone realizes the problem, and the two highest bidders are stuck. The second highest bidder (at say 90¢) realizes that 10¢ more could return a dollar and bids $1 for a dollar. The other bidder realizes the same and bids $1.10 for a dollar. This continues until someone finally gives in, usually at a cost of five or six dollars each for a dollar bill.[6]

The logic behind this game is the same as that which leads a company to invest $20 million in a product line that only has the potential of $5 million in profit. Incremental investment creeps up on it. The logic is "Well, we already have $4 million invested, we may as well invest another $2 million to get the $5 million profit." And when it has $15 million invested, it rationalizes, "We already invested $15 million, we might as well invest more to make some profit." The difficulty is that in some cases incremental investment is wise, but in others it may be wasted.

For example, one data communications company spent $80 million over four years trying to develop a new switching device. Despite knowing that a competitor would be coming out with a better performing product, sooner, and at less cost, the management team wanted to keep going because "after all, we have spent so much money on it, and we are almost there."

SPORTS STRATEGY

Strategy used in sports or games can also provide models for strategic thinking. Two very different ones have been selected here to illustrate applicability. American football is a team sport where it is necessary to lead the entire team in the same direction. Chess is a very different example. It is an old game, and sport to many, which has its very foundation in strategy.

American Football

Although American football is more a game of tactics than strategy, it does illustrate some particularly relevant strategic examples. Football, like product development, is a team game. Strategy is developed to be implemented by a team. The two following examples illustrate differing offensive strategies.

Ball-control offense.   The strategy behind ball-control offense is to use a continuous series of short-gain plays to move the ball down the field to a touchdown. Play selection is dominated by quick-hitting runs and short passes designed to get three to five yards per play. If there are no mistakes, this strategy will result in a sustained drive with a first down every three plays. As a secondary benefit, the opposing team will not get the ball as often and will have fewer chances to score.

A team using a ball-control strategy will select players and design plays to implement that strategy. Since the emphasis is on the running game, it needs a strong running back and good offensive line. Receivers need to be good blockers but do not need to be fast. The quarterback is not as critical in this offense, but the ability to run is a plus. The ball-control team's playbook focuses on running plays and short passes. Discipline is important to this strategy since a mistake or penalty will stall a drive.

The product strategy analogy to the ball-control offense is the company that focuses on a continuous stream of product variations and incremental improvements. It concentrates on relatively small, low-risk product development projects. This is a conservative strategy that will rarely produce a big-hit product yet will provide steady performance. Like the football analogy, the company selects a staff that is good at implementing this type of strategy.

Long-bomb offense. This is the opposite type of offensive football strategy. With this strategy, a football team is intent on making the big plays, typically through long passes. It needs two or three big plays to score and will make no gain on many plays. This is a high-risk strategy that will produce big results in some games and little in others.

With an emphasis on the passing game, this offensive strategy requires an outstanding quarterback and excellent pass receivers. The playbook is designed to set up and get the big play, typically a long pass play. Many plays, such as incomplete passes, result in no gain.

In product strategy, the long-bomb offense is one where a company focuses its resources on creating new products that will be a big success. It is also a high-risk strategy that will have a high failure rate. Companies that follow this strategy need to have a highly innovative development staff and need to allocate a significant portion of the development budget on innovative products and expansion into new markets. A company following a strategy similar to this needs to accept frequent failure in new products.

Chess Strategy

Chess was invented in the sixth century, giving players centuries to perfect its strategy. Strategy is the key to winning in chess, and chess masters have learned to perfect it. The two following examples illustrate some general chess strategy.

Controlling the center.   In chess, controlling the center of the board can be the key to attaining competitive advantage. The four squares in the center of the chess board (d4, d5, e4, e5) and the 12 squares immediately surrounding them offer greatest mobility. Pieces in the center have more possible moves and greater flexibility. By positioning more pieces there, a player controls the center of the board and attains competitive advantage.

The strategy of controlling the center of the board can be successful in product-line strategy as well. In launching a new product line, it is frequently best to introduce the first product in the middle range of the market rather than at an extreme such as the high or low end. This provides more flexibility to move in any direction. If the first product is introduced at an extreme such as the high end, it is much more difficult to move next to any other position than the one directly below it.

Endgame strategy.   Chess is divided into three phases, the endgame being the last. In the endgame, there are few remaining pieces left on the board, and the game is drawing to a close. The strategic characteristics are significantly different than the previous phases. Strategies that made sense in earlier phases will not work in the endgame.

High-technology markets have an endgame and, similar to chess, strategies that made sense in earlier phases of the market will not work in the endgame. These strategic differences were seen where differentiation and price strategy take on different characteristics during the decline stage of a market.

DECISION MAKING

Product strategy eventually comes down to decision making. What are the highest priorities? Which alternative vector of differentiation should be chosen? Should a new platform be introduced?

Perhaps the best analysis of the decision-making process was done by Graham Allison in 1971 in his investigation of the Cuban Missile Crisis.[7] He developed three alternative decision-making models and applied them to this event, illustrating how they worked. These same three models apply to decision making for product strategy.

These are not presented as alternatives because all three play a role in decision making. This is true for both a company and its competitors. What is important is to understand that each of these influence decisions, and in some cases it may be better to emphasize one over the other.

The Rational Model

Classical economic and modern statistical game theory states that optimal choices are made in narrowly constrained, neatly defined situations. This is the basis for the rational model of decision making.

In the rational decision-making model, a choice is made among a set of alternatives defined in any particular situation. Each alternative has an outcome or consequence that is expected if it is chosen. Rational choice consists of selecting that alternative whose consequences rank the highest in the decision maker's measure of success.

Product strategy is often thought of in terms of the rational model, and in many cases that is the preferred approach. Decision making focuses on evaluating alternatives, so the accuracy of the estimated consequences becomes critical. Unfortunately, product strategy decisions are not always rational.

The Organizational Model

The second decision-making model is based on the belief that organizations, not rational individuals, make decisions. Organizations go about making decisions in a very different way than individuals. Organizations are a coalition of participants (including customers and suppliers) with disparate demands, changing focuses and attention, and limited ability to attend to all problems simultaneously.

Decision making involves bargaining among potential coalition members to produce a set of de facto agreements that impose constraints on the organization. Organizational choice emerges as the selection of the first alternative that is seen as being acceptable. Product strategy tends to be the result of these selections.

Organizational decision making has several characteristics. First, it tends to resolve conflict among various functions, each of which has different objectives. Second, it seeks to avoid uncertainty. Third, it emphasizes solving pressing problems rather than developing long-term strategies. Finally, organizational decision making works best at solving problems rather than finding opportunities.

The Bureaucratic Model

Although related to the previous model, this model emphasizes the politics of an organization. It views decision making as a political game conducted by individual players, each of whom has his or her own agenda. Players manipulate actions with the power at their discretion for outcomes that will advance their conceptions of the company's and their own personal interests.

Players have different perceptions of what is important based on where they stand in an organization as well as on their personal aspirations. Decisions relating to product strategy emerge as a result of intricate and subtle, simultaneous, overlapping games among players located throughout the company. In this model, results are influenced more by the personality and political power of individual players than by rationality or organizational compromise.

SUMMARY

This concluding chapter emphasizes the need to think strategically in applying the concepts and strategies of the previous chapters. Without strategic thinking, a company will not achieve its potential.

Two approaches are used to stimulate strategic thinking. One is to describe what product strategy is not. It is not annual planning, sales forecasting, or product requirements specification. It is not reactive, and it is not tactical. Product strategy is not the responsibility of strategic planners, and it does not always come from brilliant ideas by brilliant people.

The other approach is to compare product strategy with strategy in other areas. Military strategy provides numerous examples of strategic thinking, and three famous writers on the strategy of war are used to illustrate some of this thinking. Game theory provides some logic on how to out-think competitors. Strategy in sports and games also provides some appropriate analogies. American football and chess illustrate very different strategic thinking. Finally, decision-making models are applied to the decision making behind product strategy.

With all the ingredients—the structure, the concepts, the strategies, the process of product strategy, and strategic thinking—a company's ability to improve its product strategy is unlimited. It will be able to grow through expansion and outmaneuver its competitors.

NOTES

1. Stradford Sherman, *Fortune,* February 22, 1993, p. 58.

2. Grolier's *Academic American Encyclopedia,* CompuServe Online version.

3. Carl von Clausewitz, *On War,* ed. Anatol Rapoport, (London: Penguin Books, 1988).

4. Sun Tzu, *The Art of War,* trans. Samuel B. Griffith, (Oxford, England: Oxford University Press, 1971).

5. Miyamoto Musashi, *The Book of Five Rings,* trans. Thomas Cleary, (Boston: Shambhala, 1993).

6. In using this with MBA classes, I found that this happened in all cases. The average bid for $1 was approximately $5.50.

7. Graham T. Allison, *Essence of Decison—Explaining the Cuban Missile Crisis* (London: Scott Foresman, 1971).

Index